Elites and Democratic Development in Russia

The transformation from Communist rule towards democratic development in Russia cannot be fully understood without taking the elites into full consideration. *Elites and Democratic Development in Russia* examines how elites support and challenge democracy and why they are crucial to Russian democracy in particular.

In this innovative volume, twelve scholars investigate how elites have affected the transition from Communist rule towards democratic development in Russia. They also discuss how the elites' behavioural and attitudinal integration on national and regional levels may constitute a main condition for the consolidation of the emerging political regime.

This book will appeal to those interested in democratization, elites, post-Soviet Russia and post-Communist studies.

Anton Steen is professor in the Department of Political Science, the University of Oslo.

Vladimir Gel'man is associate professor in the Faculty of Political Science and Sociology at the European University at St Petersburg.

Routledge Studies of Societies in Transition

1. **The Economics of Soviet Break-up**
   Bert van Selm

2. **Institutional Barriers to Economic Development**
   Poland's Incomplete Transition
   Edited by Jan Winiecki

3. **The Polish Solidarity Movement**
   Revolution, Democracy and Natural Rights
   Arista Maria Cirtautas

4. **Surviving Post-Socialism**
   Local Strategies and Regional Response in Eastern Europe and the Former Soviet Union
   Edited by Sue Bridger and Frances Pine

5. **Land Reform in the Former Soviet Union and Eastern Europe**
   Edited by Stephen Wegren

6. **Financial Reforms in Eastern Europe**
   A Policy Model for Poland
   Kanhaya L. Gupta and Robert Lensink

7. **The Political Economy of Transition**
   Opportunities and Limits of Transformation
   Jozef van Brabant

8. **Privatizing the Land**
   Rural Political Economy in Post-Communist Socialist Societies
   Edited by Ivan Szelenyi

9. **Ukraine**
   State and Nation Building
   Taras Kuzio

10. **Green Post-Communism?**
    Environmental Aid, Innovation and Evolutionary Political Economics
    Mikael Sandberg

11. **Organizational Change in Post-Communist Europe**
    Management and Transformation in the Czech Republic
    Ed Clark and Anna Soulsby

12. **Politics and Society in Poland**
    Frances Millard

13. **Experimenting with Democracy**
    Regime Change in the Balkans
    Geoffrey Pridham and Tom Gallagher

14. **Poverty in Transition Economies**
    Edited by Sandra Hutton and Gerry Redmond

15. **Work, Employment and Transition**
    Restructuring Livelihoods in Post-Communism
    Edited by Al Rainnie, Adrian Smith and Adam Swain

16. **Environmental Problems of East Central Europe: 2nd Edition**
    Edited by F.W. Carter and David Turnock

17. **Transition Economies and Foreign Trade**
    Jan Winiecki

18. **Identity and Freedom**
    Mapping Nationalism and Social Criticism in Twentieth-Century Lithuania
    Leonidas Donskis

19. **Eastern Europe at the Turn of the Twenty-First Century**
    A Guide to the Economies in Transition
    Ian Jeffries

20. **Social Capital and Democratic Transition**
    Edited by Gabriel Badescu and Eric Uslaner

21. **The Former Yugoslavia at the Turn of the Twenty-First Century**
    A Guide to the Economies in Transition
    Ian Jeffries

22. **The Former Soviet Union at the Turn of the Twenty-First Century**
    A Guide to the Economies in Transition
    Ian Jeffries

23. **Federalism and the Dictatorship of Power in Russia**
    Mikhail Stoliarov

24. **Elites and Democratic Development in Russia**
    Edited by Anton Steen and Vladimir Gel'man

Elites and Democratic Development in Russia

Edited by Anton Steen and
Vladimir Gel'man

LONDON AND NEW YORK

First published 2003
by Routledge
11 New Fetter Lane, London EC4P 4EE

Simultaneously published in the USA and Canada
by Routledge
29 West 35th Street, New York, NY 10001

Routledge is an imprint of the Taylor & Francis Group

© 2003 Anton Steen and Vladimir Gel'man for selection and editorial material; individual contributors their contributions

Typeset in Times by
Florence Production Ltd, Stoodleigh, Devon
Printed and bound in Great Britain by
Antony Rowe Ltd, Chippenham, Wiltshire

All rights reserved. No part of this book may be reprinted or reproduced or utilized in any form or by any electronic, mechanical, or other means, now known or hereafter invented, including photocopying and recording, or in any information storage or retrieval system, without permission in writing from the publishers.

British Library Cataloguing in Publication Data
A catalogue record for this book is available from the British Library

Library of Congress Cataloging in Publication Data
Elites and democratic development in Russia / Anton Steen
  and Vladimir Gel'man (eds).
  Includes bibliographical references and index.
    1. Elite (Social sciences) – Russia (Federation).   2. Political leadership – Russia (Federation).   3. Russia (Federation) – Politics and government – 1991–.   4. Democracy – Russia (Federation).   5. Postcommunism.   I. Steen, Anton, 1949–.   II. Gel'man, Vladimir, 1965–.
  HN530.2.Z9 E43 2003
    305.5'2'0947–dc21   2002153066

ISBN 0–415–30698–1

Contents

List of tables vii
List of contributors ix
Preface xi
Acknowledgements xii

1 **Elites and democratic development in Russia: an introduction** 1
  VLADIMIR GEL'MAN AND ANTON STEEN

2 **Political elite integration and differentiation in Russia** 11
  JOHN HIGLEY, OKSAN BAYULGEN AND JULIE GEORGE

3 **Russia's elites in search of consensus: what kind of consolidation?** 29
  VLADIMIR GEL'MAN

4 **The elite basis of Yeltsin's and Putin's regimes** 51
  ANTON STEEN

5 **The rise and fall of the Russian governor: institutional design vs patron/client relationships** 71
  HELGE BLAKKISRUD

6 **Between centre and regions: the State Duma deputies and Russian federalism** 92
  ANTON STEEN AND VSEVOLOD TIMOFEEV

7 **Party extinction in Russia, 1993–2002: an elite connection** 109
  GRIGORII V. GOLOSOV

8 **Local elites in Russia's transition: generation effects on adaptation and competition** 124
JAMES HUGHES AND PETER JOHN

9 **Reforms and orientations of regional elites: the case of St Petersburg** 148
ALEXANDR DUKA

10 **Elite transformation and regime change: the case of Tomsk Oblast** 168
INESSA TARUSINA

11 **Studies of political elites in Russia: an overview** 187
VLADIMIR GEL'MAN AND INESSA TARUSINA

Index 206

Tables

2.1	Types of political elites and the regime types they create	15
4.1	Support and types of legitimacy	55
4.2	Confidence in institutions. All respondents	56
4.3	Confidence in institutions by elite group	59
4.4	Inter-elite distrust	63
6.1	Confidence in central and regional institutions	95
6.2	The power of the federal government	98
6.3	The power of the regional government	98
6.4	Preferences for future power of central government	99
6.5	Preferences for future power of regional government	100
6.6	Support to special agreement and federal law	102
6.7	Controlling tax-incomes	104
8.1	Selected descriptive statistics	136
8.2	Attitudes to change by new/old elite	139
8.3	Attitudes to decentralization by new/old elite	139
8.4	Attitudes to privatization of federal property by new/old elite	139
8.5	Attitudes to privatization of municipal property by new/old elite	140
8.6	Attitudes to change by educational background	140
8.7	Attitudes to change by age	141
8.8	Persons cited as being the most influential in the city	144
9.1	Family background and identification of Russia	153
9.2	Family background and orientation towards the possible way of Russia's development	154
9.3	Orientations towards development of the Russian economy	155
9.4	Support for private ownership	156
9.5	Orientations towards economic individualism	157
9.6	Age and orientations towards private ownership	157
9.7	Communist Party official experience and orientation to economic individualism	158
9.8	Age of the respondents and negative attitudes towards the Soviet system	159

9.9 Satisfaction with the situation in the country and age 161
9.10 Experience of professional work in Komsomol and orientations towards plutocracy (a combination of membership in legislative bodies and entrepreneurship) 163
9.11 Elite of St Petersburg and Leningrad Oblast (1998) 164
9.12 Composition of sample: age and elite sectors 165

Contributors

Oksan Bayulgen is a doctoral candidate at the Department of Government and Sociology, the University of Texas at Austin, USA.

Helge Blakkisrud is head of the Centre for Russian Studies, Norwegian Institute of International Affairs, Oslo, Norway.

Alexandr Duka is deputy director of the Sociological Institute at the Russian Academy of Science, St Petersburg, Russia.

Vladimir Gel'man is associate professor at the Faculty of Political Sciences and Sociology, The European University at St Petersburg, Russia.

Julie George is a doctoral candidate at the Department of Government, the University of Texas at Austin, USA.

Grigorii V. Golosov is associate professor at the Faculty of Political Sciences and Sociology, The European University at St Petersburg, Russia.

John Higley is professor of government and sociology at the University of Texas at Austin, USA.

James Hughes is a reader in comparative politics in the Department of Government, the London School of Economics and Political Science, UK.

Peter John is professor in the School of Politics and Sociology at Birkbeck College, the University of London, UK.

Anton Steen is professor of political science at the University of Oslo, Norway.

Inessa Tarusina is a lecturer in political science, Nevsky Institute of Language and Culture, St Petersburg, Russia.

Vsevolod Timofeev is a lecturer of modern history at Moscow State University, Russia.

Preface

The purpose of the present volume is to shed light on democratic development in Russia, the argument being that the elite's behaviour and attitudes are the main determinants for the type of political regime that is taking root in Russia. The volume is the result of the seminar 'The New Elites in Russia – Consequences for Democratic Development and Economic Reforms' held in St Petersburg in September 2000, where we spent three days in fruitful discussions on a wide range of issues relating to elites and democratization.

We would like to thank the University of Oslo for travel grants that made the seminar possible. The Norwegian Research Council, the Department of Political Science at the University of Oslo and the Ford Foundation in Moscow have contributed with financial support. Thank you to John Taylor who contributed with language editing of major parts of the book. Gratitude is also expressed to the Norwegian University Center at St Petersburg for providing facilities for the seminar that made this book possible.

Oslo/St Petersburg, September 2002
Anton Steen
Vladimir Gel'man

Acknowledgements

The publishers and editors would like to thank the University of California at Los Angeles for kindly allowing us to reprint a version of 'Elite Research in Russia: Issues and Alternatives' by Vladimir Gel'man and Inessa Tarusina originally published in *Communist and Post-Communist Studies*, Vol. 33, No. 3 (2000).

1 Elites and democratic development in Russia
An introduction

Vladimir Gel'man and Anton Steen

As classics of elite theory suggest, studies of political systems are studies of political elites. This is especially true for societies undergoing 'the triple transitions', and facing complex tasks of simultaneous democratization, marketization and building of the nation-states (Offe, 1991). Russia is no exception in this respect – the post-Soviet transition in Russia, as elsewhere, to a great extent was produced by and depends upon various segments of elites. However, the outcomes of the transition process in Russia were quite different from those of most East European countries. While many post-Communist countries seem to pursue a general pattern of political development that becomes more similar to West European states, the perspectives of democratic development in Russia are still uncertain after more than a decade without Communist rule.

Most scholars, who try to explain patterns of Russia's development from early historical times until the breakdown of the Soviet Union, focus their research on the attitudes and behaviour of its rulers. The unprecedented and sudden political and economic changes in Russia after 1991 were to a great extent initiated and supported by various segments of the elites. However, elites are not operating in a vacuum; their actions are limited by a set of constraints, even in a turbulent post-Soviet environment. On the one hand, elites are constrained in their actions because their attitudes and values stem from a certain constellation of background, recruitment and ideology. In other words, these constraints have consequences for the elites' *demands*. On the other hand, elites are influenced by various incentives provided by political institutions. These institutions form a *supply* that creates certain patterns of elite thinking and behaviour. The supply/demand balance in stable political systems (whether Western democracies or Communist dictatorships) is more or less certain and known to most of elites. In contrast, post-Soviet developments in Russia dramatically changed this supply/demand equation through a series of political and economic crises and then re-equilibrations and stabilization (see, among others, Shevtsova, 1999; McFaul, 2001; Higley *et al.*, in this volume; Gel'man, in this volume).

The challenges for Russian elites that emerged in the post-Soviet period are mainly based on three major dimensions – political democratization, economic deregulation and state decentralization (or even disintegration, in the case of the collapse of the Soviet state). Despite the very fact that all these processes were initiated by elites under Gorbachev's rule, and the elites' demands heavily contributed to these changes, their consequences were rather unintended. Thus, in the 1990s until the early 2000s Russian elites were forced to change themselves through a trial and error process of adaptation to a permanent transformation of supply (for example, due to institutional changes). While democratization produced a basis of electoral contestation of elites, deregulation and decentralization played a crucial role in the formation of new segments of Russian elites, which acquired a significant autonomy from the central leadership and from each other. The emergence of new elites and transformation of old ones posed problems of elite coordination and cooperation going into the heart of Russian political agenda. While the long-term consequences still remain to be seen, the process of 'triple transition' in Russia seems to be over. Thus, time is ripe for analysing its outcomes and for assessing the role of elites in post-Soviet political changes. This is the point of departure for this volume.

The making and shaping of elites

If elites are regarded as crucial actors in political and economic developments, it is essential to be clear about their characteristics and the reasons for their importance. The social science literature dealing with elites addresses four main questions: Who are they, how unified are they, how important are they for democratization and policy outcomes, and what forces shape them?

The question of what constitutes an 'elite' has been answered differently by what might be conveniently labelled the 'power school' and the 'pluralists'. Building on the classic works of Mosca, Pareto and C. Wright Mills, the power school asserts the existence of an integrated governing or power elite that controls any modern country's political regime and makes all main policy decisions. While there are other and contesting elite groups, these manage to influence only secondary aspects of government policy. This thesis of a core power elite has been challenged sharply by scholars who depict elites in modern democratic systems as much more pluralistic (Dahl, 1961, 1971). In their view, in Western democracies there is no dominant or integrated elite but rather constantly shifting constellations and coalitions of more or less equally powerful and organizationally distinct elite groups. Elite configurations vary, and common 'elite interests' do not determine the cooperation of elites, instead it is the type of government policy that influences the interests of various elite groups.

While the pluralist model of elite behaviour is rooted in societal interests and is posited on long-term experience with Western democracies, the conditions for post-Communist elites are quite different. Because Russian democracy is new and its elites cannot clearly be classified along socio-economic cleavages, the question of elite differentiation remains an open one to be explored through empirical research. One major purpose of this volume is to provide more informed answers to the question of to what extent elite pluralism is developing in Russia. The fact that the Russian Constitution guarantees a separation of powers while also instituting a strong presidency makes it pertinent to ask if the institutional distinction between elite groups may have consequences for elite integration and fragmentation.

Higley and his collaborators have sought to combine these opposing perspectives by arguing that political elites in stable democracies are, in fact, both strongly integrated and widely differentiated or pluralistic (see Burton and Higley, 2001). They contend that such 'consensually integrated' elites are a stable democracy's *sine qua non*. However, the possible way of consensual integration of Russian elites is not so obvious. Higley argues that during decades of Communist rule the Soviet elite was rather 'ideocratic', and during Gorbachev's period it suddenly changed toward disunity and fragmentation (see Higley *et al*., in this volume; also Lane and Ross, 1999). While observers have depicted Russian elites as falling well short of consensual integration during the 1990s, the new challenges in the 2000s are even more salient for prospects of Russia's democratic development. Numerous attempts of Russian elites under Putin to overcome their fragmentation and establish a new framework of elite integration are double-edged. On the one hand, one could consider a possible danger of restoration of the omnipotent 'power elite', but on the other hand, it is hard to imagine that Russia's democratic development could have a solid basis without improvement of government performance and effective coordination of national and regional elites.

Dozens of books and hundreds of articles on Russian elites have been written over the last decade by Western and Russian specialists. There exist numerous theoretical and empirical studies, focusing on the composition of Russian elites, their recruitment, career paths, conflicts and pacts, and role in the regime change (for an overview, see Gel'man and Tarusina, in this volume), although few solid answers have so far been given about the elite's political integration and its long-term consequences for democratization in Russia. Asking 'why we need one more collection in this field' is obvious. Posing the question 'what might we learn about democratic development in Russia through the prism of studies of its elites?' is a natural further step and is the major fundament of our volume. In other words, if we would like to explain uneasy developments and problematic prospects of Russia's troubled transformation, we should look closely at the attitudes and behaviour of its elites.

From Communist elites to elitist democracy

During the 1990s the term 'elites' soon became a keyword in Russia, and was adopted as a basic focus of analysis in the public debate and in research contributions. Articles appearing in newspapers and magazines have typically blamed 'elites' for all national problems, or they see some enlightened leaders as the only hope for Russia's future. The purpose of this volume is not to join this polarized – and in our view, rather unfruitful – debate about the shortcomings and virtues of the elites. The aim is to provide empirical studies that may give some clues for a better understanding of how the elites have put their imprint on the political development in Russia.

A major characteristic of the Soviet Union was a hierarchically centralized decision-making system with carefully selected Communist elites. In particular during the last decades of Communism they formed a self-enforcing and privileged class sustained by the nomenklatura system. Surprisingly for many observers, the degree of elite turnover in post-Communist Russia was very low in comparison with East European countries (Wasilewski, 1998), and most of the new elites were deeply rooted in former Soviet nomenklatura (Kryshtanovskaya and White, 1996). However, the process of transformation of Russian elites was much more complicated. Yet, the partial reproduction of elite membership was very natural in Russia due to the lack of an alternative recruitment pool for new elites (like the dissident movement or trade unions in Poland). The demise of the Soviet Union did not imply a complete break with the past, and in particular many well-educated younger persons who had started their career during the end of the Communist era saw new opportunities in politics and the capitalist economy (Lane and Ross, 1999). We will not discuss this here, but it is clear that continuity on all levels has taken place. To what extent the uneven constellation of old and new elites contributed to democratic development in Russia is, however, an empirical question.

Even if one could trace similarities in the backgrounds of Communist and post-Communist elites in Russia, it should be noted that the institutional frameworks of elite politics are very different. First and foremost, after the bloody conflict between President Yeltsin and the Supreme Soviet in 1993, Russia adopted a new Constitution, which has not been challenged by anyone for a decade and has proved to be stable over time (McFaul, 2001). Three major pillars of the Russian constitutional order, namely, a presidential/parliamentary form of government, regular multi-party elections and federalism, provide new incentives for actions of various segments of Russian elites.

But what does this really mean? According to Schumpeter, who defined democracy as the process by which 'individuals acquire the power to decide by means of a competitive struggle for the people's vote' (Schumpeter, 1947: 269), elections are a regular feature in such a democracy. In this respect, democracy is more a device for institutionalizing the elite's competition for power than a means of mass public influence on politics and compromising politics. The Schumpeterian concept is often regarded as an 'elitist model' (Held, 1996); it considers elite contestation as a minimal necessary condition for democracy. Although modern theorists criticized 'electoralism' (Diamond, 1999) due to its insufficiency for democracy, one cannot deny that democracy without the electoral contest of elites is impossible. This critique is also relevant for Russia, because of its rather mixed record of democratization, or even 'electoral authoritarianism' (Fish, 2001). The elitist democracy in Russia is still highly fragile and vulnerable due to serious obstacles from both the demand and supply side of elite politics. As to the supply side, the institutional constraints of elitist democracy are still weak and inefficient. These weaknesses have been observed during the period of Yeltsin's presidency (Shevtsova, 1999; McFaul, 2001). But after the unexpected rise of the previously virtually unknown Vladimir Putin to presidency in 1999–2000, Russia is probably even further away from a liberal democracy. New challenges to democratic developments in Russia have appeared to stem from a more centralized leadership.

Russian elites under Putin used a similar set of institutions to that installed under Yeltsin but for different purposes: not for the destruction of the Communist regime, but for stabilization of the new order. Thus, Russia seems to have entered a period where elite relations have become relatively peaceful. Despite the fact that the trend towards centralization of elite politics contributed to their integration after more than a decade of hyper-fragmentation (see Higley *et al.*, in this volume), the democratic nature of this reintegration process casts some doubts. The attempts of elites to avoid electoral contestation both on a national level (see Gel'man, in this volume) and a regional level (see Tarusina, in this volume), the underdevelopment of political parties, especially in the provinces (see Golosov, in this volume), and the questionable merits of the restoration of federal control over regional and local politics (see Blakkisrud, in this volume), are evident. In fact, while in the early 1990s the fragmentation of elites and collapse of Soviet institutions resulted in 'feckless pluralism' of elite politics, after 2000 the integration of Russian elites accompanied by the recentralization of the institutional framework could easily return to 'dominant power' elite politics (Carothers, 2002).

From the perspective of the demand side of elite politics in Russia the situation is even more complicated. The political culture of post-Soviet elites relied heavily on the Soviet legacy, especially due to the persistence of members of former nomenklatura, who inherited attitudes and values from the Communist period (see, for example, Duka, in this volume; Hughes and John, in this volume). No wonder that their commitments are still rather illiberal, authoritarian and anti-Western. The rise of military and security elites in Russia under Putin could probably enhance this trend. On the other hand, the generational change of Russian elites has changed this gloomy picture toward more positive elites' perceptions of democracy and market economy (see Hughes and John, in this volume) as well as of cooperation with the Western countries. In fact, the elite turnover in the long run would gradually lead to the rise of young, urban-born, better educated, more internationally open elites to the apex of decision-making processes in Russia. But as yet, the uneven constellation of old and new elites in Russia is also accompanied by the uneven mixture of the orientation of elites toward major political issues, such as political regime, state, economy and international relations.

The picture presented in the recent study of Steen (2002), based on two extensive surveys of Russian elites, clearly illustrates some controversies from the demand side of the elite politics in Russia. The Russian elites do not deny the basic principles of democracy and market economy (like universal electoral suffrage or individual competition), but they are more sceptical about their major institutions (like the multi-party system and private ownership). In fact, Russian elites, both national and regional, are oriented towards state regulation as the major solution to economic and societal issues (such as income difference and welfare) and are less likely to leave such issues to market forces. Duka in his study (in this volume) observed similar orientations among St Petersburg elites, which are commonly considered as a liberal vanguard of Russia as a whole.

This mixed demand of elites is probably not surprising after ten years of output decline, high inflation and the collapse of the national currency. Consequently there are solid grounds for accepting the statement of Lane (2000), who views the future of Russian capitalism as a state-led hierarchically organized corporatism. Due to the general low level of inter-elite trust, the Russian elites put their trust in a 'strong' leader. Russian elites also have confidence in the state but are very sceptical about societal institutions (see Steen, in this volume). These demands have an impact on the elites' behaviour, instigating a principal U-turn toward the recentralization of government in Russia in the early 2000s (see Blakkisrud, in this volume), which was enthusiastically adopted by most of national elites (see Steen and Timofeev, in this volume).

The complicated combination of incentives provided by demand and supply sides of elite politics in Russia challenged a nascent elitist democracy, which is faced with a 'dilemma of leadership' (Roeder, 1994). While elites desperately need a strong leader in order to overcome current multiple crises or prevent future ones, they are also aware of the threats that this leader poses. The consequences of post-Communist attempts of Russian elites to solve such a dilemma are contradictory for democratic development. In Yeltsin's period, the solution was found on a basis of patron/client relationships at the expense of the decline of state capacity and the undermining of the rule of law (Shevtsova, 1999). In Putin's period, the solution through the 'imposed consensus' (see Gel'man, in this volume) could restore state capacity at the expense of democratic contest and political pluralism. In this respect it is unclear if the elitist democracy in Russia has become a device to preserve authoritarian elite politics while also institutionalizing democratic rule. Our main question is how such institutionalized uncertainties, as Przeworski (1991) argues are the main feature of democratic rule, have influenced the elites' ability not only to negotiate viable settlements but also to strengthen and deepen Russian democracy.

The research issues and the structure of the book

Two major challenges of Russian politics have caught the attention of the authors of this book. The first is democratization. Without doubt, a few top leaders initiated the transition from authoritarian rule to elitist democracy while democratic performance must be safeguarded by the broad national and regional elites. One main question in post-Communist Russia is how these elites may contribute to stable and pluralist democracy. The second is the impact of the reorganized federation, which brought more autonomy to regional and local elites, although under Putin central elites are pulling them back to centralized control. These crucial issues cause many problems for the Russian state, but simultaneously they open unique opportunities for social scientists to study the role of elites in societies undergoing a democratization process.

The questions are manifold: How did Russian elites, old and new, react on challenges of democratization and decentralization? Why was former Soviet nomenklatura unable either to transform itself or restore its capacities? What kind of values and attitudes shape principal choices of elites? And how did they affect the elite's practices and policies? Why did intra-elite conflicts occur in Russia, and how (and why) were they resolved? Which models of elite/mass linkages have emerged within the framework of electoral contestation? These and other issues are at the centre of attention in the chapters of this volume.

The authors from Britain, Norway, Russia and the United States present different and sometimes contending approaches, focusing on major aspects of elites and democratic development in Russia. The chapters employ various theoretical frameworks and offer perspectives of comparative analysis as well as several case studies from various Russian regions.

The chapter by John Higley, Oksan Bayulgen and Julie George considers transformation of Russian elites in a broad theoretical perspective. They link two major characteristics of elites, such as 'integration' and 'differentiation', with the corresponding types of political regimes. According to them, contemporary Russia turned from a monolith elite under Communist rule to 'fragmented' elites in the post-Communist period. This type of elite transformation is correlated with the emergence of an unstable representative regime, at least until Boris Yeltsin's resignation as President. This framework for analysis echoes in the following chapters.

Vladimir Gel'man, in his contribution, compares intra-elite conflicts and their outcomes based on case studies of the regional elite in Nizhnii Novgorod Oblast and the national elite in Russia. His conclusion is that the consequences of elite integration through 'settlements' may serve not only as a means of further democratization, but also as an obstacle towards it. A somewhat different pattern was found by Inessa Tarusina's analysis of elite changes in Tomsk Oblast where the fragmented political and business elites failed to achieve stability. Under conditions of economic crises their temporary compromises were easily replaced by new cycles of conflicts.

Other authors focus on the elite's orientations. Anton Steen examines one of the core questions of elite integration: how unified is the elite regarding confidence in political and societal institutions, and to what extent do the elite trust each other? Surveys of national and regional political, administrative and economic elites show that confidence in major political institutions like the State Duma and Federation Council, and in the President after 2000, is on a high level, while confidence is very low for societal institutions, such as private business and political parties. Further, the elite expresses little interpersonal trust. Following a decade of chaos and elite controversies, the elite now support a stronger state, which is needed to bring the fragmented society, and themselves(!), back to order. The implications are obvious: the new Russian elite consensus is as much self-imposed among national and regional elites as imposed from the top.

The chapter by Helge Blakkisrud is devoted to how institutional changes, elite bargaining and patron/client relationships may explain the changing status and political role of the regional governors in the turbulent years of the 1990s, and 2000s, after President Yeltsin's era was over. The process of regional reforms in Russia, however, is not finished yet, and Putin's attempts to transform the legal, political and economic power of regional elites are crucial for democratic developments across Russia's regions.

However, the Russian Constitution prescribes the responsibilities between central and regional government only in general terms. The actual balance between the levels of government may be seen as an ongoing 'federal bargain' between national and regional elites. Anton Steen and Vsevolod Timofeev analyse the attitudes of the State Duma deputies to the centre/regional relations. Although the major appreciation of recentralization of power among Russia's legislators is obvious, they are divided between support for a strong executive, yet also simultaneously express positive attitudes towards delegation of power to the regions.

The chapter by Alexandr Duka, based on a survey of St Petersburg and Leningrad Oblast elites, sheds additional light on controversies of political culture of Russia's elites who expressed critical views on westernization and marketization of the country. But the Russian elites, both national and regional, are not unified, and age differences, as well as nomenklatura background, have crucial importance for their attitudes, as Duka explicitly suggests. James Hughes and Peter John, who analyse elite transformation in the city of Novosibirsk, present a similar picture. The gradual replacement of the former members of the nomenklatura with new elite cohorts, which is more visible in business than in politics and government, is inevitably changing the elite orientations towards more pro-market attitudes.

In his study of performance of political parties in regional legislative elections, Grigorii Golosov shows the negligible and declining role of the parties in this process with severe implications for democratization. He focuses on institutional incentives for party formation and party affiliation, which were rather insignificant for elites over the decade of formation of regional party systems in Russia. The lack of stable partisanship among regional elites creates problems for democratic linkages, both between national and regional elites and on the elite/mass level. However, Golosov expresses some hopes about the reform of regional electoral systems, which were initiated by national elites as a major tool for promotion of national political parties.

Finally, Gel'man and Tarusina present a state-of-the-art review with analysis of the emerging field of studies of elites in Russian social science. They highlight achievements and shortcomings of major research institutions and projects, assess some findings and discuss problems and obstacles of the development of elite research in Russia. Gel'man and Tarusina pay special attention to the issue of research connections and possible integration between studies of Russian elites and broader theoretical and comparative perspectives of studies of elites and democratization. This integration has a great research potential, as Burton and Higley (2001) suggest, and most chapters in this volume are oriented to this kind of analysis.

Of course, it is impossible to provide definitive answers to the numerous research questions regarding Russia's elites and democratic development in a single seminar volume. This task has only been touched upon here. But we are confident that with the collective efforts of international and Russian academic communities one may provide at least some informed answers that enable us to better understand the prospects for a viable balance between democracy and political stability in Russia. We hope that this book might be one step toward this goal.

References

Burton, M. and Higley, J. (2001) The Study of Political Elite Transformations. *International Review of Sociology*, Vol. 11, No. 2, pp. 181–199.

Carothers, T. (2002) The End of the Transition Paradigm. *Journal of Democracy*, Vol. 13, No. 1, pp. 5–21.

Dahl, R. (1961) *Who Governs? Democracy and Power in an American City*. New Haven and London: Yale University Press.

Dahl, R. (1971) *Polyarchy: Participation and Opposition*. New Haven and London: Yale University Press.

Diamond, L. (1999) *Developing Democracy: Toward Consolidation*. Baltimore and London: Johns Hopkins University Press.

Fish, M.S. (2001) *Authoritarianism Despite Elections: Russia in Light of Democratic Theory and Comparative Practice*. Paper prepared for delivery at the APSA annual meeting, San Francisco.

Held, D. (1996) *Models of Democracy*. Cambridge: Polity Press.

Kryshtanovskaya, O., and White, S. (1996) From Soviet Nomenklatura to Russian Elite. *Europe-Asia Studies*, Vol. 48, No. 5, pp. 711–733.

Lane, D. (2000) What Kind of Capitalism for Russia? A Comparative Analysis. *Communist and Post-Communist Studies*, Vol. 33, No. 4, pp. 485–504.

Lane, D., and Ross, C. (1999) *The Transition from Communism to Capitalism: Ruling Elites from Gorbachev to Yeltsin*. New York, St Martin's Press.

McFaul, M. (2001) *Russia's Unfinished Revolution: Political Change from Gorbachev to Putin*. Ithaca, NY and London: Cornell University Press.

Offe, C. (1991) Capitalism by Democratic Design? Democratic Theory Facing the Triple Transition in East Central Europe. *Social Research*, Vol. 58, No. 4, pp. 865–892.

Przeworski, A. (1991) *Democracy and the Market: Political and Economic Reforms in Eastern Europe and Latin America*. Cambridge: Cambridge University Press.

Roeder, P. (1994) Varieties of Post-Soviet Authoritarian Regimes. *Post-Soviet Affairs*, Vol. 10, No. 1, pp. 61–101.

Schumpeter, J. (1947) *Capitalism, Socialism, and Democracy*. New York: Harper and Row.

Shevtsova, L. (1999) *Yeltsin's Russia: Myths and Reality*. Washington, DC: Carnegie Endowment for International Peace.

Steen, A. (2002) The Post-Communist Transformation: Elite Orientations and the Emerging Russian State. *Perspectives on European Politics and Society*, Vol. 3, No. 1, pp. 93–126.

Wasilewski, J. (1998) Hungary, Poland and Russia: The Fate of Nomenklatura Elites, in M. Dogan and J. Higley (eds) *Elites, Crises and Origins of Regimes*. Lanham, MD: Rowman and Littlefield, pp. 147–167.

2 Political elite integration and differentiation in Russia

John Higley, Oksan Bayulgen and Julie George

Introduction

Most lasting democratizations have originated in deliberate and sudden compromises of core disputes among political elites – in 'elite settlements' (Higley and Burton, 1998, 2000). Such settlements lay the basis for elite consensus about the worth of governmental and other institutions, and they create shared codes and rules for restrained political competitions. In this way, elite settlements tame politics, which is the *sine qua non* for lasting democratization. For a settlement to occur, however, there must be a long experience of costly but inconclusive elite conflict, an abrupt political crisis that threatens to enflame this conflict, inter-elite negotiations aimed at defusing the immediate crisis and avoiding future ones through compromises on basic issues, as well as authoritative and skilled leaders who can get allies and supporters to accept such compromises.

Most observers of Russian politics since 1991 agree, we believe, that no elite settlement has occurred and no basically consensual, power-sharing elite configuration has so far emerged. Accordingly, Russia's new democracy is still at risk. But different reasons for why this is so are given. In one view, excessive elite integration, which is a residue of the Soviet state socialist period, prevents any substantial autonomy and voluntary accommodation among main elite groups. Populated heavily by holdover personnel from the old Soviet elite, most Russian elites remain tied to, and dependent upon, the State. Because of this dependence, the elites have few autonomous power resources with which to check and balance each other and the state. Until this situation changes and elites become more autonomous and separately powerful, a 'demo-elite' formation that would tame Russian politics and stabilize the democratic regime will not emerge (Etzioni-Halevy, 1993).

In a second and diametrically opposing view, excessive elite differentiation and conflict, bordering on the chaotic, militates against elite accommodation and consensus and, thus, against stable democracy. Business and parastatal elites constantly seek to undermine each other (as in the 'bankers war' during 1997); party elites squabble incessantly and their parties are mostly short-lived; military and state security elites are internally divided; powerful provincial governors and regional elites go their separate ways; trade union and agricultural elites lobby strenuously for their conflicting interests; the autonomy and effectiveness of important state agencies like the Central Bank are uncertain; media elites are harassed and shrill; the resurgent Orthodox Church is a political wild card; and there are organized and powerful criminal groups that lie beyond anyone's control. All of these elites struggle with each other to control the assets of a 'soft state' that is largely unable to enforce its laws and decrees (Remington, 1997). What is needed is more, not less, elite integration, and this can be achieved only through a strengthened national state that creates a clearer hierarchy of elites and restores order to Russian politics.

We argue that the extent and character of political elite integration and differentiation are the key research questions about Russian politics today. Whether there is too much or too little integration and differentiation, and how each is likely to change, are crucial issues. We begin with an analytical framework in which to address them. We then assess recent English-language analyses that bear on Russian elite integration and differentiation. We conclude with a discussion of where the elites may be headed in these respects. Throughout, we highlight puzzles for further research and analysis.

Elite integration and differentiation

Political elites are the several thousand persons in a country the size of Russia who hold top positions in large or otherwise powerful organizations and movements and who participate in or directly influence national political decision-making. They include not only the familiar 'power elite' triumvirate of top business, government and military leaders, but also top position holders in parties, professional associations, trade unions, media, interest groups, religious, and other powerful and hierarchically structured organizations and sociopolitical movements. It is plausible to presume that all such persons participate in or directly influence national political decisions, even if some do so mainly by blocking or countering decisions. Put most simply, political elites are those persons who have the *organized capacity* to make real political trouble.

The key variables in the structure and functioning of political elites are the extent of their integration and differentiation. Integration is extensive when there are inclusive formal and informal networks that tie elites together and give them access to the most important decision-makers. Integration is also extensive when there is a political *modus operandi* and set of game rules about which elites agree and to which they adhere in their competitions. Differentiation is extensive when elites are organizationally diversified, functionally specialized, and have relative autonomy from each other and from the state – in a word, when they are significantly plural.

Four basic types of political elites can be distinguished according to the extent of their integration and differentiation.

Strong integration and wide differentiation

Elites are enmeshed in dense and interlocked networks that cut across factional and sector boundaries and provide connections and access to key decision-makers. There is a rough consensus about the rules and codes of political competition and behavior, and over time this creates an ethos of restrained partisanship and a tamed politics. That is, elites recognize each other as legitimate players in the political game, they generally regard their competitions as positive-sum bargaining exercises, and they cooperate, often tacitly, to contain or avoid explosive issues and conflicts. Although usually well institutionalized, the integration of elites is at base voluntary, so that we may speak of an elite united through consensus – a *consensual elite*.

Strong integration and narrow differentiation

Elites belong to a single and strongly centralized party or movement that controls the state and constitutes a semi-formal but inclusive hierarchy of elite authority. A far-flung network structure radiates out from this hierarchy, with those who are uppermost in it being the network's central nodes. Elites publicly and uniformly profess allegiance to the ideology, religious doctrine, or ethnic creed with which the party or movement justifies its power monopoly. Common membership in the party or movement, the encompassing but centralized network that it constitutes, and the uniform profession of the party or movement's belief system allow little real organizational diversity, functional specialization, or autonomy. We may again speak of a united elite but this time on the basis of an enforced ideocratic system – an *ideocratic elite*.

Weak integration and wide differentiation

Elites are arrayed across numerous competing and conflicting factions and functional domains. Networks of contact and access do not cut across these factions and domains in any dense and interlocked way. There is no underlying consensus on political codes and game rules, nor is there a single hierarchy of elite authority. Instead, elites are deeply opposed in their beliefs and goals, which they often pursue in an unrestrained manner. However, elite pluralism is great enough to prevent any one faction or coalition from gaining assured power over all others. We may thus speak of an elite that is disunited and badly fragmented – a *fragmented elite*.

Weak integration and narrow differentiation

Elites are clustered in two or three distinct and well-organized camps, each of which is fundamentally opposed to the other(s). Networks do not cross camp boundaries and there is no game-rule consensus or single belief system to restrain elite competitions. Even more than in a fragmented elite, power struggles have a no-holds-barred, violent character. At any given time, and perhaps for a long period, one camp is ascendant and it uses the state apparatus and its own coercive forces to repress opponents, though, unlike in an ideocratic elite, opponents are clearly visible and they actively seek, often from underground or exile, to destroy the ascendant camp. We may speak of a disunited elite in which two or three camps confront each other across deep divisions – a *divided elite*.

Each of these four political elite types creates a distinctive type of political regime, defined as the patterns by which government executive power is *actually* organized, exercised and transferred (irrespective of what a constitution, charter or set of foundational laws stipulates). Two considerations lead us to distinguish types of regimes according to criteria other than their democratic or non-democratic character. The first is that regimes are structures of power and no known type embodies 'democracy', which we regard as more a normative than an analytical concept. The second is the morass of adjectives and diminished subtypes that bedevil distinctions among regimes that are labeled 'democratic' (Collier and Levitsky, 1997). Wanting to skirt these problems, we simply distinguish regimes according to whether and how the political elites in them do or do not have *mutual access* to the organization, exercise and transfer of government power. In some regimes elites compete for and take turns dominating one or another kind of representative body that is the basis of executive power. In other regimes one elite faction or camp monopolizes access so that there is no important representative body and, therefore, no serious competition to dominate it. We label the former type of regime *representative* and the latter *unrepresentative*. Among both types, we further distinguish regimes that are *stable* from those that are *unstable*, as indicated by the recent occurrence or widely expected occurrence of irregular seizures of government executive power by force.

The twin typologies of political elites and political regimes that we propose are charted in Table 2.1.

Annotating Table 2.1, a *consensual elite* creates a *stable representative regime* in which government power is centered in some representative body and transferred from one faction to another through regular competitions for electoral support. Irregular seizures of power by force are recently unknown and not widely expected. However, the extent to which elite competitions for electoral support are open to all citizens and devoid of manipulative practices varies widely over time. An *ideocratic elite* creates

Table 2.1 Types of political elites and the regime types they create

		Elite integration	
		Strong	Weak
Elite differentiation	Wide	Consensual elite Stable representative regime	Fragmented elite Unstable representative regime
	Narrow	Ideocratic elite Stable unrepresentative regime	Divided elite Unstable unrepresentative regime

a *stable unrepresentative regime* in which a single party or movement monopolizes power, so that power exercises and transfers involve jockeying for position within the party or movement's uppermost body. Because of the party or movement's crushing dominance, overt seizures of government power by force have not recently occurred and are not widely expected. A *fragmented elite* creates an *unstable representative regime* in which power is at least partly located in a representative body and transferred between factions according to competitions for electoral support. However, the absence of agreed elite game rules and the multiplicity of conflicting factions that typify elite fragmentation mean that the representative body is frequently circumvented, electoral competitions display much chicanery and fraud, and an irregular and forcible seizure of executive power, whether by an executive coup or an open one, has recently occurred or is widely regarded as likely. Finally, a *divided elite* creates an *unstable unrepresentative regime* in which power is centered in and transferred irregularly among the members of an ascendant camp or family dynasty so long as opponents are harshly repressed and kept on the run.

Our thesis is that the Soviet political elite long approximated the narrowly differentiated and strongly integrated ideocratic type, with a stable but thoroughly unrepresentative regime being its principal creation. During the 1970s and early 1980s this elite-regime configuration gradually changed as elite differentiation increased. Gorbachev's reforms after 1985 were aimed, *inter alia*, at institutionalizing this increased differentiation without undermining elite integration, though in this respect his reforms ultimately failed. During 1990–1991, elite differentiation, mainly in the form of autonomy-seeking regional and republic elites, together with bitter ideological conflicts between CPSU 'hard-liners' and 'soft-liners' and the emergence of relatively powerful anti-Communist movements, destroyed elite integration. Consequently, the Soviet Union's collapse during the last months of 1991 gave rise, in Russia, to political elites of the fragmented type: weakly integrated but widely differentiated. They constructed an unstable and loosely representative regime. However, new insights about Soviet elite integration and differentiation are offered by several recent studies, and the debate over how best to conceive the Soviet elite's downfall continues. It is, therefore, useful to revisit briefly the changing configuration of elites during the Soviet period.

An ideocratic elite and a stable unrepresentative regime

The Soviet political elite's dominant feature was its ideocratic uniformity. Drawn exclusively from members of the Communist Party, the elite did not permit competition by other parties or organizations. Under the CPSU's anti-factionalism rule, moreover, no internal differentiation of the Party elite, other than that corresponding to administrative/territorial divisions, was tolerated. The political elite was undivided, committed to one ideocratic belief system, and had but a single interest – to maintain its power. Consistent with its mono-organizational base, the elite was arrayed in a seamless and strict hierarchy that ran from the Party's top leadership directly down to regional and local actors. Decision-making was highly centralized, and the autonomy of elite groups below the highest Party-state leadership was sharply limited. The control of higher officials by the top leadership was secured through the nomenklatura system of elite recruitment and appointments, which made officials at each organizational level directly dependent on those above them. Elite hierarchy and centralization were sustained by the Party's behavioral norms, which were inculcated through intensive ideological indoctrination and socialization. Commitment to the Party's values and behavioral code was exhibited through unquestioning obedience, self-sacrifice, and, particularly during the Soviet Union's early decades, a revolutionary élan and a constructed 'revolutionary elite' self-identity (Easter, 2000).

Although to outside observers the elite's uniformity seemed complete, it always masked much mistrust among key position-holders. Hidden from public view, elite power struggles frequently approximated a zero-sum game in which competition was non-iterative: winners won everything, losers lost all and were destroyed or permanently expelled from politics. Elite insecurity was, thus, deep and pervasive. The top Party elite's reliance on hierarchy and fear to control lower-level elites and cadres produced unintended behavioral consequences. Lower elites and cadres created informal circles of camaraderie and patronage to shield themselves from high Party authorities, carve out personal domains relatively immune from central control, and compete with other mid-level actors for higher positions. A 'formalized informalism' – in which social proximity to key leaders was the route to power – developed (Kullberg et al., 1998: 111). The prevalence of these behaviors and norms fostered corruption, and this undermined state socialism's performance, especially in economic matters.

In a study that breaks new ground in the analysis of Soviet elite structure, Gerald Easter (2000) focuses on Provincial Komitetchiki (PK) leaders to examine changing relations between regional and center elites. During the crucial decade between the mid-1920s and mid-1930s, PK leaders controlled the Soviet Union's major agricultural and grain-producing regions, and they were charged with the task of developing the state's capacity for territorial administration. They led the campaigns for collectivization and provided the state with the means for extracting revenues from the countryside. In short, they were the main link between the central state and the territorial political/administrative apparatus.

Easter has investigated the networks of personal influence and dominance among PK elites, and his main finding is that these had a distinct 'outward' structure. Instead of being confined to each Soviet region, the PK networks were cross-regional and their core members (nodes) were located in the center, in Moscow. The outward PK networks thus constituted an informal structure for coordinating the allocation of resources and for administration, and in these respects they were the principal means by which the Soviet state secured control of its vast territories. Translated into our terms, the networks that Easter traces were the mechanism that enabled the Soviet political elite to become strongly integrated and to construct a stable but unrepresentative regime.

While Easter's study sheds much light on how the ideocratic Soviet elite was constructed, its real significance for our purposes is his thesis that, once Stalin consolidated his power in the late 1930s, the outward network structure of PK elites was eclipsed by a much more coercively centralized network that approximated bureaucratic absolutism. The political machines run by PK elites in the regions were crushed and forcibly subordinated to the center, notably in the Great Purges of 1936–1938 when most PK leaders were labeled and then liquidated as 'enemies of the people'. In place of the outward networks through which regional PK elites had oriented themselves to each other and to their key members in the center, a bureaucratically structured network now radiated outwards from the center and pervaded all regional elites. Elite status became a strict attribute of position – what Mawdsley and White (2000) call the 'job-slot system' – rather than a mark of heroic service in the revolutionary struggle and Civil War. But after Stalin's demise and after a cabal of regional and military leaders overthrew Khrushchev and put Brezhnev and his 'stability of cadres' policy into power, the informal elite networks gradually became more 'inward'. That is, regional elites entrenched themselves through patrimonial practices, over which the center exerted less and less control. During the long Brezhnev period, power flowed away from the center so that an array of personal political machines that were increasingly insular and particularistic became conspicuous in the regions – a trend that Valerie Bunce (1999) highlights in her elegant study of why and how the Soviet Union collapsed. In our terms, overall political elite integration weakened while differentiation increased.

Easter and Bunce both argue persuasively that it was these 'forces from within' (rather than forces 'from above' or 'from below') that were the primary cause of the Soviet Union's collapse. After 1985, Gorbachev tried mightily to overcome the entrenched and patrimonial regional political machines that flourished during the Brezhnev decades. He sought to impose a more centralized and rationalized bureaucratic structure – what another scholar, Robert V. Barylski (1999: 210–212), has characterized as an 'authoritarian socialist meritocracy'. Gorbachev's reforms did much damage to the patrimonial regional power structures, but he had no means with which to rebuild the networks that in the PK period had emanated outward from the regions and that were oriented cross-regionally and toward the center.

By the end of the 1980s, the results of Gorbachev's reforms were a weak central state and a chaotic array of inward-oriented and highly resentful regional elites. This was the card that Yeltsin played against Gorbachev by promising Russian regional and other Soviet republic elites still more autonomy in exchange for supporting his drive for Russian independence. 'In the end', Easter writes, 'the Soviet state lacked the capacity to stave off its own territorial demise . . . [T]he diffusion of power along informal lines was a precondition of state collapse' (Easter, 2000: 170; see also Barylski, 1999 and Bunce, 1999).

It is important to note that Easter's network explanation of why and how Soviet elite integration weakened and, therefore, of why the collapse occurred is not supported by data. It is, instead, a plausible conjecture by Easter, whose data on networks cover only the PK elites during the Soviet Union's early years. Whether there is solid evidence for his thesis that 'inward' rather than 'outward' networks came to the fore under Brezhnev and became even more pronounced under Gorbachev is an open research question. To answer it, an investigation of Party and government communications between the center and regions during the Brezhnev and Gorbachev years would be necessary. Nevertheless, Easter's thesis strikes us as highly plausible, and it dovetails with our conceptualization of how strong or weak integration and wide or narrow differentiation shape basic types of political elites and the kind of regime each type creates.

To summarize, the postrevolutionary elite self-identities and the outward networks of PK leaders were crucial to the formation of the ideocratic Soviet elite and the stable unrepresentative Soviet regime. After the Stalinist interlude, which entailed erasure of the PK leaders as a self-identified postrevolutionary elite, the 'licensing' of elite status through the nomenklatura system, plus the gradual shift of networks from outward to inward, eroded the elite's ideocratic features, and weakened the state's capacity to control the regions. This moved the elite configuration toward the fragmented type (weakly integrated but widely differentiated), which in turn created an unstable though more or less representative regime that has been 'democratic' in form and to some extent practice, but with irregular power seizures still being regarded as distinct possibilities.

That Soviet-Russian elites moved from the ideocratic to the fragmented type concomitant with the Soviet Union's collapse is disputed by some scholars. For example, David Lane and Cameron Ross (1999) argue that by the 1980s the Soviet elite was already more weakly integrated and widely differentiated than is compatible with the ideocratic type. Lane and Ross speak of a 'segmented' Soviet elite in which the several bureaucratic entities of both Party and state were substantially autonomous from each other as a consequence of growing economic and societal complexity. They claim that 'departmentalism' and corruption spread through Soviet structures during the 1970s and 1980s and stemmed from the operational independence of functionally defined elite groups and power hierarchies. Lane and Ross thus raise the possibility that the Soviet-Russian elite displayed a fragmented configuration well before the elite and regime collapse in 1990–1991. It must be asked, however, just what 'bureaucratic autonomy' meant in the Soviet system, even during its last years, because personal wealth and power continued to depend upon one's status in the Party and its 'job-slot' system. In other words, it was precisely the *lack* of autonomy from Party control that fueled the drive for an 'elite emancipation' that destroyed the regime. As Barylski phrases this thesis:

> The Communist Party's national development strategy created a Soviet managerial and administrative elite, but it denied Soviet elites the type of personal autonomy and security that comes from owning and controlling assets and from living under a system of limited government. Elite emancipation required that the elite privatize economic assets and break the Communist Party's ability to deprive it of those gains. Many Soviet professionals were angry that their country's institutional structures and practices – *their system* – encouraged and supported the idea of systemic reconstruction, which is precisely what the Russian term *perestroika* means. Gorbachev gave hope that such a future could be attained and he broke through the main barriers that had been blocking progressive reformation. However, Gorbachev was stymied by his deep personal commitment to preserving the Soviet Union and reforming its one-party system, instead of jettisoning it altogether.
> (Barylski, 1999: 227, italics in original)

The claim by Lane and Ross that elite fragmentation predated the Soviet Union's collapse by a good ten years is also thrown into doubt by a new and exhaustive study of the entire CPSU Central Committee membership – some 1,932 persons – from 1917 to 1991. In this study, Evan Mawdsley and Stephen White (2000) show that although Gorbachev engineered a significant turnover in the Central Committee's makeup in March 1986 (45 percent new members and candidate members), he did not equal the 53 percent turnover that occurred at the postwar Party Congress in 1952 – the first Congress since 1939 and one that reflected the tremendous personnel changes wrought by the war, Stalin's repressive apparatus, and the sheer passage of time – or the 50 percent turnover that was achieved by

Khruschev in 1961. Under Gorbachev and at the highest Party level, in other words, elite persistence still outweighed elite change so that 'the Central Committee was able almost to the end to retain its position as the locus of moral authority within the Party, and as a community of influentials among whom it might hope to rediscover a sense of purpose' (Mawdsley and White, 2000: 239).

Mawdsley and White likewise show that CPSU membership did not undergo serious decline until the start of 1990, and that internal disputes and discontents did not surface publicly until the 28th Party Congress in July of that year. They argue that it was only at the July 1990 Congress that the Central Committee elite began to disintegrate, with 88 percent of its members and candidate members being 'new faces' and with a series of resignations and expulsions from the Central Committee beginning six months later, in January 1991. Through research in newly opened CPSU archives, moreover, Stephen White (1994) has established that expressions of discontent by middle-echelon CPSU officials became a drumbeat only during the year that followed the 28th Congress. Mawdsley and White (2000: 237) conclude that the Central Committee elite was 'losing its cohesion' during the twelve-month period that started with the Committee's massive turnover in July 1990, that this loss continued with a series of highly confrontational meetings during the rest of 1990 and the first half of 1991, and that it culminated in the Committee's last plenum in July 1991 and the August State coup that came a few weeks later.

A fragmented elite and an unstable representative regime

Elite transformations are such basic and complex processes that it is silly to think of them as happening on a given day or in a few weeks. In our view, the Soviet-Russian elite transformation began in mid-1990 and it unfolded over the following year and a half. The failed state coup in August 1991 was the point of no return. It triggered the well-known series of events that led, over the next four months, to the Soviet Union's collapse: Ukraine's immediate declaration of independence, suspension of the CPRF, the Party's banning three months later and the peremptory (apparently drunken) 'pact' of early December, in which Yeltsin and the Party leaders of Belarus and Ukraine agreed on the USSR's dissolution.

In the years since, scholars have exhibited much uncertainty about just what type of elite and regime has emerged in Russia. One reason for this uncertainty is the lack of an agreed typology of elites and associated regimes, such as we have outlined. But another reason has been the striking 'reproduction' of Soviet-era elites in post-Soviet Russia. With little or no evidence that a sweeping elite circulation has occurred, most scholars have been reluctant to speak of a new type of elite in Russia. They have instead engaged in a major research effort and debate about the actual extent of elite circulation or reproduction from the Gorbachev to the Yeltsin years. The main findings, as well as their disputed interpretation, are well summarized by Mawdsley and White (2000: 288–302; among pertinent English-language publications, see also Higley *et al.*, 1998; Gill, 1998; Wasilewski, 1998; White and Kryshtanovsksaya, 1998; Lane and Ross, 1999; Shlapentokh *et al.*, 1999).

The research and debate about elite turnover since 1991 do not need to be rehearsed here. It is sufficient to mention the conclusion of Mawdsley and White that change in Russian elite composition was more 'partial' than in the Czech Republic, Hungary and Poland. Specifically, 'The leading figures in Russia's post-Communist politics had often, even typically, been members of the Gorbachev nomenklatura; at the same time their views and affiliations had changed, and their position was now dependent on a popular mandate rather than the directives of a monopolistic party' (Mawdsley and White, 2000: 300–301).

It is possible that too many research resources have been expended studying Russian elite circulation and reproduction during the past dozen years. The more important questions are about the attitudes, networks and actions of elites that have found themselves in entirely new circumstances. Research on elite attitudes has, of course, been a cottage industry, one not much smaller than that on elite circulation and reproduction. Gel'man and Tarusina (in this volume) discuss many of the survey studies that have been conducted, mainly by Russian scholars. While we have by no means dug through the mountain of data that these surveys have produced, the ones we have seen leave us with two impressions. First, the questions typically asked are either too policy-specific or too doctrinal/philosophical in nature to reveal much about elite integration and differentiation. Second, the brevity and simplicity of most surveys, in which forced-choice questions of the 'agree/disagree' and 'too much/not enough' kind have been the standard technique, have vitiated the surveys' value. On the other hand, where less structured and more in-depth interview studies have been conducted, small N's and highly diverse responses have prevented confident generalization.

As regards the study of Russian elite networks and modes of interaction, our impression is that research is still in its infancy. Gel'man (1999) has taken a solid first step by studying the differing interaction patterns among four of Russia's most important regions. In a recent study of interactions between the oil elite and the Russian state, David Lane (2000) charts the existence of considerable mutual elite hostility and suspicion. A recent book by Anton Steen (2003: Chapter 8), whose two-wave survey of Russian elites in 1998 and 2000 promises to shed much light on their networks and interactions, sketches a network structure that accords, at least broadly, with our thesis of fragmentation.

Judgments about the type of elite that existed in Russia after 1991 have thus had to rest, in the main, on inferring the extent of integration and differentiation from elite actions and political events. A new assessment of these during the 1990s, by Graeme Gill and Roger Marvick (2000), helps considerably. They argue that an initial but fragile elite unity, which was probably based more in a negative consensus about the Soviet past than in a common view of the post-Soviet future, was shattered by the Yeltsin government's 'shock therapy' economic policies during 1992 and early 1993. These turned elites that were based in the Supreme Soviet and Congress of Deputies against the president, creating a deep division between those who favored a presidential and those who wanted a parliamentary form of government. Seeing the parliamentary elite camp as an obstacle to rapid marketization and economic growth, Yeltsin and the presidential camp sought hegemony. They prevailed by force in the October 1993 crisis and in the dubiously legal constitutional referendum that adopted a strong presidential form of government two months later.

After the dramatic 1993 events, the axis of elite power struggles shifted. Whereas the main struggle was earlier over the new Russian government's form, struggles now took place within the presidential and government apparatuses themselves, fueled by economic disputes and needs. The presidential apparatus wanted to pursue strict monetarist policies accompanied by voucher privatization; most of the so-called 'branch ministries' (for example, in the energy and communications sectors) wanted a less harsh monetary regime, greater protection of domestic industries, and the promotion of large financial/industrial conglomerates.

These post-1993 struggles among governmental elites were paralleled by struggles among the new business elites. Yeltsin's defeat of the parliamentary elite camp in 1993 amounted to the open victory of the financial and resources elites that supported him over the industrial elites that supported the parliamentary forces. Following the rouble's dramatic devaluation on 11 October 1994 ('Black Tuesday'), and, with it, the collapse of the Chernomyrdin government's anti-inflationary policies, a further struggle between banking and energy sector elites broke out. The issue was the course of privatization, and its eventual resolution was the 'loans for shares' scheme that secured Yeltsin enough backing by business elites to win the 1996 presidential election over a determined CPRF opposition.

That Russian elites formed coherent and opposing camps – and thus the divided type of elite (weakly integrated and narrowly differentiated) – must be doubted, however. The multiplicity of competing elites was too great. Al-though attention focused on Yeltsin and his 'all-powerful presidency', Yeltsin in fact presided over a greatly weakened state and he never enjoyed solid social or political support within the population. Consequently, he had no alternative but to enter into compromises with a galaxy of elite groups in order to stagger on in office. For example, Yeltsin felt compelled to repay the business oligarchs for their crucial support in the 1996 presidential election campaign by appointing two of them – Vladimir Potanin and Boris Berezovsky – to key government positions. But if Yeltsin and his presidential entourage lacked solid mass support, so did the financial and business oligarchs and all other important elites except the Communists. In one way or another, all were dependent on the Russian state's dwindling patronage and resources. This pervasive elite weakness intensified the 'clanization' of Russian politics, its corruption, and its cascading feuds and palace conspiracies. The most that can be said is that elite relations during the Yeltsin years approximated a series of moving equilibria, each of which was but another iteration in the always very tenuous dependence of weak elites on a weak state.

Nevertheless, no overtly authoritarian regime eventuated; the Yeltsin government's ability to control political and economic developments simply deteriorated. The nadir was reached in the wake of the Asian economic crisis that began in August 1997. Not only did this shrink Russia's crucial commodity export markets, but the Asian economic collapse drove the prices of oil and other commodities to unprecedented lows, with oil selling for $10 per barrel in March 1998. By August 1998, the Russian state was effectively bankrupt, unable to pay the interest on its international loans and unable to secure new loans. Stocks on the Moscow exchange had lost 80 percent of their value during the preceding ten months and the state's desperate attempts to raise revenues by auctioning shares in state-owned oil companies failed.

Increased political turbulence was the result. Yeltsin sacked Chernomyrdin and Anatoly Chubias in March 1998, replacing Chernomyrdin with the young and untested Sergei Kirienko. Unable to staunch the economic crisis, Kirienko lasted in the prime minister's office a mere five months. Yevgeny Primakov was then installed but was himself fired in March 1999, with Sergei Stepashin, the Minister of Internal Affairs, becoming prime minister. Stepahsin was in turn sacked and replaced by Vladimir Putin a few months later. However, despite this musical chairs rotation in the penultimate political position, indicators of the polarized conflict among two or three deeply opposed camps that is typical of a divided elite remained faint at best. Given the plethora of business, party, and parastatal elites competing against each other, differentiation was too great for such polarization to occur. Moreover, few of the newly 'emancipated' elites had any interest in restoring an authoritarian regime that would surely have created such polarization by choking the autonomy of financial oligarchs and regional elites and by stripping opposition Communist and other party elites of their ability to make electorally lucrative denunciations of the central government.

The main elites were thus content to allow competitive, if democratically quite blemished, elections for the Duma in December 1995 and 1999, and for the presidency in June 1996 and March 2000. Dire forecasts that the 1996 presidential election would be canceled or thoroughly rigged proved incorrect, though Yeltsin has revealed in his published memoirs that he came within an ace of canceling the election and declaring emergency rule. Together with wide elite differentiation, these nerve-wracking and precarious contests, coupled with Yeltsin's erratic behavior and the social tensions that arose from severe economic difficulties, indicated a fragmented elite configuration and an unstable representative regime.

The current direction of elite change in Russia

Can one foresee a transformation of Russian elites from the fragmented to the consensual type? In our terms, this means asking if substantially greater elite integration is on the cards. One possibility is that the severe economic and financial crisis of 1998–1999 served as a wake-up call for the principal economic and political elites. Having consolidated their privatized holdings, but having also experienced a dramatic reduction in the value of those holdings, the financial oligarchs may have recognized that greater elite cooperation and a stronger national state are necessary for economic stability. Already in April 1996, thirteen prominent oligarchs, led by Boris Berezovsky, urged political leaders to negotiate a power-sharing pact that would approximate an elite settlement: 'Russian politicians must be induced to make very substantial mutual concessions and to conclude strategic political accords and to codify them in legal form. There is simply no other way out' (Berezovsky et al., 27 April 1996, quoted by Barylski, 1999: 222). In a similar vein, upon becoming prime minister in June 1999 Stepashin met with some fifty top business and financial leaders and extracted their promise not to raise prices and to pay taxes more regularly.

Vladimir Putin also adopted such a stance when he began his widely noted meeting with twenty-one oligarchs in July 2000 by saying:

> You built this state yourself, to a great degree through the political or semi-political structures under your control. So there is no point in blaming the reflection in the mirror. So let us get down to the point and be open and do what is necessary to do to make our relationship in this field civilized and transparent.
>
> (*New York Times*, 29 July 2000)

Putin was reported to have proposed a deal whereby his government would refrain from examining the privatization processes through which the oligarchs acquired their wealth if they would refrain from further political interventions. In the last months of 2000, on the other hand, Putin and his entourage launched a criminal case against Berezovsky, who promptly left Russia, and they harried another oligarch, Vladimir Gusinsky, in an eventually successful battle to liquidate his Media Most press and television empire.

But what Putin's government intended as regards its relations with business and other elites remained uncertain. Andrei Ryabov, a scholar at the Carnegie Foundation's Moscow Centre, framed this uncertainty well: 'Yeltsin's style was feudal, but it worked. And now Putin is trying to completely change this whole relationship between the state and the elites. No one knows what the new relationship will look like' (*Financial Times*, 18 July 2000). Unlike Yeltsin, Putin enjoyed a popular mandate from voters who were less anchored in the Soviet past. Not only did he win election in the first March 2000 election round with 52.9 percent of the vote, but he also secured majorities in 84 of the 89 regions. This impressive victory marginalized various key leaders of the old 'party of power', such as Yuri Luzhkov and Yevgeni Primakov. It also enabled Putin to distance himself from a number of powerful elites and to truncate incestuous ties between oligarchs and state officials, not least in the presidential administration itself. Also unlike Yeltsin, who treated the state bureaucracy that he inherited from the Soviet period with disdain, Putin recognized that he needs a strong federal bureaucracy and he took dramatic steps to strengthen its presence in the regions. Putin also moved to establish firmer control over the military, removing half a dozen older generals and attempting to strike a better balance between the military's conventional warfare and missile branches. Most important, Putin enjoyed increased latitude of action owing to much higher prices for Russia's oil exports and the State Duma's passage of a long-awaited tax reform that enhanced state revenues.

Still, one swallow does not make a summer. We began by observing that a fundamental elite settlement has been the origin of most lasting democratizations, but that no such settlement has occurred in Russia. If we go down the checklist of conditions for settlements and the processes they entail, a Russian settlement remains unlikely. First, though conflicts between elites have been pronounced, they have been comparatively brief and not all that costly. Very nearly all elite actors have survived the conflicts and the incentive for orchestrating a basic change in elite relations is, thus, fairly weak. Second, except for the October 1993 confrontation, recurrent crises have not been of a magnitude that might trigger elite negotiations aimed at a settlement, though the 1998–1999 financial crisis was certainly a sobering experience. Third, the elites are not arrayed in two or three well-organized camps with authoritative and skilled leaders who might be able to impose a settlement on their colleagues. Fourth, there is no clear set of core disputes that involve deeply principled positions, out of which might come the basic compromises that constitute a settlement.

It is worth considering, however, that a national elite of the consensual type, giving birth to a stable democratic regime, may yet emerge through a gradual convergence of the fragmented elites. This could occur as a consequence of regular electoral competitions. Specifically, if several competing factions form a broad electoral coalition that enables them to win elections and government power repeatedly, the components of this coalition would gain assured protection from other hostile elites. Over time, successive electoral defeats and exclusion from government power might persuade the latter elites to moderate their sharply dissident and more or less anti-system stances in order to attract voters outside their customary class, ethnic or regional followings. Once this happens, the deep conflicts that mark fragmented elites would attenuate and power competitions would be confined increasingly to regular electoral contests under agreed game rules (Higley and Burton, 2000).

Is such an elite convergence underway at present in Russia? The half dozen competitive and regular national elections that have been held since 1993 would seem to go some way toward meeting the first condition for a convergence. On the other hand, the second condition, namely, a coherent party system and the formation of a winning electoral coalition has as yet been less clearly met. To be sure, the 1999 Duma election featured repeat appearances by four parties: the Communists, the Union of Right Forces, Yabloko and the Liberal Democratic Party. But the election was also preceded by the sudden and dramatic emergence of a new party, Unity, that supported Putin and that won nearly a quarter of the popular vote. Another new party, Fatherland, which Putin endorsed, took a further 8 percent.

For a convergence to occur, these new parties must each show that they are not just a flash in the pan; they or other parties must form a winning electoral coalition. The drastic federal election law that was adopted by parliament in July 2001 may help greatly in this regard because it makes the entry of new parties more difficult and it discourages the splintering of those that exist. Indeed, the readiness of the existing parties to impose the electoral law and thereby consolidate their bases of support may itself be a sign of established elites wanting to reduce fragmentation. More important still, the law tends to spur party amalgamations in order to meet its requirements for nationwide party organization. Thus, Unity has merged with the Fatherland and All Russia parties, while the Union of Right Forces has reconstituted itself as a single party. As a possible sign of things to come, the four national parties participating in the Moscow City Duma election of December 2001 put together an agreed list of candidates in order to divide the Duma's seats among themselves. These are indications that the formation of a winning coalition capable of dominating successive elections and, thereby, inducing opposing and more or less non-allegiant parties, such as the CPRF, to moderate their stances in order to compete more effectively for government power may be at hand. This would signal a graduate convergence from the fragmented to the consensual elite type.

Several additional developments lend credence to the proposition that an elite convergence may be starting. Altered relations between the presidency and parliament is one. Lilia Shevtsova (2000) has noted that where Yeltsin routinely invoked anti-Communism in his confrontations with the State Duma, Putin has instead denigrated ideological crusades and portrayed himself as willing to work with anyone, not least the CPRF. Before and after his election in March 2000, Putin consulted and cooperated with the Communists on a range of issues, from continuing the war in Chechnya to greater support for the military-industrial complex, the intelligence services, and various market and state reforms. He sought to extend his political base beyond the circle of governors, military generals, and security officials who supported him initially in order to encompass the center-right, some nationalists, and even some elements of the Communists' constituency. In response, the Communist elite moderated the hostile stance it had taken toward the Yeltsin presidency, and several of its key leaders in the Duma became willing participants in, and supporters of, the established political order. One key aspect of elite fragmentation in Russia – the struggle between Communist and anti-Communist elites – began to attenuate. Another and concomitant development has been deepening fissures within the Communist elite itself, as factions aligned with the two Gennadiis – Seleznev and Zyuganov – have increasingly squared off against each other, with the Seleznev faction arguing for a more moderate and profitable electoral posture. This movement by part of the most outspokenly dissident elite toward a pragmatic competitive position accords fully with the convergence thesis.

Finally, the Al Qaeda attacks on New York and Washington on 11 September 2001, appear to have had as deep an impact on Russian elites as on their American and West European counterparts. During the months that followed 9/11, informed commentaries on Russian political and foreign policy developments were rife with speculation that the attacks constituted a historic watershed for Russian elites, one in which they had to choose between remaining a lone actor in world affairs and joining, once and for all, the European cum Western camp. In a series of dramatic actions, Putin and his Kremlin entourage clearly chose the latter course, aligning Russia with the United States, the European Union, and, even, with its former enemy, NATO. Although some members of the foreign policy and military/security elites questioned this basic change, widespread elite opposition to Putin's actions was conspicuous by its absence. It is not far-fetched to conclude that the exogenous shock of 9/11 may have greatly spurred an elite convergence and fundamental taming of Russian politics.

References

Barylski, R.V. (1999) The Russian Case: Elite Self-Emancipation, in M. Rimanelli (ed.) *Comparative Democratization and Peaceful Change in Single-Party-Dominant Countries*. New York: St Martin's Press, pp. 201–236.

Bunce, V. (1999) *Subversive Institutions: The Design and the Destruction of Socialism and the State*. New York: Cambridge University Press.

Collier, D. and Levitsky, S. (1997) Democracy With Adjectives: Conceptual Innovation in Comparative Research. *World Politics*, Vol. 49, No. 3, pp. 430–451.

Easter, G.M. (2000) *Reconstructing the State: Personal Networks and Elite Identity in Soviet Russia*. New York: Cambridge University Press.

Etzioni-Halevy, E. (1993) *The Elite Connection*. London: Polity Press.

Gel'man, V. (1999) Regime Transition, Uncertainty and Prospects for Democratisation: The Politics of Russia's Regions in a Comparative Perspective. *Europe-Asia Studies*, Vol. 51, No. 6, pp. 939–956.

Gill, G. (ed.) (1998) *Elites and Leadership in Russian Politics*. London: Macmillan.

Gill, G. and Marvick, D. Roger (2000) *Russia's Stillborn Democracy? From Gorbachev to Yeltsin*. New York: Oxford University Press.

Higley, J. and Burton, M. (1998) Elite Settlements and the Taming of Politics. *Government and Opposition*, Vol. 33, No. 1, pp. 98–115.

Higley, J. and Burton, M. (2000) Elite Transformations in Democratization's Three Waves. Paper presented to IPSA World Congress, Québec, 2 August.

Higley, J., Pakulski, J. and Wesolowski, W. (eds) (1998) *Postcommunist Elites and Democracy in Eastern Europe*. London: Macmillan.

Kullbeg, J., Higley, J. and Pakulski, J. (1998) Elites, Institutions and Democratisation in Russia and Eastern Europe, in G. Gill (ed.) *Elites and Leadership in Russian Politics*. London: Macmillan.

Lane, D.S. (2000) Russia: The Oil Elite's Evolution, Divisions, and Outlooks, in J. Higley and G. Lengyel (eds) *Elites after State Socialism: Theories and Analysis*. Lanham MD: Rowman & Littlefield, pp. 179–198.

Lane, D.S. and Ross, C. (1999) *The Transition from Communism to Capitalism: Ruling Elites from Gorbachev to Yeltsin*. New York: St Martin's Press.

Mawdsley, E. and White, S. (2000) *The Soviet Elite from Lenin to Gorbachev: The Central Committee and its Members, 1917–1991*. London: Oxford University Press.

Remington, T.F. (1997) Democratization and the New Political Order in Russia, in K. Dawisha and B. Parrot (eds) *Democratic Changes and Authoritarian Reactions in Russia, Ukraine, Belarus, and Moldova*. New York: Cambridge University Press, pp. 125–146.

Shevstova, L. (2000) Can Electoral Autocracy Survive? *Journal of Democracy*, Vol. 11, No. 1, pp. 36–38.

Shlapentokh, V., Vanderpoll, C. and Doktorov, B. (eds) (1999) *The New Elite in Post-Communist Eastern Europe*. College Station TX: Texas A&M University Press.

Steen, A. (2003) *Political Elites and the New Russia. The Power Basis of Yeltsin's and Putin's Regimes*. London: Routledge-Curzon.

Wasilewski, J. (1998) Hungary, Poland, and Russia: The Fate of Nomenklatura Elites, in M. Dogan and J. Higley (eds) *Elites, Crises, and the Origins of Regimes*. Lanham MD: Rowman & Littlefield, pp. 147–168.

White, S. (1994) Communists and Their Party in the Late Soviet Period. *Slavonic and East European Review*, Vol. 71, No. 4, pp. 644–663.

White, S. and Kryshtanovskaya, O. (1998) Russia: Elite Continuity and Change, in M. Dogan and J. Higley (eds) *Elites, Crises, and the Origins of Regimes*. Lanham MD: Rowman & Littlefield, pp. 125–146.

3 Russia's elites in search of consensus
What kind of consolidation?

Vladimir Gel'man[1]

INTRODUCTION

It is commonly accepted that different segments of the elite are major actors in regime transition and consolidation. Most scholars of democratization believe that substantial compromises among elites is a necessary (although not the only) condition of successful 'transitions to democracy'. However, evidence from Russian politics casts some doubt on this proposition. At least, as yet, several attempts of elite consolidation on a basis of consensus have not led to successful democratization. According to the recent Freedom House survey, the rating of democratic development in Russia is similar to that of Jordan and Malaysia, and behind its neighbours Ukraine and Georgia (Karatnycky, 2002: 108–109). Thus, the study of elite interactions and their impact on transition process in Russia might be useful for understanding the limits of elitist models of democratization. The following analysis consists of three sections. In first section, I shall discuss some elements of theoretical schemes of impact of intra-elite conflict and consensus on the regime transition process as well as their application to contemporary Russia. The second section is a case study of regime transition on the level of subnational politics in Russia in Nizhnii Novgorod Oblast during 1991–1998. The final section reflects some considerations on developments of national elites in post-Soviet Russia and speculations about possible implications of Russia's experience for further analysis of the role of elites in regime transition processes.

Elite consensus: *Pro et contra*

Although the very idea that the achievement of consensus among different factions of elites is a breakthrough in the process of transition to democracy was formulated a long time ago (Rustow, 1970), the elitist concept of democratization was elaborated in the 1980s and early 1990s. The 'transitologists', who analysed the process of democratization in Latin America and Southern Europe, introduced the model of successful transition to democracy via a 'pact' between the moderate wings of the ruling elite and opposition (O'Donnell and Schmitter, 1986; Przeworski, 1991: 51–99). Almost simultaneously, elite theorists, who analysed regime transitions in a comparative-historical perspective, developed a similar concept (Field et al., 1990; Burton et al., 1992). The analysis of regime transitions by elite theorists started from a typology of political elites and corresponding political regimes. The scholars determined three ideal types of elites based on the different types of elite structure (see Field et al., 1990: 154–158):

1   'Disunified elite' characterized by a minimal level of value consensus and cooperation among elite factions in regard to existing political institutions, and by unlimited political struggle according to a zero-sum game principle. This type of elite exists in unstable political systems – both democratic and authoritarian.
2   'Consensually unified elite' characterized by value consensus and cooperation among elite factions in regard to existing political institutions in the framework of which political conflicts are carried out in a positive-sum game. This type of elite exists in stable representative regimes, 'at least nominally democratic in nature'.
3   'Ideologically unified elite' characterized by a value consensus and cooperation among elite factions with regard to existing political institutions; this cooperation is assured by the presence of a dominant elite faction: its ideology determines the character of official political discourse. This type of elite exists in stable non-representative regimes; where despite the presence of democratic institutions, political competition among elites for mass support does not exist.

According to the elitist concept, the main development trend is the transformation of elite and political systems from a disunified elite towards a consensual unified elite. In a comparative-historical perspective elite theorists make the distinction between two different models of elite transformation: long-term 'elite convergence' and short-term 'elite settlement' (Burton et al., 1992). To some extent, the 'elite settlement' model is close to the model of a 'pact'. 'Pact' as a mode of transition is based on a compromise among elite groups regarding the major political institutions (i.e. the set of formal and informal norms and rules, which constrains activities of political actors (North, 1990: 3)). A precondition for the achievement of such consensus is a conflict between elite factions that results in heavy losses for all sides. In a situation where a compromise strategy produces lower costs to the actors than does the threat of loss in the case of a force strategy, the reach of an agreement and the formation of an 'elite settlement' become the most rational choice for all actors (Marks, 1992).

Yet, the origins of the above-mentioned scheme of transitions have their roots in the deep crises of previously existing non-democratic regimes and attempts of elites to overcome such crises, minimizing their transaction costs. But the outcomes of those crises and their consequences might be quite different. Thus, scholars need to focus their attention not only on 'success stories' of 'pacts'/'elite settlements', but also on some other, relatively neglected 'stories' of elite consensus. Indeed, two partially overlapping research questions deserve to be placed on the agenda: (1) what are the consequences of elite consensus, if transitions from non-democratic regime occur by another means than 'pacts'/'elite settlements'? (2) Does achievement of consensus among elites inevitably lead to successful democratization or are other outcomes of regime change also possible?

Both of these research questions could be crucial in the application of a study of post-Soviet politics. The principal distinction of the breakdown of the Soviet regime (and of the subsequent collapse of the Soviet Union) from the 'pacts'/'elite settlements' is obvious. The Soviet regime failed in August 1991 as a result of unilateral conflict between different elite factions, resolved as a zero-sum game. In terms of typology of models of transitions, such an outcome of crisis fell into the category of 'imposition' (Karl and Schmitter, 1991: 275). With respect to the case of Russia, the following crisis in October 1993 is a repeated model of the previous crisis of 1991: the conflict between President Yeltsin and the Supreme Soviet has been resolved as a zero-sum game as well. At first glance, this experience is an explicitly demonstrated triumph of the use of force strategies by 'winners' of intra-elite conflicts. However, by mid-2002 elite dissent in Russia's national politics – at least at the behavioural level – has been significantly minimized, if not eliminated. The label of 'imposing consensus' seems to be appropriate for evaluation of such developments.

Meanwhile, in the broader perspective, the elitist concept of democratic transition is vulnerable in at least two principal points. First, based on the typology of political elite structures, one could theoretically speculate about a distinctive fourth type of elite structure. In this type the combination of two features occurs: (1) a value consensus and cooperation among elite factions in regard to existing (merely informal) political institutions, while political conflicts follow the model of a 'positive-sum game'; (2) the existence of a dominant elite faction that determines the official political discourse either through its ideology or by other means. This type of elite structure can exist under a political regime where competition among actors is restrained. William Case, for example, discovered similar characteristics of 'semi-democracy' in his analysis of elites and regimes of South-East Asian countries (Case, 1996).

Second, the elitist concept of transition almost entirely excludes the content of the 'pacts'/'elite settlements' themselves from the analysis; they are perceived only as a movement towards 'democracy by non-democratic means' (O'Donnell and Schmitter, 1986: 38). However, it remains unclear why the very concept presupposes democratic potential of 'pacts'/'elite settlements' virtually by default, despite some objections (see Przeworski, 1991: 90). What would move the elites towards democracy from the perspective of contestation and accountability, which includes the threat of their loss of power? On the contrary, the most rational decision guaranteeing preservation of the actors' power positions under conditions of 'pact' is a division of spheres of influence among the elite groups with the goal of excluding the chance of an invasion by political outsiders, i.e. non-participants of the 'pact'/'elite settlement'. In the conditions of market economy such a cartel agreement between the companies is no less common than open competition (which, by the way, is usually encouraged by the state). The metaphor 'cartel of anxiety', used by Ralf Darendorf in his critical analysis of West German elites in 1960s (Darendorf, 1967: 256), is quite typical for this kind of elite consensus, which might correspond with possible consolidation of new (certainly non-democratic) regimes. This is not the case for established democratic systems, but might be a serious challenge for so-called 'new democracies'. This is especially important for post-Soviet societies with their previous long-term record of lack of both elite differentiation and law-bounded state. Thus, one can assume that the participants of these 'pacts'/'elite settlements' find themselves interested not in democracy, but in non-competitive regimes. The analysis of deals of Mexican elites in the late 1920s (Knight, 1992), opens up alternative perspectives for assessments of political consequences of 'pacts'/'elite settlements' as an obstacle toward further democratization.

In the light of the above considerations, the practices of intra-elite relations in post-Soviet Russia might be to encourage the special interest of scholars. Various assessments of the impact of intra-elite interactions in Russia were quite controversial (for an overview, see Gel'man and Tarusina, in this volume). However, no special studies of elite consensus in Russia have been made as yet. The next parts of this chapter intended to fill this gap, looking first at subnational political developments, and then at national elites under Yeltsin and Putin. One could say that any consideration about regional political elites and regimes would be incorrect without taking into account the dependence of regions on national political developments. It is true, but why not say the same about dependence of nation-states on international influence? However, such an international influence is certainly not an obstacle to the study of national politics. Given the fact that in the 1990s, the degree of political autonomy of Russia's regions has increased, while the federal influence on regional politics became less significant until the early 2000s, for analysis of regional political elites regimes in Russia, it is possible to identify regional entities as if they were nation-states. Within this framework, federal authorities (as well as other actors outside a particular region) may be regarded as 'external' actors, or as if one was analysing the impact of international influence on national polities. This assumption allows us to turn to a case study of 'pact'/'elite settlement' in Nizhnii Novgorod Oblast in the 1990s.

'ELITE SETTLEMENT' AND LIMITS OF DEMOCRATIZATION: NIZHNII NOVGOROD OBLAST

Governor Nemtsov and regional elite bargaining

The liberalization and subsequent decline of the previous political regime characterized political developments in the region during the opening of the Soviet system in the late 1980s (for details of these and subsequent events, see Stoner-Weiss, 1997; Gel'man *et al.*, 2000: 146–180). In this period regional democratic movement gained sufficient influence to engage in public political competition with the authorities and managed a mass mobilization that resulted in the triumphal election of the leader of the local democrats, young scientist Boris Nemtsov, as Russia's Congress deputy. They also received 52 of 280 mandates to the Oblast Soviet and formed the 'Democratic Reform' group in the Oblast Soviet, whose main activity was a struggle with Communists, led by their regional leader, Gennadii Khodyrev, represented in the Soviet by the 'Union' group.

The breakdown of the previous regime, however, although caused by external circumstances, led to the failure of the Communists in the region. During the August 1991 putsch the Oblast leaders showed loyalty to the putschists, while the democrats strongly supported Yeltsin and the Supreme Soviet of Russia. After the suppression of the putsch and the banning of the Communist Party, Khodyrev and other Oblast Soviet leaders were replaced by democrats. Nemtsov was appointed as Yeltsin's representative in the region. The 'imposition' in this case was imposed from the outside, and the conflict in the region with its disunified elite structure ended as a 'zero-sum game': the democrats took the key power positions and completely ousted their Communist opponents.

In the autumn of 1991, a struggle broke out around the nomination to the post of head of the regional administration. Although the appointment was made by the Russian President, the candidate had to be approved by the Oblast Soviet. As the 'Union' group did not support the nomination of democrats, he had no chance of receiving a majority of the deputies' votes. Nemtsov made use of this situation. Supported by Soviet chairman Evgenii Krest'yaninov, Nemtsov managed to reach an informal agreement with the 'Union'-backed candidate, Ivan Sklyarov, on the division of powerful positions. Sklyarov agreed to Nemtsov's nomination as the head of the regional administration on the condition that his own nomination should be Nemtsov's first deputy. As a result, the overwhelming majority of deputies recommended Nemtsov to the President and he was soon appointed as the head of the regional administration. He also retained his post as presidential representative as well (Stoner-Weiss, 1997: 96).

The Nemtsov–Sklyarov 'pact' was not just a tactical alliance reached out of personal interests. On the contrary, after approval by their political supporters in the regional Soviet, the 'pact' became the foundation of an 'elite settlement' in the region, based on the cooperation of representatives of the old and new elite groups. Both principal factions of the regional elite, which had previously been in serious confrontation with each other, now agreed on both the new configuration of actors and the new institutions, thus overcoming the uncertainty that had arisen after August 1991. But in contrast to the 'pact' model described above serving as a means of democratization, the Nizhnii Novgorod 'elite settlement' was based on the actors' agreement not over the definition of formal institutions, but over the informal institutions that determined the redistribution of resources among them. Nevertheless, the Nizhnii Novgorod 'pact' created the foundation for the establishment of a new – and in practice relatively stable – regional political regime.

Nemtsov, a political outsider in relation to the former elite, did not have his own crew of administrators and faced the necessity of choosing a political strategy. It goes without saying that Nemtsov's most important political resource was in his influence at the Centre, primarily, his close links with the President of Russia. However, Nemtsov's effective use of this resource was possible only if there was stability in the region. Nemtsov rewarded posts in administration only to some of his supporters, while keeping and appointing former elite members. In the regional administration, members of former party-Soviet nomenklatura made up 40 per cent of the high-level officials and 75 per cent of mid-level officials (Gel'man et al., 2000: 157). The most significant new appointment Nemtsov made was the promotion of Dmitrii Bednyakov, who previously served as a professor of the local police academy, as the mayor of Nizhnii Novgorod in December 1991.

On the other hand, Nemtsov managed to neutralize the most influential actor of the region – the directors of large industrial enterprises after concluding several informal agreements on cooperation with them (Stoner-Weiss, 1997: 175–176). Nemtsov, using his ties in Moscow, managed to arrange for part of the tax payments from large enterprises to be paid into an extra-budget fund for conversion. In response, some of the directors provided political support and helped to consolidate the legitimacy of the new political regime; others at least did not oppose the administration. As a result, some enterprises obtained informal access to the administration's decision-making process, and the assistant to director of car plant GAZ was appointed vice-governor for external economic relations. Thus, Nemtsov, who did not have sufficient resources to control this group, managed to ensure his own security against possible conflicts with this group.

Nemtsov also enlisted the support of a number of new entrepreneurs. Andrei Kliment'ev (a friend of Nemtsov from his childhood), who had earlier been convicted of fraud and who became a businessman after he was released from prison, launched an initiative in spring 1992 to found the Council of Entrepreneurs under the governor. According to Nizhnii Novgorod experts, the members of this Council received some preferences from the administration, although this was not a matter of corruption, but a case of face-to-face negotiations used to interest entrepreneurial groups in participating in regional programs.

The Oblast Soviet supported Nemtsov not only on his appointment but in his further activities as well. Mostly thanks to the influence of Krest'yaninov, who controlled the majority of the deputies, Nemtsov was provided by the Soviet with additional legitimation for many of his decisions. In June 1992 Nemtsov proposed the establishment of the regional Coordinating Council to organize support for decisions concerning the implementation of reforms. This Council included the heads of the regional and city of Nizhnii Novgorod administrations and the chairmen of the regional and city Soviets. Although some deputies opposed this move, since the leaders of the region were in favour of the idea, the opinion of the assemblies was not taken into consideration. After the new regional Legislative Assembly was elected in 1994, Nemtsov's authority grew even greater. Almost half of its deputies were executive officials subordinated to Nemtsov.

Subsequent events consolidated Nemtsov's dominant position in the elite of the region. In December 1993 Nemtsov and Krest'yaninov, balloting in the Federation Council elections in a two-mandate district, received 66 per cent and 57 per cent of the vote respectively. It should be noted that no other alternative candidates attempted to compete with them in this election. In order to ensure a formally competitive vote, a puppet candidate was put up. During the 1993 elections to the State Duma that took place at the same time, a 'Vybor' ('Choice') foundation was set up under Nemtsov's patronage. It ran candidates in five out of six single-mandate districts in the region and coordinated their campaigns. Election returns showed four out of the five 'Vybor' candidates claiming victory in their districts, one of them ran second; and a candidate received one more mandate also loyal to Nemtsov.

If such support of the 'elite settlement' was mainly due to an effective resource exchange between the dominant actor, other (subordinate) actors and the regional population, then the maintenance of the actors' status within the framework of the 'elite settlement' was a result of Nemtsov's strategy of accumulating maximum resources. After having reconfirmed his legitimacy on the electoral field Nemtsov acquired the means to eliminate or neutralize those members of the 'elite settlement' who did not have sufficient resources to compete with him for influence over regional politics. The subordinate actors, in turn, claiming autonomy within the limits of the 'elite settlement', found themselves restrained in implementing their strategies. This constellation determined the outcome of a series of conflicts between Nemtsov and other actors in 1994–1995.

The first of those conflicts arose between Nemtsov and Bednyakov during elections for mayor of Nizhnii Novgorod in 1994. In addition to the objective divergence between regional and city authorities over how to use the resources of the regional centre (primarily property and finances).

Moreover, a popularly elected city mayor would acquire the status of a legitimate autonomous actor who would be potentially capable of competing with the dominant actor for control. Under strong pressure from Nemtsov, Krest'yaninov also announced his candidacy for mayor. On the eve of the election, when, according to survey estimates, both candidates' chances were equal, Krest'yaninov withdrew. Since there was no other candidate registered (except for Bednyakov), the election was cancelled. Two days after the cancelled elections and on Nemtsov's initiative Bednyakov was fired and replaced by Sklyarov by Yeltsin's decree; Krest'yaninov was quickly rewarded – he was given Nemtsov's post of Yeltsin's representative to the region.

During this conflict Nemtsov broke with the leaders of GAZ over the issue of privatization of the enterprise. The GAZ directors tried to take control of a 50 per cent stake in the company, but Nemtsov was opposed to these plans. After a court found in favour of GAZ, Nemtsov agreed to a compromise: the controlling stake was formally left in the hands of GAZ management, and GAZ's managing director retained his position; however, he soon retired. Shortly thereafter a former GAZ director and former USSR minister, who later became a strategic ally of Nemtsov, occupied a new position of president of the joint-stock company GAZ. If in the case of Bednyakov, a Nemtsov opponent was totally removed as a political actor, then the GAZ leadership was neutralized. This conflict demonstrated the limits of both Nemtsov's and the directors' opportunities. On the one hand, the directors could be content with the status of subordinate actor within the 'elite settlement' framework; on the other hand, Nemtsov, as dominant actor, was limited in his ability to apply force strategies to other actors and was not able to accumulate all the resources.

A short time later, Nemtsov initiated another conflict with far-reaching consequences for the region. At the beginning of 1995, Nemtsov declared that Kliment'ev, who had earlier actively supported Nemtsov in all his activities, had misused a part of the credits allocated from the federal budget for the modernization of one of the regional factories. Kliment'ev in turn claimed that it had been the administration itself that had deliberately imposed conditions that made it impossible to return the credit. The conflict quickly grew into a political opposition. Kliment'ev announced his intention to run for the post of governor in the elections. A criminal case was then opened against Kliment'ev, who was arrested.

While the above conflicts may have seemed to be undermining stability in the region and breaking down the 'elite settlement', in reality they allowed a consolidation of the political regime. Consensus and interaction between elite factions in relation to existing political institutions were not only weakened but also in fact strengthened. In any case, the majority of the 'elite settlement' participants took Nemtsov's side in these conflicts and his position as dominant actor remained indisputable. Nemtsov, as he gradually removed potential challengers, became independent in implementing his politics, as he had no obligation to the 'elite settlement' participants and was no longer bound by the terms of the initial 'pact'.

Finally, Nemtsov's most successful public action was the December 1995 gubernatorial election. Nemtsov won 58.4 per cent of the votes, more than twice the amount of his nearest competitor, the entrepreneur Vyacheslav Rasteryaev, who was supported by the left-patriotic bloc 'Nizhegorodskii krai' (26.2 per cent). According to Nizhnii Novgorod experts, the main issue in the governor's elections was not an ideological conflict between the liberal reformer Nemtsov and his main rival, but rather the loyalty of the electorate to Nemtsov's regime. The results of simultaneous mayoral elections in Nizhnii Novgorod were very important for Nemtsov. Sklyarov claimed a convincing victory over Bednyakov.

Thus, the 'elite settlement' formed in 1991 led to consolidation of the actors of the regional political regime that was maintained throughout the entire period of Nemtsov's governorship – until spring 1997 (when Nemtsov was appointed as first deputy prime minister of the Russian government and moved to Moscow). This consolidation was based on a resource exchange system among actors ('bargaining'). It provided mutual advantage for the participants of the 'settlement' and was able to maintain stability in the region.

From 'elite settlement' to a new elite fragmentation

While evaluating the effect of the 'elite settlement' on the process of democratization, one should take into account the most important dimensions of the political system introduced by Robert Dahl – contestation and participation (Dahl, 1971: 3). From this point the Nemtsov regime in Nizhnii Novgorod Oblast may be viewed as one with hybrid or mixed features. Although mass political participation was not obviously limited, its effectiveness (both in the sense of vertical and horizontal accountability of authorities) declined as the set of political alternatives narrowed. The 'elite settlement' in Nizhnii Novgorod Oblast set limits for the process of democratization in the region in three essential dimensions: (1) restriction of competition among political actors; (2) exclusion of some actors from the process of decision-making; (3) dominance of informal institutions of the political regime.

The restriction of competition was established when the 'pact' had been achieved, because the distribution of positions between Nemtsov and Sklyarov was based not on a coalition victory in competitive elections, but because these positions were assigned to them by the decision of the regional Soviet and by subsequent presidential decree. In the course of the 1993 and 1995 elections, Nemtsov did not face any serious challenge from his competitors, and, in turn, did not need to form the political parties on the basis of the ruling group. As a result, the party system in Nizhnii Novgorod Oblast experienced a deep crisis even in comparison with the weakness of parties in other regions of Russia. It is enough to note that there was only one deputy from all political parties elected in 1994 and 1998 in the regional legislature.

The exclusion of some participants from the 'elite settlement' (with the non-intervention of other actors) served not only to consolidate Nemtsov's position but also to legitimize the regime, as a peculiar substitute for accountability. At the same time, an increase in the influence of political outsiders was inevitable, as the price of a 'divide and rule' strategy, which led the authorities to limit the effect of mass political participation. What were the alternatives to the dominant actor governing through an 'elite settlement'? Obviously 'pact' participants could have been given certain guarantees through a collective leadership mechanism on both the informal and formal institutional levels. In this connection pacted transitions are predisposed to corporatist forms of interaction among actors (Karl, 1990: 15). The one-party regime in Mexico that evolved from an 'elite settlement' provides an example of the benefits of collective leadership. However, corporatism in its essence presupposes, at least, guarantees for all actors, and this in itself is in obvious contradiction to the position of Nemtsov as the dominant actor.

Philip Roeder considered this contradiction as a 'dilemma of leadership': the elites' need for a strong leader is coupled to the threat that this leader constitutes to them (Roeder, 1994). In post-Soviet society this dilemma is resolved through clientelism and integrating a system of 'checks and balances' into the executive branch of power. In Nizhnii Novgorod Oblast the 'clientelist' mechanism of intra-elite interactions was implemented as an alternative to corporatism under Nemtsov. Frequent changes in the structure and staff composition of the administrative apparatus, and Nemtsov's conflicts with other actors, became the main tools in elaborating this mechanism. Simultaneously the effective clientelist mechanism between the 'elite settlement' and the population provided mass support for the regime in elections, where votes were the 'currency' of the electorate in the system of resource exchange (Putnam, 1976: 158).

However, the institutionalization of informality by the Nizhnii Novgorod regime, based on the dominance of informal practices in adopting exclusionary decisions to the detriment of formal structures and procedures, seems to be its most important feature. The foundations of informal institutionalization were based on the patron/client interactions between actors. The Coordinating Council together with Nemtsov's 'inner circle' made up of his fellow students at the university who took a number of prominent posts with his help, had a significant effect on the process of decision-making in Nizhnii Novgorod Oblast. In contrast, the role of legislative assemblies in the region, not to mention judicial branch of power, was insignificant. Moreover, the norms of regional laws had been constantly changed to please the political conjuncture. A certain informal contract was in force in relations between Nemtsov and the federal Centre, guaranteed, first of all, by Yeltsin. At the same time, Nemtsov's interactions with the directors of enterprises, entrepreneurs, parties, public associations, the mass media and the population he was entrusted with were based on a similar model of informal contract, this time guaranteed by Nemtsov himself. Thus, the main features of the regional political regime could be described as: (1) the dominance of the executive over representative branch of power; (2) the contract of mutual loyalty between the Centre and the head of the regional executive; (3) indirect control by the executive over mass media; (4) the neutralization or suppression of real or potential centres of opposition in the region; (5) patronage exercised over public associations (both political and those of the 'third sector') by the regional executive in exchange for the public support of the latter (Gel'man et al., 2000: 168).

The appointment of Nemtsov led to the migration of part of Nizhnii Novgorod's elite to Moscow, where they took a number of government posts (including Krest'yaninov). In the absence of other important actors, only Sklyarov could provide for the continuity of the 'elite settlement'. Sklyarov ran in the gubernatorial elections of June 1997 as the official candidate supported by the regional 'elite settlement' (and by Nemtsov as well). Sklyarov won elections in the second ballot, but in fact Nemtsov's departure weakened the new political regime that he had created in the region. This weakening was related not only with the matter of leadership and change of regional elite composition, but with the very fact that Nemtsov's skills in bargaining with external actors (i.e. federal authorities) made possible a resource inflow to Nizhnii Novgorod, while Sklyarov was unable to provide sufficient resources into the exchange system both to elites and masses. In the wake of ongoing economic crisis in Russia, this was a crucial point of regional political development.

In March 1998, elections for the legislative assembly were held simultaneously with mayoral elections in Nizhnii Novgorod to replace Sklyarov, who had become governor. The threat to the 'elite settlement' arose from the fact itself of popular elections for the regional centre's mayor – the only political actor in the region with access to economic resources comparable in volume to the resources controlled by the governor. In this sense the victory of a candidate loyal to the Nizhnii Novgorod 'elite settlement' in the mayoral elections was of extreme necessity. However, Kliment'ev, who at the same time was the major figure in a scandalous legal case initiated when the electoral campaign was in full swing, and his candidacy thus received additional publicity, buried these hopes. The race resulted in a victory for Kliment'ev with a slim margin. The city electoral commission declared the elections invalid due to violations of law in the course of the campaign. The next day, following this decision, Kliment'ev was arrested. The presidential representative in the region, Yurii Lebedev, was forced to resign from his post after he accused the authorities of attempting to falsify the results in the mayoral elections.

Although the Nizhnii Novgorod 'elite settlement' attempted to survive in the post-Nemtsov period, the cost of survival was the denigration if not the total denial of the formal institution of elections that confronted the 'elite settlement' with a challenge to or loss of its authority. These attempts, however, could not preserve the regional political regime. The mechanism of resource exchange – formed under Nemtsov – had been undermined and open electoral political competition led the actors to return to their autonomous state. The by-elections for mayor of Nizhnii Novgorod in September–October 1998 led to the complete breakdown of the 'elite settlement'. Although the imprisoned Kliment'ev had been excluded from the election struggle this time, the conflict between actors exceeded the limits of the 'elite settlement'. The new challenger was Lebedev who became a candidate from a kind of coalition of negative consensus – some directors and entrepreneurs, who claimed independence from the regional administration, and a number of federal politicians, including Nemtsov himself, who by that time had already lost his post as first deputy prime minister of the Russian government. No wonder that Lebedev claimed victory and immediately after the election launched a series of critical attacks on Sklyarov, and in so doing began preparation for the struggle for the post of governor in new elections. Thus, the Nizhnii Novgorod 'elite settlement', and, consequently, the post-Nemtsov political regime were conclusively broken. The intra-elite agreements on the division of authority were replaced by an open competition between actors for the control of resources in a situation of new uncertainty, which was ended in the next gubernatorial elections in July 2001. Surprisingly, Sklyarov lost elections to Khodyrev, who returned to power after ten years of post-Communist developments. This power shift that resulted from a high fragmentation of regional elite, however, might be viewed as a sign of democratic development, at least in terms of democratic institutions.

NATIONAL ELITES IN RUSSIA: TOWARD CONSOLIDATION?

Elite coalitions and rivalry: 1993–2000

The previous analysis is useful for explaining the reasons behind the impact that intra-elite relations had on the transition in national politics in 1993–2000 (for details, see Shevtsova, 1999; McFaul, 2001). As noted above, the October 1993 putsch and decisive zero-sum game victory of Boris Yeltsin could be evaluated as a typical 'imposition' mode of transition. The following adoption of the new Constitution on December 1993 by national referendum increased Yeltsin's gains, granting him extraordinary powers (see Robinson, 2000), and limiting potential dangers to existing ruling groups. However, the further use of the force strategies would be costly, first of all, due to the emergence of new formal institutions in Russia, such as multi-party elections and (to lesser extent) federalism.

The December 1993 elections clearly showed the limits of the influence that the ruling group had on popular will: opposition of different political persuasions won nearly half the seats in the State Duma (Gel'man and Golosov, 1999: 34–35; McFaul, 2001: 268–278). The idea of denouncing election results, although discussed among Russia's rulers, was buried due to the simultaneous holding of the constitutional referendum. Thus, the winners of the 1993 conflict who gained the status of the dominant actor were turned towards more or less peaceful cohabitation with the opposition(s).

For their part, opposition parties and politicians found themselves facing the following dilemma: either to follow, employing an 'irreconcilable' strategy, without realistic chances of gathering sufficient resources for victory (and even to be threatened by new oppression from the ruling group), or to consider implementing a new political system (see Przeworski, 1991: 89). But within the new institutional environment the latter choice meant that the opposition(s) agreed to be subordinated to a dominant actor, i.e. to the Russian president. Since the opposition(s) has no opportunities either to change the constitution (this would be possible only in the case of broad consensus of virtually all Russia's political class), or to win presidential elections (this would be possible only in the case of support of majority of votes in the second ballot of national elections), the opposition(s) would gradually be eliminated.

In comparison with the post-1991 Nizhnii Novgorod case, the post-1993 developments in Russian national politics appear similar, although the 'pact'/'elite settlement' in the latter case was never discussed in explicit form. However, Yeltsin's camp initiated the signing of the so-called 'Treaty on Public Accord', which serves as a substitute for the 'pact'. While within the model of 'transition to democracy', contents of 'pacts' are clearly focused on conditions of establishing a new (presumably democratic) regime; in Russia's case the major goal of the treaty was the preservation of status quo post-1993 regime. According to the draft treaty, Yeltsin had promised not to dissolve the State Duma, and Duma factions had promised not to implement non-confidence votes in the government and/or initiate impeachment of the President. Early elections of both President and State Duma were also excluded. Yeltsin and 245 representatives of parties, regional governments, and major interest groups signed this treaty in April 1994, although both the Communist Party of Russian Federation (KPRF) and Yabloko refused to sign it. Nevertheless, in practice such a status quo 'imposed consensus' is still to be realized. The principal turn from 'war' to 'bargaining' was a determinant of Russia's national political developments in 1994–1995.

At the same time, the dominant actor achieved Russia's national 'imposed consensus'. But it was too fragile and (contrary to the Nizhnii Novgorod case) unable to secure stability of the newly emerged political regime. In search of the causes of the diverse outcomes of these similar elite developments, one could consider the impact of the different styles of Yeltsin's and Nemtsov's leadership. Yet, while Nemtsov actively built up capacities for effective resource exchange, established new and maintained old ties within and outside his polity, Yeltsin was merely inactive and sought to balance the different elite groups that were competing with each other for his favours (see Shevtsova, 1999). In addition, Yeltsin's poor health and habit of heavy drinking certainly undermined his leadership capacity. In terms of the above-mentioned 'dilemma of leadership' (Roeder, 1994) Yeltsin demonstrated another kind of 'bad equilibrium' regarding Nemtsov: the former was unable to perform well; the latter abused his dominant position and purged subordinated actors. But ineffectiveness of the new regime was even more threatening to the survival of the 'imposed consensus' than weak leadership. The escalating economic crisis, unfinished Chechen war (launched in late 1994), and growing unpopularity of the ruling group as well as the general decline of popular trust in existing political institutions, challenged the political elite, particularly on the eve of the presidential elections, which were scheduled for June 1996. The decisive victory of the KPRF in the December 1995 parliamentary elections, when the Communists and their allies achieved more than 40 per cent of State Duma seats, was a clear sign of such a challenge.

Thus, the 1996 presidential elections played a crucial role for the survival of Russia's national elite and political regime. According to the institutional design, presidential elections were a zero-sum game: their results meant either fully fledged domination or a loss of power for the ruling group. Prospects of electoral defeat were unlikely, not only for Yeltsin's survival as a political actor, but also even for guarantees of his personal security. Thus, the political dilemma of the abolishment of elections, or of denouncing their results in the case of defeat, became (and still are) an element of the Yeltsin campaign (Gel'man and Golosov, 1999: 35–37; McFaul, 2001: 300–304). However, the survival of the ruling group by refusing to hold presidential elections after seven years of electoral experience and after holding two parliamentary elections could undermine the legitimacy of the regime and make the intra-elite conflict even deeper – worse than that of 1991 and 1993. Thus, the presidential team was forced to choose elections as the lesser evil; in other words, the establishment of a 'cartel of anxiety' imposed elite consensus again.

No wonder Yeltsin's team effectively mobilized virtually all resources in the cause of their electoral victory, including the administrative capacity of the state apparatus, the control over most of the media, and with almost unlimited financial resources. Entrepreneurs seized former state property on the basis of loan-for-shares auctions. Yeltsin granted more powers to influential leaders of Russia's regions. The academic and cultural intelligentsia had been intimidated by horrors in the event of the Communists' return to the power. Some of Yeltsin's competitors were involved in his campaign or had been strongly pressured and given limited access to the media. Yeltsin's major rival, Communist leader Gennadii Zyuganov, had been obstructed and discredited in the media. During the campaign period TV news on the three major national channels, the balance of positive and negative assessments of Yeltsin and Zyuganov was +492 and −313, respectively (White et al., 1997: 252). Observers evaluated the campaign of Zyuganov as being sluggish and colourless, and even proposed some hypotheses of behind-the-scene deals between Yeltsin's team and the left-wing opposition (Fadin, 1996). Last, but not least, electoral fraud in favour of Yeltsin had been revealed, although there are no data of crucial importance of these matters.

The change of the political strategy of the Communist opposition was one of the immediate consequences of the elections. In August 1996, the opposition adopted the new approach of 'implementation into power'; due to lack of resources for mass mobilization, they were finally integrated into the political system within the framework of the existing regime. The danger to the transition process from anti-system political forces seemed to be exhausted, but the stabilization of the political regime remained too fragile and too partial; it was based on an understanding of short-term common goal of elites, i.e. survival of the 'cartel of anxiety', rather than on acceptance of common norms and practices. Soon after the election the 'grand coalition' of negative consensus disappeared, and an 'imposed consensus' easily turned into a new struggle between elite factions for the position of the (new) dominant actor, especially on the eve of the next elections, which would inevitably lead towards a new presidency. As a result, intra-elite relations again soon turned from 'bargaining' to 'war'. These open conflicts among national elites definitely undermined the fragile legitimacy of Russia's national political regime. But the impact of the economic crisis on the regime of 1998 was even more dramatic in terms of its inefficiency.

These developments found Yeltsin's 'family' in similar circumstances to those of Gorbachev in late 1991, when negative consensus among both masses and elites left him no space for his political survival. However, contrary to the days of Gorbachev, Yeltsin still had administrative resources under his control. In August 1999, he appointed as Prime Minister the former head of the Federal Security Service, KGB colonel Vladimir Putin. Most observers agreed that such a replacement made no sense in terms of the survival of Yeltsin's regime. But, in fact, Putin's appointment was probably the most successful cadre decision throughout all Yeltsin's political career.

Soon after Putin became Prime Minister, bomb explosions in Moscow and some other Russian cities killed several hundred people. Public opinion suggested that these explosions were commonly associated with Chechen terrorists (although no documented evidence of their involvement has been provided as yet). Putin, who promised to kill bandits wherever they arose, successfully mobilized the wave of popular fury against terrorists. In September 1999, the Russian army launched new attacks on Chechen paramilitary troops and then transformed this operation into a fully fledged war. While the Chechen war of 1994–1996 was unpopular among Russians, the new campaign was merely recognized as a requital for the bombing; thus the war was 'justified' in the eyes of both masses and elites. Due to its overwhelming resource domination, the Russian army had soon taken over most of the Chechen territory, although it never realized real control over this area. However, in the short-term perspective of the 1999–2000 elections, military euphoria was helpful for Putin and his allies. All Russia's parties except Yabloko supported military actions against Chechnya.

At the same time Putin, thanks to efforts of the presidential administration and remaining supporters of the 'family', effectively maintained a pro-government (really pro-Putin rather than pro-Yeltsin) parliamentary campaign. The newly emerged electoral coalition 'Unity' received economic resources and administrative support that was incomparable to any of Russia's parties. Under strong pressure from the Kremlin, most regional and business leaders changed their preferences to 'Unity' during the campaign. In sum, electoral results were quite favourable to Putin: his vehicle 'Unity' and its allies won about one-third of the State Duma seats. The Communists and their allies won nearly the same proportion of seats; while the remaining one-third of seats was distributed among the four other parties. Due to the composition of Duma, the presidential administration could easily control parliamentary agenda and outcomes.

These successes of Putin allowed Yeltsin to make his next positive step. On 31 December 1999 he resigned from his presidential post and passed his powers to Putin as acting President. An early election was scheduled for March 2000. Against the background of growth of mass support for Putin, his electoral chances were beyond discussion. Although Zyuganov and other politicians participated in the presidential race, virtually all elite groups expressed their loyalty to Putin. Without significant resistance and even with a relatively modest campaign, Putin achieved 53 per cent of votes in the first ballot, marking the end of Yeltsin's epoch.

National elites under Putin: imposed consensus

As one can see, attempts to achieve national elite consensus in Russia (even though in 'imposed' form) – in 1993–1994 and 1996–1997 – failed for two reasons: (1) the absence of a dominant actor due to the leadership of Yeltsin, who serves as 'a hegemonic President without a hegemonic project' (Robinson, 2000: 28), and (2) the ineffectiveness of the efforts of elites to maintain effective resource exchange system, mainly due to lack of stable mass support (thus undermining the legitimacy of elites and the regime as such), limited state capacity and economic crises. However, since late 1999, these circumstances have changed and become much more favourable for the consolidation of national elites in a similar way to Nizhnii Novgorod Oblast under Nemtsov.

First and foremost, Putin launched his presidency on decisive claims for revitalizing state capacity. In fact, the military operation in Chechnya and attempts to use (or abuse) military and security forces as a tool in domestic as well as in foreign policy – whether successful or not – have some impact on remobilizing the administrative capacities of the state. Even if one could trace the roots of this U-turn to the role of the state in Putin's KGB background, the consequences of such a U-turn were much broader. It meant not only an increase in military and security elites (who definitely played a limited role in Russia's politics after 1991) as well as their integration into new resource exchange system, but also an increase in military and security elites as a powerful tool of the dominant actor. This strategy was double-edged. Although quite costly in economic terms, the military/security-dominated revitalizing of state capacity gave some opportunities for Putin to maintain a balance between different segments of national elites as well as a tendency to increase his popularity.

Second, the conjuncture of the world market (high oil prices) allowed Putin and his government to solve – at least in short-term perspective – such problems as stabilization of public finances, currency exchange rate, payment of pension debts, obligations before the IMF etc. In the summer of 2000, Russia's government adopted an ambitious programme of economic reforms based on similar approaches to those of the early 1990s. Some liberal economists were promoted to key posts in Russia's government and the Presidential Administration.

Finally, Putin was able to gain electoral legitimacy. In contrast to the re-election of Yeltsin in 1996, this resulted not only from negative consensus provided by the 'cartel of anxiety', but was mainly due to mass support. While the incumbent vote in the presidential election of 1996 was merely anti-Zyuganov, in 2000 it was a pro-Putin vote. At least as yet, no visible challenges for Putin's high popularity emerged. Thus, Putin's claim to the position of dominant actor is based on fertile grounds of both intra-elite and elite/mass relationships.

Despite the difference in initial conditions as well as immediate consequences, in general, the emergence of 'elite settlement' in Nizhnii Novgorod Oblast and of 'imposed consensus' of Russia's national elites under Putin is based on similar principles: (1) the existence of agreement between dominant and subordinate actors on power-sharing; (2) the maintenance of the resource exchange system between them; and (3) the prevalence of informal institutions. Since the appearance of Putin as Prime Minister, his dominant position was never seriously challenged, while other actors either agreed to be subordinate to him or have been targeted by the dominant actor. Those actors who seek their autonomy outside the 'elite settlement' in terms of political influence (or, moreover, those actors, who tried to maintain the alternative resource exchange system) were either integrated within the 'elite settlement' or targeted as well. In fact, during Putin's presidency the degree of actors' autonomy and contestation among elites has been limited.

As noted above, the national parliament of 1993–1999, especially the State Duma, serves as a base of opposition(s) of different colours. By contrast, after the 1999 election the pro-Putin 'Unity' and its allies consolidated one-third of the seats, at least serving as a veto group. At the very beginning of parliamentary sittings, 'Unity' and KPRF, with strong support of Putin's administration, achieved an informal agreement for sharing most of the powerful positions within Duma: the Communists secured the post of chairman of Duma, while pro-Putin factions gained control over most of the committees. The remaining minor factions received almost nothing. Although two liberal parties, 'Yabloko' and Union of Right-Wing Forces, tried to protest against these deals, they were forced to agree with the new rules of the game. Moreover, since important posts rewarded some liberals, they voted in favour of Putin in the Duma. No wonder the Duma supported virtually all bills provided by the President and the government, including new budgets and tax reform. In 2002 'Unity' and their allies, backed by the Kremlin, changed the State Duma leadership, and the Communists lost chairmanship in all parliamentary committees.

This success in the Duma was a great help to Putin, who targeted other fluent autonomous actors, the regional elites. In May 2000, Putin established seven federal districts across all Russia's territory and appointed his envoys, who obtained control over branches of the federal ministries as well as control over the use of federal property and finances from the federal budget. Thus, resources of regional leaders, who previously had almost unlimited power in their fiefdoms on the manner of 'feudalism' (see Solnick, 1999: 805–812), were restrained to some extent. However, the legal basis of autonomous regional leaders was based not only on their broad powers but also on the ex officio principle of representation in the upper chamber of the Russian parliament, the Federation Council, which comprised chief executives and heads of legislatures from each region. Meanwhile, Putin proposed a bill on the reform of the Federation Council, the major goal of which was to remove regional leaders from the upper chamber and replace them with permanent parliamentary members, although these were to be nominated by the regional governments. Another bill gave the right to Putin to dismiss regional legislatures and/or chief executives in case of violation of federal laws (in some circumstances, even without decisions of the courts). These bills were enthusiastically adopted by loyal Duma. Regional leaders were forced to agree to this subordinated status.

Simultaneously, Putin launched attacks on the independent media, primarily TV (radio and newspapers, not to mention the Internet, have limited circulation). Among three national TV channels, state-owned RTR and joint stock ORT with 51 per cent of state-owned shares were politically loyal to Putin. But NTV, controlled by Media-Most holdings, was the only national TV that criticized Putin openly. In May 2000, the law enforcement agencies launched a series of attacks on NTV and other Media-Most companies, culminating in the seizure of Media-Most by state-owned giant Gazprom.

Relations between the state and major business leaders, or tycoons (so-called 'oligarchs' in Russian slang), developed according to the familiar 'sticks and carrots' scheme. The prosecutors and tax police targeted some banks and oil companies due to underpayment of taxes and other violations of the law. Although Putin declared an 'equidistant' approach of the state towards business, these attacks were in fact clear indications of the attempts to restrain the political autonomy of big business and to limit their influence as independent actors. Almost all business leaders soon declared their loyalty to the new regime, thus agreeing to subordinate status.

As to another principle of 'imposed consensus', such as prevalence of informal institutions in national politics, at first glance this contradicts the very idea of 'dictatorship of law' announced by Putin. However, the 'dictatorship of law' is distinct from the principle of 'rule of law'. In practice, 'dictatorship' means the purely instrumental use of legal norms as a tool (or even coercion) within the resource exchange system. These legal norms and rules, imposed on Russia by the dominant actor, tend to serve as a façade of informal practices of arbitrary rule rather than to the installation of a framework of formal institutions as a basis of 'rule of law'.

So, 'imposed consensus' seems to have been adopted by Russia's national elites as a major tool for elite integration (or reintegration). In this respect, we could even call it a 'self-imposed consensus'. This mode of elite integration may survive under Putin's leadership, if this were to help Russia's modernization. Thus, as Juan Linz noted, referring to post-1964 Brazil, 'such a process, combining administration, manipulations, arbitrary decisions, false starts, and frequent changes of personnel might be successful as long as the economy goes well' (Linz, 1973: 254). This scenario might be successful in terms of Russia's economic growth and rise of its international influence, but it might be worse for the future of Russia's democracy, finally undermining incentives for future emergence of political contest within the framework of formal institutions under the principle of rule of law. In this respect, Linz mentioned that such an 'authoritarian situation' would be 'leaving a frightful political vacuum for the future'. However, it seems unclear what kind of political regime would fill such a vacuum, and what kind of consolidation would follow an accordance with elite consensus.

Tentative conclusions: some theoretical implications

In the context of analysis of regime transitions, the case of 'pact'/'elite settlement' of Nizhnii Novgorod Oblast and possible developments of 'imposed consensus' in Russia's national politics under Putin demonstrate the limits of the applicability of the elitist model of 'transition to democracy'. Contrary to theoretical models, those 'pacts'/'elite settlement' led to restrictions on actors' contestation. Thus, a consolidation of the elite might be achieved as an obstacle to further democratization. However, the political regime based on such an 'imposed consensus' revealed itself to be weak. Without a comparative study of this 'imposed consensus' it is difficult to properly judge their impact on regime transitions and consolidation. But the practice of the political regime in Nizhnii Novgorod Oblast as well as some trends in Russia's national politics under Putin provide some grounds for certain theoretical generalizations.

We cannot say that the effect of the elite consensus influence on the process of regime transition, as shown above, totally contradicts the elitist concept of transition. On the contrary, the elite theorists notice that 'pacts'/'elite settlements' may lead to the creation of 'limited democracies' and 'pseudo-democracies' (Burton *et al.*, 1992: 22, 34), but they do not study the consequences of this kind of elite transformation. Meanwhile, the question that arises in a comparison of 'transition to democracy' with Russia's experience is why, at the stage of the breakdown of the previously existing ancien regime, the elite consensus serves as a means of democratization, while at the stage of installation of the new regime – as a means of pending democratization.

The achievement of the elite consensus at the stage of exit from uncertainty in Nizhnii Novgorod in 1991 as well as in Russia under Putin's rule in 2000 had different costs for its participants. The strategy of 'bargaining' for both parties was clear even before the conclusion of the intra-elite agreement. The subordinated actors agreed to the 'imposed consensus', because it seemed to be the only way to retain their status as a political actor, or the lesser evil in comparison to other variants of political developments. For dominant actors like Nemtsov or Putin, the 'imposed consensus' was the most effective way to establish a 'minimal winning coalition' and thus maximize their gains. In such a situation the terms of the consensus reflected uneven constellation of actors' resources and consolidated the status of Nemtsov and Putin as the dominant actor. But the possible change of this constellation doomed the 'imposed consensus' to instability, as it was in the case of Nizhnii Novgorod, where the departure of the dominant actor led to a new elite fragmentation. Thus, we may assume that the initial strategies and positions of the actors and the procedural conditions for reaching 'pact'/'elite settlement' predetermine its consequences for the new political regime.

The analysis of Russia's cases within the comparative framework of studies of elite consensus allows us to reach some tentative conclusions and formulate hypotheses for further comparative studies on the differences in the conditions of elite consensus from the perspective of its consequences for democratization:

1   The elite consensus that emerges when one of the actors has a dominant power and that consolidate the dominance of informal institutions contribute to the establishment of hybrid and unstable political regimes.
2   The elite consensus that emerges when the actors' powers are balanced or when the constellation of their resources is uncertain and that are

based on defining formal institutions are able to create conditions suitable for the emergence of democratic political regimes.

Notes

1 The early version of the chapter appeared as a journal article in *Demokratizatsiya: The Journal of Post-Soviet Democratization* (2002), Vol. 10, No. 3.

References

Burton, M., Gunther, R. and Higley, J. (1992) Introduction: Elite Transformations and Democratic Regimes, in J. Higley and R. Gunther (eds) *Elites and Democratic Consolidation in Latin America and Southern Europe*. Cambridge: Cambridge University Press, pp. 1–37.
Case, W. (1996) Can the 'Halfway House' Stand? Semidemocracy and Elite Theory in Three Southeast Asian Countries. *Comparative Politics*, Vol. 28, No. 4, pp. 437–464.
Dahl, R. (1971). *Polyarchy: Participation and Opposition*. New Haven and London: Yale University Press.
Darendorf, R. (1967) *Society and Democracy in Germany*. Garden City, NY: Doubleday.
Fadin, A. (1996) Obshchestvennoe soglasie v tselom dostignuto. *NG-scenarii*, No. 4, p. 1.
Field, L.G., Higley, J. and Burton, M. (1990) A New Elite Framework for Political Sociology. *Revue Européene des Sciences Sociales*, Vol. 28, No. 88, pp. 149–182.
Gel'man, V. and Golosov, G.V. (eds) (1999) *Elections in Russia, 1993–1996*. Berlin: Edition Sigma.
Gel'man, V., Ryzhenkov, S. and Brie, M. (eds) (2000) *Rossiya Regionov: Transformatsiya Politicheskikh Rezhimov*. Moscow: Ves' Mir.
Karatnycky, A. (2002) The 2001 Freedom House Survey: Muslim Countries and the Democracy Gap. *Journal of Democracy*, Vol. 13, No. 1, pp. 99–112.
Karl, T. (1990) Dilemmas of Democratization in Latin America. *Comparative Politics*, Vol. 23, No. 1, pp. 1–21.
Karl, T.L. and Schmitter, P. (1991) Models of Transition in Latin America, Southern and Eastern Europe. *International Social Science Journal*, Vol. 43, No. 128, pp. 269–284.
Knight, A. (1992) Mexico's 'Elite Settlement': Conjuncture and Consequences, in J. Higley and R. Gunther (eds) *Elites and Democratic Consolidation in Latin America and Southern Europe*. Cambridge: Cambridge University Press, pp. 113–145.
Linz, J. (1973) The Future of an Authoritarian Situation or the Institutionalization of an Authoritarian Regime: The Case of Brazil, in A. Stepan (ed.) *Authoritarian Brazil. Origins, Policies, and Future*. New Haven and London: Yale University Press, pp. 233–254.
Marks, G. (1992) Rational Sources of Chaos in Democratic Transition. *American Behavioral Scientist*, Vol. 35, No. 4/5, pp. 397–421.
McFaul, M. (2001) *Russia's Unfinished Revolution: Political Change from Gorbachev to Putin*. Ithaca, NY, and London: Cornell University Press.
North, D. (1990) *Institutions, Institutional Changes, and Economic Performance*. Cambridge: Cambridge University Press.

O'Donnell, G. and Schmitter, P. (1986) *Transitions from Authoritarian Rule: Tentative Conclusions About Uncertain Democracies*. Baltimore and London: Johns Hopkins University Press.

Przeworski, A. (1991) *Democracy and the Market. Political and Economic Reforms in Eastern Europe and Latin America*. Cambridge: Cambridge University Press.

Putnam, R. (1976) *The Comparative Study of Political Elites*. Englewood Cliffs, NJ: Prentice-Hall.

Robinson, N. (2000) The Presidency: The Politics of Institutional Chaos, in N. Robinson (ed.) *Institutions and Political Change in Russia*. Basingstoke and London: Macmillan, pp. 11–40.

Roeder, P. (1994) Varieties of Post-Soviet Authoritarian Regimes. *Post-Soviet Affairs*, Vol. 10, No. 1, pp. 61–101.

Rustow, D. (1970) Transitions to Democracy: Toward a Dynamic Model. *Comparative Politics*, Vol. 2, No. 3, pp. 337–363.

Shevtsova, L. (1999) *Yeltsin's Russia: Myths and Reality*. Washington, DC: Carnegie Endowment for International Peace.

Solnick, S. (1999) Russia's 'Transition': Is Democracy Delayed Democracy Denied? *Social Research*, Vol. 66, No. 3, pp. 789–824.

Stoner-Weiss, K. (1997) *Local Heroes. The Political Economy of Russian Regional Governance*. Princeton, NJ: Princeton University Press.

White, S., Rose, R. and McAllister, I. (1997) *How Russia Votes*. Chatham, NJ: Chatham House Publishers.

4 The elite basis of Yeltsin's and Putin's regimes

Anton Steen

Introduction[1]

While mass confidence in state and societal institutions is often considered the hallmark of democratic governance, elite support has been less studied. The Russian change of regime in 1991 was a process initiated and dominated by the elite, and apathy among the masses remained widespread even once democracy had been established. Thus, the problem of legitimacy in Russia should also be analysed from an elite perspective. One should ask whether the elite support institutions and leaders, and what implications such support has for democratic stability. The purpose of this study is not so much to identify a single 'power-elite'. By comparing a large number of elites reflecting basic values and orientations, the aim is to map out some aspects of Russian political culture related to democratic performance.

Following the demise of Communism, for the first time the Russian elites could openly express critical attitudes towards institutions and their leaders – the main feature of the democratic process. However, there is a dilemma in that stable democracy also requires a certain level of support for political and societal institutions and their leaders. Stable institutions are a prerequisite for democracy, and they acquire legitimacy only through general approval. In the Russian case the problem is how such support is possible when economic reforms, poverty and a weak state undermine the incentives for regime approval.

The main question here is what was actually the level of support following this change of basic institutions and how elite attitudes may have altered after Vladimir Putin's more centralized rule was introduced. Has the level of confidence among the elite increased because of more authoritarian central leadership? And what are the implications for the type of democracy which is developing in Russia?

Support may be 'diffuse' and related to the value of the institution as such, or it may take the form of more specific support for the leaders of the institution in question and the actual outputs they produce. Most would agree that for democracy to be stable, leaders and the masses must have a minimum level of confidence in institutions, and members of the elite must have a basic level of trust in each other. A change of regime away from authoritarian rule makes such support crucial since democracy requires backing, particularly from its leaders.

Method and data

Elite surveys raise the question of which persons shall be included and the validity of the results will depend largely on the sampling of the respondents (Hoffman-Lange, 1987). However, in seeking to cope with the complexities of the real world, elite studies necessarily involve a considerable amount of ad hoc choices when it comes to selection (Moyser and Wagstaffe, 1987). In this study, pragmatic considerations of what is possible in practical terms have been combined with more theoretical considerations as to which institutions are important in decision-making processes. The main selection criterion has been to include leaders from the institutions with the greatest political importance. It might be argued that, in aggregate, the respondents constitute not only a representative sample of the national and regional elites but approximate a sort of universe of those elites not directly affiliated with the president and the executive power.

Structured face-to-face interviews were conducted with a total of 1585 respondents in leading positions in 1998 (980) and 2000 (605).[2] The following eight institutions are included, with number of respondents interviewed at the two points in time in brackets: prominent politicians in the State Duma (100); members of the Federation Council (30); leaders in the federal administration and ministries (100); heads of state enterprises (50) and private businesses (50); leaders of educational, cultural and media institutions: cultural elite (50); and political/administrative leaders at the regional levels (1998: 600; 2000: 225). In the 2000 survey, the number of regional elite was reduced but covered the same kinds of regions as in 1998. The selection of institutions and elites conforms to what has been defined as *strategic elites* (Keller, 1972). Such elites are institutionally diverse and exert various functions but all exercise influence, directly or indirectly, on decision-making. However, these elites are institutionally distinct from the president entourage, i.e. the policy-leadership consisting of the President, the presidential administration and the cabinet.

In selecting respondents, several criteria were employed. *Political elites* in the State Duma and the Federation Council were easy to identify. Emphasis was placed on obtaining a representative sample in terms of political affiliation; further, that those selected should hold positions of leadership within the party group or in main committees in the State Duma. The greatest challenge lay in the selection of respondents from private and state business activity, because the ownership structure may be unclear. Available business directories were used which list the names of firms and their directors. An enterprise was defined as 'state-owned' if more than 50 per cent of the shares in that company were in the hands of the state.

Including all the 89 regions of the Russian Federation was clearly unfeasible. Five main types of regions were chosen: geographically central, geographically peripheral, reform-oriented, regions marked by stagnation, and regions with large ethnic minority groups. The interviews were conducted in the period June–September 1998, with the bulk of the interviews being carried out in June and July; and in June–September 2000. On average, each interview lasted one hour and the response levels were high, exceeding 90 per cent for most questions.

Political support – implications for democracy

According to Higley and Burton (1989), the development of legitimate and stable political regimes in Western countries initially depended on 'consensually unified' elites who, while divided over political issues, agreed on common norms concerning institutional support and mutual trust. These norms developed gradually over a long period and were absorbed into Western political culture. The post-Communist countries, particularly Russia, are quite different in this respect.

Institutions, be they parliament, ministries or political parties, are the arenas for mobilizing and regulating conflicts among the elites. 'Institutions' may also, however, be taken to mean functions like law enforcement by the judiciary, the police or the military; socialization carried out by educational institutions; or the market as an institution for distribution of resources. Pluralist societies should develop critical attitudes towards these institutions. Democracy is founded on criticism, but if that criticism goes beyond 'sound scepticism', which is not easy to define, it obviously has implications for the capability of the institutions and in the longer run for political stability.

Trust between leaders lends much of the substance to the functioning of political and social systems. In informal relations and networks, trust among the participants is a basic element for a stable exchange of views, information and give-and-take agreements. The inter-personal aspect of legitimacy is especially relevant in the Russian context, where the rules of the game and the institutions are not yet a fully integral part of political culture.

Democratic government requires in particular elite support in order to perform vital state functions.[3] But what are the roots of legitimacy – are they to be found in support for institutions ('the form') or in support for leaders and their decisions ('the content')? Easton (1975) and Gabriel (1992) assert that the most basic kind of legitimacy comes from support for institutions *as such*, irrespective of policy outputs and leader success. According to Offe (1997), confidence in democratic institutions should be 'diffuse' because these are valued for their own sake. In this type of paradigm, confidence is understood as fundamental and diffuse attitudes. Confidence in institutions means that people have trust in basic structures and processes that by their very nature sustain vital functions or have the potential to do so. Confidence results more from a general adherence to political and societal symbols than from satisfaction with policy output or popular leaders.

The alternative 'specific support' approach presupposes that elites and the mass public act in response to how institutions contribute to their own well-being and the kind of opportunity structures they provide. Therefore, one would expect the output of institutional activities and the leaders responsible for decisions to determine the pattern of attitudes. According to Barry (1970), the policy *performance* of democratic institutions over a period of time gives legitimacy to the political system. Therefore, as Smith (1972: 9) asserts, 'value-related explanations take on a subordinate role' for legitimacy and support.

If trust arises from the ability of institutions to produce positive policy outputs, confidence will depend upon how the outputs from institutions meet the expectations of the elite and the masses. Low confidence will stem not from distrust in institutions as such, but from poor performance feeding back to the institutions. 'Specific' support is instrumental and directly related to how performance meets short-term expectations and implies a substantial destabilizing potential in times of economic crisis. Economic recession and malfunctioning in society may therefore reduce belief in institutions, but not necessarily lead to a desire to change them. A real crisis occurs when the elite proposes to replace one institution with another. According to Mishler and Rose (1999) the foundation of legitimacy differs between new and established democracies. New democracies are supported mainly for what they *do*, while established democracies are valued also for what they *are*, because of long-term political socialization.

In one sense leaders are 'specific', easy to identify and therefore prone to be blamed or praised for decisions and results. However, some leaders may acquire an 'institutional aura', whereby their acceptance is based more on charisma than on performance. Max Weber's distinction between 'charismatic', 'traditional' and 'legal/rational' forms of governance points to the fact that legitimacy may be derived from several sources. System legitimacy may come both from institutional arrangements and from leaders with special personal qualities. In the following the main focus is on 'legal/rational rule' which implies confidence in institutions, and on one aspect of 'charismatic rule' – trust among leaders. The main forms of legitimacy are illustrated inTable 4.1.

A consolidated democracy will score high on both counts (Type 1), while in a less consolidated system the elite will have low trust in both leaders and institutions (Type 4). Since trust in institutions is an effect of socialization of democratic symbols over time, one would expect 'diffuse support' to be low in Russia. Further, the high level of elite-competition and many zero-sum games is conducive to lower 'specific support'. The general hypothesis is that Russia ends up as Type 4, marked by a low level of confidence in institutions and low inter-elite trust.

Table 4.1 Support and types of legitimacy

Trust in leaders	Confidence in institutions	
	High	Low
High	Type 1	Type 2
Low	Type 3	Type 4

Confidence in institutions

The large number of institutions included here makes it useful to identify some main categories. The distinction between *public* and *private* or *government* and *non-government* is often used in the study of support for institutions in Western countries (Rose, 1984). Listhaug and Wiberg (1995) propose an empirically reductionist approach and differentiate between 'order institutions' (such as the police and the army), and others. In a study of mass confidence in institutions in the Baltic states a distinction was drawn between 'old' and 'new' institutions and between 'policy-making' and 'policy-implementing' institutions (Steen, 1996). It was found that institutions with a direct effect on people's lives, like the bureaucracy and the market, were more prone to low confidence than institutions with less tangible and more symbolic functions, like the Church and educational institutions. Keeping these ways of differentiating institutions in mind, I will also focus on how the open conflicts between institutions in Russia, especially the struggle between the State Duma and the President during Yeltsin's period, may influence confidence. Further, how did the new State Duma and President Putin impinge on the political climate among the elite? Table 4.2 shows the Russian elite's confidence in various political and societal institutions.

For the average of all institutions the elite is split approximately down the middle for both years, with one half expressing some confidence and the other half exhibiting low or no confidence. On average, only 5–6 per cent of all institutions have full confidence for the two years. The highest score in this category is for the Church and armed forces with 10–13 per cent. At the other end of the scale we find that about one-fourth have no confidence at all in the presidential administration, political parties, the press, TV and radio and police.

Separating the institutions into government and non-government shows that confidence in *government* institutions is split. As of 1998 the Federation Council and, in particular, the regional and local governments, enjoy a high level of confidence. The State Duma also has a relatively high degree of support.[5] By contrast, the executive power – consisting of the President and his administration, the cabinet, civil servants and the judiciary – enjoy considerably less confidence. In fact, the President and the presidential administration during Yeltsin's period had an extremely low loyalty score

Table 4.2 Confidence in institutions. All respondents (%)[4]

	Full confidence 1		Quite a lot confidence 2		Not very much confidence 3		No confidence at all 4		Mean values	
	1998	2000	1998	2000	1998	2000	1998	2000	1998	2000
Average all institutions	5	6	42	44	38	37	15	13	2.6	2.6
Presidential administration	2	3	24	30	46	42	28	24	3.0	2.9
Political parties	2	1	19	24	55	54	24	20	3.0	2.9
President	3	17	30	58	40	21	28	4	2.9	2.1
Private business	1	2	28	37	53	47	18	14	2.9	2.7
Press	1	1	25	24	53	52	21	24	2.9	3.0
TV and radio	1	1	25	24	53	51	21	25	2.9	3.0
Trade unions	1	1	30	33	49	45	19	20	2.9	2.8
Civil servants	1	0	35	31	48	54	16	15	2.8	2.8
Police	2	1	34	30	43	44	21	25	2.8	2.9
Cabinet	2	3	40	62	45	31	13	4	2.7	2.4
Judiciary	3	2	41	31	41	47	15	21	2.7	2.9
State Duma	5	4	52	52	33	37	10	7	2.5	2.5
Church	11	13	46	53	28	21	15	12	2.5	2.3
Regional government	11	8	58	56	25	31	6	6	2.3	2.4
Federation Council	7	6	64	58	24	30	5	6	2.3	2.4
Armed forces	10	12	53	63	29	20	8	5	2.3	2.2
Local government	11	7	62	55	22	31	5	6	2.2	2.4
Education system	11	9	72	75	14	14	3	2	2.1	2.1

Response rate 1998: 94%–98% for all questions, except for 'Church' with 90%. $N = 980$.
Response rate 2000: 93%–98% for all questions, except for 'Church' and 'Political parties' with 91%. $N = 605$.

among the Russian elite. Later, the confidence in the President was dramatically changed under Putin. From a low position in 1998 the President attained the highest score in 2000, with an increase in the confidence score from 33 per cent to 75 per cent. Putin was the man the elites had been waiting for.

The administrative apparatus of the state, including the presidential administration, civil servants and the judiciary, have not benefited from change of President. They seem to be in a permanent crisis of confidence reflecting a deep traditional Russian suspicion of the bureaucratic apparatus.

The low level of confidence in the executive combined with a fairly strong belief in elected institutions and regional government underscores the main tensions between Russian government institutions as of 1998. In 2000 this was turned upside down: the elite has more trust in the central power and became more sceptical to regional and local government although these institutions still enjoy a relatively high level of support. The elite quite clearly want a firmer hand in the central power but not necessarily a return to authoritarian rule.

Singling out the *order institutions*, 36 per cent of the elite supported the police in 1998, but just 31 per cent in 2000. The army has a quite high confidence level, which increased from 63 per cent to 75 per cent in this period. Allegations of a corrupt and inefficient police force may explain the low level of confidence in the police, whereas the economic crisis and the decline in morale among the soldiers and officers have obviously not had any substantial impact on the confidence of the elite in the armed forces *as an institution*. The widespread desire to preserve the Russian Federation and avoid further fragmentation after the Chechnya problem obviously mobilized national feelings and support for the main integrative power instrument of the state: the military.

Among state institutions that are not so easily classifiable as 'government' or 'order', the education system has a very high confidence score in both years, with 83–84 per cent. The elites interviewed here are themselves very well educated – more than 90 per cent have a university degree – and during the Soviet period the education system had a reputation for high quality. This sector has probably come through the transition period more unharmed than other institutions, which may explain the high support level.

Elite support for *non-government* institutions is in general low. Confidence in political parties is extremely meagre, with only 21 per cent of the elite expressing some confidence, although increasing to 25 per cent in 2000. A minority also expressed positive attitudes towards private business, in 1998 29 per cent, but increasing to 39 per cent two years later. Business under a firm central hand seems to be more attractive than the chaotic capitalism under Yeltsin. The press, radio and TV have especially low and stable confidence scores with 25–26 per cent. Confidence in trade unions is also scanty. The only exception among non-government institutions is the Church. This enjoys quite a high level of trust, 57 per cent rising to 63 per cent in the period. Obviously, the symbolic aspects of this institution have strong appeals to religious and traditional feelings among the elite, even after 70 years of atheist rule, and many regard the Church as compensating for a lack of basic societal norms that disappeared with Communism.

Since political parties are a key institution in any democracy, and private business is the backbone of a market economy, the low level of support for these institutions is a cause for concern. It says something essential about the type of political and economic system that is emerging from the legacy of totalitarian rule and the centrally planned economy. Market economy and a multi-party system were introduced as Yeltsin's key reforms, and yet a decade later the elite are still very sceptical about these new basic institutions.

Elite integration and confidence

The Russian elite is not a uniform group. Even during the Soviet period, there was a certain degree of pluralism among competing elite groups within the centralized nomenklatura system. Elite differentiation was often connected to regional interests and clan traditions. Since the change of regime, the institutionalization of heterogeneous elite groups has formalized new arenas for the elite. When they used the term 'consensually unified elites' to describe stable Western democracies, Higley *et al.* (1998) were referring to commonly held attitudes among the elite regarding support for democratic institutions. As shown in Table 4.2, Russian federal elected institutions enjoy considerable support among the elite, while the others have low confidence.

If confidence in institutions across elite groups is one main requirement for consensually unified elites, it is important to know which elite groups support which institutions. One may assume that elites will primarily rally around their own institution and that they will trust their own sector more than others. Elites with positions in government institutions will tend to trust other government institutions and be more critical of non-government activities. On the other hand, elites in the non-governmental sector may be expected to be sceptical towards public institutions and have a higher level of trust in private sectors. Table 4.3 compares confidence in some selected institutions among the eight groups of respondents. Shaded figures show *internal* confidence inside the same elite group or between similar groups.

Central representative institutions

A large proportion of the central political elite (members of the State Duma and the Federation Council) has confidence in the *State Duma*, and the legislators are quite confident in themselves. Support from leaders of state enterprises and private business is much lower. The State Duma is under attack not only from the economic sector but also from some governmental institutions, but it seems to face this criticism with a high level of self-confidence. There is little variation in support for the *Federation Council* in 1998 which was the most popular institution among all groups except for the cultural elite. Moreover, its members are almost unanimous in their support for their own institution and as one should expect in regional government. The status of the Federation Council changed two years later where especially leaders of state enterprises and private businesses became more negative.

The central government sector

Confidence in the *cabinet* among the State Duma deputies is very low in 1998 (23 per cent) compared with other elite groups and rose as high as 60 per cent in 2000. There is also a sharp increase in confidence in the cabinet among all the other elite groups. As might be expected, the deep conflicts of the final years of Yeltsin's presidency had profound effects and confidence in the *President* among the deputies in the Duma was at a very low level with only 13 per cent confidence in the President in 1998. It was also low or moderate among other elite groups, with the exception of the deputies of the Federation Council where a majority supported the

Table 4.3 Confidence in institutions by elite group (%)[6]

Confidence in:		1	2	3	4	5	6	7	8	9	10
Elite group:											
State Duma	1998	84	70	23	14	11	20	54	26	46	16
	2000	77	62	60	71	26	31	57	33	40	12
Federal	1998	69	97	61	56	46	50	100	45	34	10
Council	2000	60	100	83	86	55	47	100	59	32	25
Federal admin-	1998	48	65	61	40	31	48	54	20	22	14
istration	2000	58	68	78	80	31	41	67	22	23	24
State enter-	1998	41	63	43	29	17	21	64	32	13	34
prise	2000	30	48	64	64	17	15	53	41	2	33
Private	1998	30	60	34	33	21	12	64	70	21	34
business	2000	30	47	59	57	20	16	46	70	21	35
Culture	1998	46	48	38	34	24	17	64	26	14	38
	2000	46	58	58	78	24	18	47	43	16	32
Regional	1998	58	74	42	35	27	41	73	26	18	27
government	2000	60	65	63	79	44	36	69	39	27	22
Total elite	1998	57	71	42	33	25	36	69	29	21	25
	2000	56	64	65	75	34	32	63	39	25	24

Column headings: 1 = State Duma, 2 = Federal Council, 3 = Cabinet, 4 = The President, 5 = the President's administration, 6 = Civil servants, 7 = Regional government, 8 = Private business, 9 = Political parties, 10 = The press.
Response rate 1998: 94%–98% for all questions, except for 'Church' with 90%. $N = 980$.
Response rate 2000: 96%–98% for all questions, except for 'Church' with 91%. $N = 605$.
Grey shading indicates confidence between leaders of the same or similar institutions; other figures indicate confidence across different institutions.

President. As a consequence of Vladimir Putin's recentralization policies the popularity of the presidency skyrocketed to between 71 per cent and 86 per cent confidence among all elite groups, even for those who might fear less power than before, regional leaders for example.

The material exhibits an interesting change of attitudes in the bureaucracy. In 1998 the leaders in the ministries express quite high trust in the Federal Council and the cabinet but only a minority has confidence in President Yeltsin and his administration. In 2000 the bureaucrats evidently found Vladimir Putin much more attractive by doubling the level of confidence from 40 per cent to 80 per cent but they still are quite critical of his administrative apparatus.

The *presidential administration* and the *civil servants* scored very low among the Duma deputies in 1998. Elite groups in private business and state enterprises were also very critical. While the level of support is still moderate in 2000 the increase in support comes mostly from the Federation Council, the State Duma and leaders in regional government. The support for a stronger presidency spills over to more acceptance also of Putin's administrative apparatus but only among the central and regional political elites. The same positive tendency cannot be said about civil servants in general. Confidence remains at a low level and is also declining among some elite respondents.

Regional government enjoys considerable support among all elite groups, in particular the Federation Council. The 100 per cent confidence rating may no doubt be attributed to the fact that the members are recruited directly from the regions as governors or leaders of regional parliaments. While over time leaders of federal administrations have an increasing trust in regional government the trend is negative for private business leaders, leaders of state enterprises and cultural institutions which lost a lot of confidence in the regional government during the end of the 1990s.

The non-government sector

Private business scored a very low level of confidence among all respondents in 1998, except for business leaders themselves – 70 per cent of whom trust their own sector – and among the respondents in the Federation Council. Two years later, private business is obviously more accepted among most elite groups, with an extraordinarily high score among cultural and regional elites. *Political parties* in general enjoy the least confidence of all institutions. An exception is the somewhat higher level of support they get from deputies in the State Duma and the Federation Council since these naturally have closer relations to the parties than other elite groups. However, there are few indications of any substantial rise in popularity during the period. *The press*, too, has a very low standing among all central, regional and local governmental elites. However, it does get some support from the cultural elite, private business and state enterprise leaders. The support by cultural leaders may be explained by the direct connections between this group of respondents (which includes leaders of the mass media and newspapers) and the media sector. The relatively high level of confidence among leaders in private business may be related to the close investment links between business and the media in Russia. Why leaders of state enterprises are relatively sympathetic towards the press may be explained by the blurred borderline between private and state business which both see the media sector as a partner.

The variation in levels of confidence in institutions between elite groups indicates a fascinating pattern of conflicting and converging interests among Russian elites. There are considerable anomalies in the extent to which government institutions in Russia trust each other. While very few deputies in the State Duma in 1998 say they have confidence in executive institutions, members of the Federation Council are quite positive towards the executive, including the President and his administration as well as civil servants. However, the State Duma deputies trust the Federation Council, despite its positive relations with the President under Yeltsin. This confidence pattern illustrates the central position of the Federation Council during the 1990s as a mediator between the critical Communist opposition in the State Duma and a reform-oriented unpopular President.

Concluding remarks

Are these patterns of orientations indicating a trend from elite fragmentation to elite integration? In terms of legitimacy the Federation Council is a very fascinating case during the turbulent period around 1998, enjoying a high level of confidence by all elite groups in the government and non-government sectors. By and large this confidence is reciprocated on the part of the council deputies. While the Federation Council members continue to express trust in other institutions also in 2000, several of these leaders have become more sceptical to the Federation Council indicating a declining status after 2000. These more sceptical attitudes fit well in with President Putin's strategy of reducing the influence of the governors.

The attitudes support the widespread impression that by 1998 the regions had attained a fairly strong position, while the regional elite expressed critical attitudes to the centre, except for the Federation Council. However, after 2000 the attitudes of regional leaders to the political centre are becoming increasingly more positive. Although attaining regional autonomy during the 1990s the chaotic Yeltsin period obviously had its costs. The regional elite wants a more stable and predictable central power and is consequently enhancing their support for the President, his administration and the cabinet quite dramatically.

One may conclude that central governmental institutions connected with the President, and in particular non-government institutions, faced a deep crisis of legitimacy in 1998. This fits in with the widespread picture of Russian politics during that period as having a fragmented centre with a lack of power instruments and independent regions that were assuming increasing responsibility for policy-making and implementation. The pattern reported here also coincides with many reports during the 1990s of frequent controversies between the State Duma and the President, regions striving for more autonomy and a society with weak civic values.

At the same time, some of the attitudes expressed indicate some degree of integration, in particular with regard to the Federation Council. As both a focus of elite confidence in Russian politics and as an institution that itself has a high level of confidence in governmental and non-governmental institutions, the Federation Council was in a potentially strong position to mediate between fragmented elites. The governors in the Federation Council built coalitions between the regions and President Yeltsin and made controversial decisions that instigated many conflicts between the State Duma and the executive powers. These extremely resource-demanding adversary processes could not continue and the Russian elite had by 2000 achieved the stronger central power they desired. With the new President starting his programme of strengthening the central authorities, it is not only the actual locus of power that has changed. More important, the wave of enthusiastic support from leaders in both the state and non-state sectors has made the central power legitimate, thereby enhancing the possibilities for stable rule while power centralization has made the prospects for democracy less definite.

Trust among elites

There is a notable lack of systematic empirical studies that address the issue of trust among elites. In the tradition of Almond and Verba (1965) and later Putnam (1993), a certain level of basic trust in other persons is a prerequisite for a democratic political culture. Studies of mass attitudes in post-Communist societies shows the trust level is low and some argue that trust in others is less significant for democratic development than the 'political culture' approach suggests (Miller, 1993; Miller et al., 1997). If inter-personal trust on the mass level is not crucial for democratic rule, we would argue that trust between elites is more essential. In particular when institutions are weak, new democracies require an elite which can cooperate and solve problems based on a minimum amount of mutual confidence.

Given a situation where a new generation of ambitious, well-educated young 'westernizers' is challenging the former nomenklatura, one might expect elites to be especially critical of each other. Lane and Ross (1999) attribute the disruptive forces in Russia mainly to conflicts between the new ascendant class of intellectuals who have adopted Western-style, market-oriented thinking, and the conservatives in the central and regional bureaucracies. After comparing elite configurations in several post-Communist countries, Higley et al. (1998) were less categorical about elite fragmentation, and came to the more cautious conclusion that even if the Russian elite appears fragmented and unstable, it also has the potential for consensus and unity. But how to operationalize 'trust' is not an easy task and the inter-personal distrust among the elite shown in Table 4.4 is measured by attitudes to two statements.

In general, members of the elite exhibit very sceptical attitudes, with more than two-thirds of the respondents expressing distrust in other leaders.[8] The respondents particularly agreed with the statement that politicians put their own interests before those of the country. Thus, at face value the overall figures indicate quite a fragmented elite with low internal cohesion and such attitudes are stable and independent of who is the acting President. The national and regional political leaders seem to integrate over time under the umbrella of a more authoritarian executive. The bureaucracy is increasingly alienated about the dealings of political leaders, and the new business class is the most frustrated about politicians and public leaders who seem to think more about their own interests than in creating predictable conditions for business activities.

Looking at the various elite groups, the situation in 1998 was as follows: the central political elite in the Federation Council and the State Duma, and local government leaders tend to be the most trustful. Bureaucrats in ministries and regional government leaders form a second group which

Table 4.4 Inter-elite distrust (%)[7]

	Average (1) + (2)		Agree with statement (1)		Agree with statement (2)	
	1998	2000	1998	2000	1998	2000
Total elite	67	65	70	66	64	64
State Duma	63	57	68	65	59	48
Federal Council	54	41	76	53	33	28
Federal administration	70	75	73	75	67	74
State enterprises	77	73	76	70	77	76
Private business	80	85	77	84	83	85
Culture	84	70	83	69	85	71
Regional government	67	65	69	68	62	61

Response rate 1998: 94%–97%, $N = 980$; response rate 2000: 94%–96%, $N = 605$.

express somewhat more mistrust. Leaders in the cultural sector, in state enterprises and private businessmen have a considerably lower trust score than the other elites.

The elites are somewhat more sceptical to 'politicians' than other 'public leaders'. The members of the Federation Council tend to be considerably less critical to 'public leaders' than to 'politicians', underscoring their role as more understanding with the executive than the State Duma during Yeltsin's period. Even if elites in general have little trust in other leaders, the central politicians in the State Duma and especially in the Federation Council had a larger potential for integration during the 1990s. Two years later the political elite has moved towards somewhat extended accommodating attitudes, especially in the Federation Council. On the other hand, distrust has increased among bureaucrats and private business leaders. Then, what may explain these differences?

The ranking seems to be connected to proximity to political decision-making. Those who are on the sideline of the political process and operating in mass media, education, culture and in the new economy feel particularly alienated towards other leaders involved in politics. Those involved in political decision-making know the processes better from their own experience with elite bargains than the 'outsiders'. Here, criticism probably stems more from mass media coverage and general impressions than from personal knowledge of political life.

Since bureaucrats traditionally regard politicians as adversaries and the new business leaders are forced to engage in strategic games in a volatile and hostile political environment they have not many political friends and few incentives for trusting others. On the other hand, the leaders of state enterprises and private businesses are dependent on the state to regulate the legal and economic framework in which they operate. The new state-market companionship has obviously not been conducive to trust between the business leaders and politicians, and why should it be? Since few institutions regulate the interface between the state and society, the privatization of state responsibilities creates what Grabher and Stark (1997: 15) have called 'flexible opportunism', a strategy for survival not very conducive to trustful relations with politicians and state officials.

How important is inter-elite trust for democracy? Miller *et al.*'s (1997) conclusion in their study of Russian and Ukrainian elites that 'trust in others plays a less important role in the establishment of a democratic political culture than previously suggested' is relevant here. Those who were less trusting of others actually saw democracy as providing institutions that would regulate the harsh forms of elite competition. Paradoxically, those who distrusted elites expressed confidence in democratic institutions. Distrust between elites, which is a form of 'personalized orientation', may be separated from the more 'diffuse' and basic confidence in democratic institutions. The significance of an institution is not necessarily associated with the quality of its leaders.

Thus, going beyond cultural determinism, an optimist interpretation is that as long as institutions have a certain degree of confidence, distrust in leaders can be regarded not as a sign of crisis but of sound scepticism in particularly turbulent political processes inside the framework of an emerging democracy. If trust in public leaders indicates 'cohesion', then, strange as it may seem, data show that the political elite comprises the most integrated group. From a political integration point of view the main problem is not the political elite that over time tends to harmonize but the state bureaucrats and elites outside the traditional state sphere. Their increasing level of distrust in politicians and public leaders illustrates a deep cleavage both inside the state and between state and society.

Conclusion: hope for the state – crisis for society

Stable democracy must be established on a minimum level of confidence in institutions among the elite, and trust among members of the elite. The topic here has been trust in the new Russian democracy and the results raise three fundamental problems: how to *measure* trust and identify trust 'paths' (who trusts whom and what?); how to *interpret* levels of trust (what are our points of reference?); and how to *evaluate* varying levels of 'diffuse' and 'specific' trust in terms of implications for democracy and political stability.

The findings reveal a rather complex picture of attitudinal integration among elites. When we speak of the legitimacy of a political regime we may be referring to the acceptance of a specific political order or else to support for institutions and particular leaders and what they can deliver. The study draws a distinction between on the one hand the elite's 'confidence in institutions' and 'trust in leaders' where both are seen as intrinsic to democratic stability. One feature of post-Communist countries with weak institutions and often strong leader-figures are cases of 'personalized institutions' where ordinary people may not be able to distinguish between the two. On the other hand, one may assume that the elite are more able not to associate leaders with institutions.

One approach argues that legitimacy and political stability is based on 'diffuse support' for institutions that have an intrinsic value, irrespective of their output. Huntington (1991) maintains that, while the legitimacy of an authoritarian regime is dependent mainly on performance, the legitimacy of a democratic regime rests more on acceptance of procedures and institutions. As Offe (1997) and Mishler and Rose (1999) emphasize, in the West, political and economic institutions have become socialized over time into the general political culture and adopted as part of a values system. In post-Communist countries they were established in a rather artificial manner by instrumental 'shortcuts' and to some extent copied from abroad. In the long run institutions cannot survive only on the basis of an instrumental rationality – i.e. because they are beneficial in some sense or have a charismatic leader. Since all institutions experience periods when they are unable to fulfil expectations or fail completely, 'the only thing that can ensure their continued validity and recognition is a firmly entrenched system of beliefs that supports them – not for the reason that they are useful, but because they are 'right' and hence intrinsically deserving of support' (Offe, 1997: 66). While Offe and Huntington have mass support in mind, their argument applies even more forcefully to the *elite's* orientations towards institutions.

The alternative to the 'intrinsic value approach' is that political support is specifically related to outputs. The very understanding of 'democracy' is relevant here. Among the Russian elite, and in particular among the masses, a common idea of what justifies a political regime is its ability to produce material well-being. As asserted by Lukin (2000), one widespread definition of democracy among Russians is as a means of achieving prosperity. Accordingly, only the ability of the system to provide economic growth and necessary public goods gives legitimacy to the regime. Inglehart (1999) found that the correlation between non-authoritarian orientations and economic growth in 57 countries was substantial, suggesting that when the economy is growing, authoritarian attitudes tend to decline. Russia is among those countries scoring high on 'respect for authority' and having a low GNP per capita.

Although Inglehart's analysis did not measure support for institutions or leaders, he clearly indicates that the public's acceptance of the regime is related to economic performance. When democratic Russia remains poor, some elites may mobilize mass support to achieve economic well-being by other means, for example by resorting to the 'Chinese solution' where successful economic development has been attained by an authoritarian regime. In fact, when asked in 1998 which country should serve as a model for Russia, 33 per cent of the Russian elite named China as the best solution, considerably higher than Germany, the second most-named country on the list.[9] The Russian comprehension of a political regime is obviously associated with certain institutional outputs. However, if economic decline may lead to authoritarian attitudes the democratic institutions are not necessarily jeopardized. Elections and strong leadership may very well work in tandem.

It is difficult to construe whether confidence comes from intrinsic democratic ideas, the leaders' charisma, their decisions or actual outputs. The data indicate that it will stem from all these, but to different degrees depending on the kind of institution in question and on how that institution, its leaders and performance affect the special interests of elites and social groups. The relatively high level of support among the elite for central and regional representative institutions (the Federation Council, the State Duma and regional government), during the Yeltsin period and later under Putin, can hardly be explained by successful performance. Why, then, so much support? One explanation is the tradition of representative institutions under previous Soviet and Russian regimes. Another is that a kind of 'legal/rational thinking' prevails among a major part of the elite, whereby these main state institutions came to be regarded as valuable because of their potential collective and integrative functions.

Second, supporting representative institutions is also in the elite's own interests, since they are a counterweight towards a powerful presidency. Democracy 'Russian style' implies certain elements of pluralism safeguarding the influence of the strategic elites and serves as a guarantee towards a too strong centralization of power.

A third explanation draws the attention to the distinction between support for representative institutions having more diffuse results and support for the economic and administrative sectors where expectations are directly related to outputs impinging on the citizen's interests. The argument that poor system outputs determine fragile support seems to apply best to the business, state bureaucracy and 'order' institutions, where performance is more visible and direct. The high level of distrust in these institutions could be interpreted as a desire to replace them with something else, or at least introduce more state control through a stronger presidency as happened with the election of Vladimir Putin.

One major cleavage in Russian politics during the Yeltsin period was the very low level of confidence expressed in the President and his administration. Distrust in the President and widespread suspicion of public leaders more generally, as shown in the data, scarcely indicates a liberal attitude. A large majority of the Russian elite (78 per cent in 1998) regarded the idea of a 'strong leadership' positively.[10] However, the dissatisfaction with the President was a reflection not of criticism of this powerful institution as such but of scepticism towards the poor effects of the liberal economic policies of President Yeltsin, lack of law and order, and fears of fragmentation of the Russian Federation.

The underlying problem in Russia during the late 1990s was that poor economic performance and market failure split the elite over economic issues. The leaders who supported the President tended to have positive market preferences, while those who trusted the State Duma were sceptical towards the market. This means that attitudes to the market, based on the elite's experiences either as part of the 'newly rich' class or as representatives of the poorer segments of the population, spill over into confidence in institutions. The institutional constellations in Russia, where radical economic reforms were implemented by the President and his administration while the State Duma was intent on restricting these reforms because in the short run they benefited only a few, illustrate a rather paradoxical situation of the late 1990s. The poor consequences of the market reforms do *not* seem to have undermined the elite's support for representative institutions, but rather to have sustained them. The economic conflict went right between the Presidency and the State Duma. Many of the deputies and other elites regarded the Duma as the main stronghold for counteracting 'raw capitalism'.

President Putin's more state-oriented economic policy has been favourably received by most elites and the masses. The policies of combining state responsibilities for welfare with constraining market reforms gained considerable support. It reflects that members of representative institutions and other elite groups have fallen into line with the President's centralization policies. Support for the state's executive institutions and their leaders have increased tremendously and may be favourable to stability but will not necessarily lead to a more democratic process. Many Russians would argue that first of all the country needs stability and that a more predictable and national-oriented regime is a considerable achievement.

The main problem in Russia after Putin is not lack of support for representative and governing state institutions but the considerable scepticism towards non-government institutions. A political culture in which the status of non-state institutions like political parties and business are seriously undermined is not conducive to the development of either civic values or a functioning market. The data indicate that while the legitimacy of state institutions is increasing, there is a long way to go before a viable civil society is established. In essence, civic values and market transactions are questions of inter-elite trust. As long as personal trust remains scant the prospects for the market as an institution seem less positive. Returning to the categories of Table 4.1 one may cautiously conclude that the legitimacy of the Russian state institutions as of 2000 has come closer to Type 3 than the Type 4 situation characteristic of the late 1990s, while in the non-government sector legitimacy still remains of Type 4.

Particularly deep dissatisfaction with the new market institutions and political parties that form the core of a pluralistic society is likely to lead to more state involvement in the economic sector and further centralization to bring society back to order. However, as long as the Constitution of 1993 is respected, the 'new order' does not mean a return towards an authoritarian regime of the old type. The elite's orientations presented here bode more for political integration under a stronger presidency which needs support from the elites in representative institutions and makes possible a fairer distribution of resources and economic development not only to the advantage of the upper part of society.

One important question is whether the solid beliefs in political institutions will spill over to society and the market. If Putin's state-oriented capitalism is successful general prosperity may increase elite and mass support for the market and thereby sustain a more viable democracy rooted in societal and economic interests. Even for a patient and understanding elite, in the longer perspective legitimacy of a democratic regime derives not only from the 'intrinsic value' of institutions but also from actual experiences with system performance.

Notes

1 I am grateful for comments on an earlier draft from Vladimir Gel'man and Ola Listhaug. This chapter draws partly on Steen (2001).
2 Interviewing and coding of the questionnaires were carried out by ROMIR (Russian Public Opinion & Market Research), one of the leading Russian opinion survey institutes based in Moscow. The interviewers were especially instructed about how to conduct these interviews and several had experience with such interviews from previously.
3 Political support among the public has been the focus of several population surveys. In Western countries the tendency over time has been an erosion of public support (Pharr and Putnam, 2000). Listhaug and Wiberg (1995) paint a less pessimistic picture, claiming that there was no general decline in public support for governing institutions during the 1980s.
4 Question: 'Please, tell me how much confidence you have in each of the institutions listed. Choose among the four alternatives, where 1 is "full confidence", 2 is "quite a lot", 3 is "not very much" and 4 is "no confidence"'. 'Don't know/no answer' is treated as missing values. The institutions with low confidence are at the top (high mean) and those with high confidence are at the bottom end of the table.
5 The core institution of any democracy is the elected national assembly. Mass surveys have shown a low level of confidence among the general public in national parliaments in East European countries. Mishler and Rose (1995), who looked at nine countries not including the Baltic states and Russia, found that 91 per cent of the public expressed distrust or scepticism, and only 9 per cent full trust. In 1994, 72 per cent of the public in Russia expressed distrust in the parliament (State Duma) (Rose, 1995). Wyman (1997) reports in a survey conducted in September 1994, that only 25 per cent of Russians expressed trust in their parliament. Steen (1997) reports from 1994 that in the three Baltic states – Estonia, Latvia and Lithuania – an average of 28 per cent of the public and 53 per cent of the elite had confidence in parliament. Three years later, in 1997, popular confidence had fallen to 25 per cent, while among the elite it had increased to 63 per cent. The elite's confidence in the parliament is especially high in Estonia.

Comparing the elite's attitudes in the present study with population surveys (Whyte et al., 1997) shows that such positive trade-offs are absent in Russia for societal and government institutions, except for the State Duma and the cabinet. Thus, the Russian elite represents at least a certain guarantee for stable core democratic institutions (Steen, 2001).
6 Only institutions directly connected to the political process and basic institutions following transition to market economy and democracy, like business and the press, are included here. The vertical list of institutions does not correspond to the horizontal list because the interviewees from the eight respondent-groups were also asked to express views on other institutions. The categories 'full confidence' and 'quite a lot of confidence' are merged.

7 Statements (1) 'politicians cannot be trusted to care for the good of the country'; (2) 'public leaders think more about their own gain than about the interests of the people'. The attitudes were measured on a scale from 1 to 4, where 1 was 'fully agree' with the statement, 2: 'somewhat agree', 3: 'somewhat disagree' and 4: 'fully disagree'. In the table, values 1 and 2 are merged into a single category consisting of those agreeing with the statements and therefore expressing 'distrust' in leaders.
8 Distrust between elites is not only a Russian phenomenon. The elites in the three Baltic states also have a low level of trust in each other. The orientations of the Baltic elites (fieldwork in 1993–1994) have been analysed in Steen (1997). A comparison of Baltic and Russian elites is made in Steen (2000), with fieldwork in 1997–1998.
9 Unpublished data. Steen, A. (1998). The Russian Elite Study. Mimeo.
10 'Strong leadership' was measured on an index consisting of five statements on authoritarian attitudes. Compared with the Baltic leaders, the Russian scores are not extraordinarily high (Steen, 2000).

References

Almond, G. and Verba, S. (1965) *The Civic Culture: Political Attitudes and Democracy in Five Nations*. Boston: Little, Brown & Company.
Barry, B. (1970) *Sociologists, Economists and Democracy*. London: Collier-Macmillan.
Easton, D. (1975) A Re-assessment of the Concept of Political Support. *British Journal of Political Science*, Vol. 5, Part 4, pp. 435–457.
Gabriel, O.W. (1992) Values, Political Trust and Efficacy. Paper prepared for the Fifth Meeting of the Subgroup 'Impact of Values', European Science Foundation Scientific Program on Beliefs in Government, Colchester, Essex.
Grabher, G. and Stark, D. (1997) Organizing Diversity: Evolutionary Theory, Network Analysis, and Post-socialism, in G. Grabher and D. Stark (eds) *Restructuring Networks in Post-Socialism. Legacies, Linkages and Localities*. Oxford: Oxford University Press.
Higley, J. and Burton, M.G. (1989) The Elite Variable in Democratic Transitions and Breakdowns. *American Sociological Review*, Vol. 54, No. 1, pp. 17–32.
Higley, J., Pakulski, J. and Wesolowsky, W. (1998) Introduction: Elite Change and Democratic Regimes in Eastern Europe, in J. Higley, J. Pakulski and W. Wesolowsky (eds) *Postcommunist Elites and Democracy in Eastern Europe*. Houndmills: Macmillan Press.
Hoffman-Lange, U. (1987) Surveying National Elites in the Federal Republic of Germany, in G. Moyser and M. Wagstaffe (eds) *Research Methods for Elites Studies*. London: Allen & Unwin.
Huntington, S. (1991) *The Third Wave. Democratization in the Late Twentieth Century*. Norman and London: University of Oklahoma Press.
Inglehart, R. (1999) Postmodernization Erodes Respect for Authority, but Increases Support for Democracy, in P. Norris (ed.) *Critical Citizens. Global Support for Democratic Government*. Oxford: Oxford University Press.
Keller, S. (1972) Elites, *International Encyclopedia of the Social Sciences*, Vol. 5. London: Macmillan, pp. 26–29.
Lane, D. and Ross, C. (1999) *The Transition from Communism to Capitalism. Ruling Elites from Gorbachev to Yeltsin*. New York: St Martin's Press.
Listhaug, O. and Wiberg, M. (1995) Confidence in Political and Private Institutions, in H.-D. Kligemann and D. Fuchs (eds) *Citizens and the State*. Oxford: Oxford University Press.

Lukin, A. (2000) *The Political Culture of the Russian 'Democrats'*. Oxford: Oxford University Press.
Miller, A.H. (1993) In Search of Regime Legitimacy, in A.H. Miller, W.M. Reisinger and V.L. Hesli (eds) *Public Opinion and Regime Change. The Politics of Post-Soviet Societies*. Boulder: Westview Press.
Miller, A.H., Hesli, V.L. and Reisinger, W.M. (1997) Conceptions of Democracy Among Mass and Elite in Post-Soviet Societies. *British Journal of Political Science*, Vol. 27, Part 2, pp. 157–190.
Mishler, W. and Rose, R. (1999) Five Years After the Fall: Trajectories of Support for Democracy in Post-Communist Europe, in P. Norris (ed.) *Critical Citizens. Global Support for Democratic Development*. Oxford: Oxford University Press.
Moyser, G. and Wagstaffe, M. (1987) Studying Elites: Theoretical and Methodological Issues, in G. Moyser and M. Wagstaffe (eds) *Research Methods for Elite Studies*. London: Allen & Unwin.
Offe, C. (1997) How Identity Politics and Imported Liberalism Conspire to Frustrate Successful Reform. Cultural Aspects of Consolidation: A Note on the Peculiarities of PostCommunist Transformations. *East European Constitutional Review*, Vol. 6, No. 4, pp. 64–68.
Pharr, S.J. and Putnam, R.D. (2000) *Disaffected Democracies. What's Troubling the Trilateral Countries?* Princeton: Princeton University Press.
Putnam, R.D. (1993) *Making Democracy Work. Civic Traditions in Modern Italy*, Princeton, NJ: Princeton University Press.
Rose, R. (1984) *Understanding Big Government*. London: Sage.
Rose, R. (1995) Russia as an Hour-glass Society: A Constitution without Citizens. *East European Constitutional Review*, Vol. 4, No. 3, pp. 34–42.
Smith, G. (1972) *Politics in Western Europe. A Comparative Analysis*. London: Heinemann.
Steen, A. (1996) Confidence in Institutions in Post-Communist Societies. *Scandinavian Political Studies*, Vol. 19, No. 3, pp. 205–225.
Steen, A. (1997) *Between Past and Future: Elites, Democracy and the State in Post-Communist Countries. A Comparison of Estonia, Latvia and Lithuania*. Aldershot: Ashgate.
Steen, A. (2000). What Kind of Light in the End of the Tunnel? Democratic Norms, Market Orientations and Political Socialization. A Comparison of Elites in Estonia, Latvia, Lithuania and Russia, in J. Frenzel-Zagorska and J. Wasilewski (eds) *The Second Generation of Democratization Elites in Central and Eastern Europe*. Warsaw: Polish Academy of Sciences.
Steen, A. (2001) The Question of Legitimacy: Elites and Political Support in Russia. Europe–Asia Studies, Vol. 53, No. 5, pp. 697–718.
Whyte, S., Rose, R. and McAllister, I. (1997) *How Russia Votes*. Chatham: Chatham House Publishers, Inc.
Wyman, M. (1997) *Public Opinion in PostCommunist Russia*. Houndsmills: Macmillan Press Ltd.

5 The rise and fall of the Russian governor
Institutional design vs patron/client relationships[1]

Helge Blakkisrud

Introduction

In the spring of 1999, the Russian and Western media brought reports about a new phenomenon in Russian politics. For the first time, the regions, or rather their governors, seemed to emerge as major power-brokers in Russian politics. As the Yeltsin era was clearly drawing to a close, the Russian governors (in tandem with the republican presidents) looked destined to play the role of kingmaker. A year later, however, in the summer of 2000, the governors lay with broken backs on the political battlefield. Not only had they failed to influence the election of Yeltsin's successor, they had also been deprived of much of their formal, not to mention informal, power.

The rise and fall of the Russian governor must undoubtedly be seen against the backdrop of transition of executive power at the federal level. The governors' pursuit of power in early 1999 was clearly related to the evolving power vacuum around President Yeltsin, just as their subsequent fall coincided with the consolidation of Putin's presidency. To understand the causes and consequences of this process, there is, however, also a need to examine the development of the institution of governors itself, as well as the institutional and political context within which the powers of the governors evolved.

One way to explain the rise and fall of the governors would be to follow a neo-institutionalist approach. Russia's institutions are in a state of transitional flux, and throughout the last decade the state has alternated between periods of de- and recentralization. The institution of governors is itself still in the making, having undergone several important changes since it was first established. Is it hence possible that the sudden unravelling of the governors' position could be ascribed to in-built weaknesses in the attempt at institutionalizing devolution of power? That is, was the seemingly successful institutionalization of the governors' power in the middle of the 1990s a mere façade concealing the inherit propensity for a strong centre, so visible throughout Russian history? Could it be that a failure to sufficiently entrench the governors' powers through legislative processes and/or to clearly delineate the division of powers and responsibilities between the federal and regional executive left the governors exposed to a counterattack from a reinvigorated federal centre and, subsequently, to their downfall?

Another option would be to look for answers outside the formal structures (i.e. outside the legislative and institutional framework). Parallel to the institutionalization of the new state, the tradition of conducting politics outside the formal political/administrative structures persisted. Political patronage became a well-known characteristic of Russian politics in the 1990s. This development was due not least to President Yeltsin's inclination towards reliance on *ad hoc* and personalized relations in his dealings with the governors. When political power relies heavily on informal practices and networks, a transition of power at the apex will have repercussions throughout the structure. Could the governors' loss of power thus alternatively be explained by a breakdown of patron/client relations in connection with the transition to the new presidency?

In the following I will briefly describe the evolution of the institution of governors in the 1990s before turning to a discussion of the two proposed explanatory factors to see whether they can help us understand the 1999–2000 debacle. Through examining the bearings of the legislative framework and the institutional design, as well as the impact of intra-elite relations, I hope to shed some light on the processes that led to the rise and (apparent) fall of the Russian governor as well as its impact on democratization in Russia.

The appointed governor

The institution of governors first came into being on the eve of the dissolution of the Soviet Union. In the Soviet period the Oblast and krai Soviets had formally combined executive and legislative power. As part of the institutional perestroika of the Russian administrative system, and as a measure to introduce separation of powers at the regional level, President Yeltsin sought to transfer executive power from the executive committees (*ispolkomy*) of the Oblast and krai Soviets to the new heads of administration (*glavy administratsii*). The August 1991 coup, in which some of the regional leaders sided with the plotters, spurred the introduction of the new 'executive vertical'. On 22 August, immediately after the putsch had been suppressed, Yeltsin issued a decree establishing a hierarchic structure of regional executive institutions.[2] The new heads soon came to be known by the name of their pre-revolutionary predecessor, i.e. governors (*gubernatory*).

One of the most controversial issues related to the new administrative reform was connected with the way in which the new regional executives were to be selected. Yeltsin had decreed that the heads of administration should be appointed by the President in consultation with the regional Soviet. On 6 September, however, the Presidium of the Supreme Soviet decided to call elections to the posts of head of administration. In the political and institutional turmoil that followed the August coup, Yeltsin nevertheless succeeded in winning the Congress of People's Deputies' approval for temporarily appointing the governors by presidential decree.[3] The measure was justified by the need for preserving central control during the transition period (Gel'man, 2000: 92).

In spite of the parliament's initial approval, the President's right to appoint regional executives was contested. At the federal level, the Supreme Soviet came to see a prolongation of this practice both as being in violation of the fundamental rights of the citizen and as a way to strengthen the presidency in the brewing power struggle between the executive and legislative power. At the regional level, the Oblast and krai Soviets opposed the practice of parachuting in governors-appointees. In a number of regions, the Soviets sought to have Yeltsin's choice replaced, usually by the former leader of the *obl-* or *kraiispolkom*.[4] In the end, Yeltsin was forced to agree that the appointment of governors was subject to the approval of the Oblast or krai Soviets and thus had to give up the attempt at fundamentally altering the regional political map through appointments (Slider, 1994: 256).[5]

The question of appointment vs election was resolved only after the final showdown in the conflict between the President and the Supreme Soviet in the autumn of 1993. After having crushed the Supreme Soviet's opposition, Yeltsin in October 1993 reasserted his control over appointments and dismissals of governors. Popular elections were postponed and, according to a new decree adopted in October 1994, to take place only with Moscow's explicit approval.[6] Once the Supreme Soviet was replaced by a more pliant State Duma (the latter having its powers severely curtailed compared with its predecessor) no one seriously challenged Yeltsin's right to appoint governors. As a result, between 1993 and the onset of his second period in office in the summer of 1996, Yeltsin allowed only 16 regions to organize gubernatorial elections.

The October 1993 presidential 'putsch' can therefore be seen as a crucial divide in the process of defining the position of the governor. Until then the institutional design had been in flux and the delineation of power unclear. This put the governor under pressure from a number of actors interested in limiting their powers, most importantly the regional Soviet. Nevertheless, the institutional confusion also meant that the governors' dependence on the President could be partially offset by other alliances.

After October 1993, the executive branch became the pivot of power, whereas the legislatures at federal and regional levels were relegated to a secondary place. This made the governors more powerful within their own region but also more vulnerable *vis-à-vis* the President. It nevertheless seems that a *modus vivendi* was achieved. The governors accepted their position and chose not to challenge the President openly, while Yeltsin on the other hand seldom used his prerogative to sack governors.

The elected governor

The second phase of the development commenced with the presidential election in the summer of 1996. Yeltsin's re-election paved the way for organizing the long-postponed gubernatorial elections. Whereas only 21 Oblasts and krais had elected governors in June 1996, by the end of October 1997 all but one of the 89 federal subjects had elected heads of the executive branch (i.e. governors or presidents).[7]

The gubernatorial elections had several important implications. First of all, they heralded a further consolidation of the governors' position. The fact that the governors now could refer to a popular mandate rather than a presidential decree as their source of legitimacy undoubtedly strengthened their independence as well as their status within their constituencies. Although the balance of power had tipped in favour of the governors long before the elections, the regional Dumas had until this point at least been able to argue that they better reflected popular attitudes. Now the governors established themselves as the undisputed number one at the regional level.

The elections also reduced the governors' dependence upon the Kremlin. The governors could no longer be dismissed, and the presidential administration had to rely on carrots such as federal transfers rather than the stick when seeking to implement federal policies. Although a majority of the regions were net-recipients over the federal budget and thus needed to maintain good relations with the Kremlin, the centre by its 'move away from a short administrative leash towards a loose and long financial one' (Petrov, 1999: 23) gave up its main control mechanism. Finally, the governors' new ex officio representation in the Federation Council[8] meant better access to federal agencies and an improved bargaining position.

Parallel to the introduction of gubernatorial elections, the centre opened up for negotiating bilateral treaties with the regions to regulate powers and responsibilities. (This practice had previously been restricted to the republics.) Moreover, after the completion of the first electoral cycle, the August 1998 economic crisis presented the governors with yet another set of opportunities to challenge Moscow's authority (e.g. through the introduction of trade barriers and price controls) (Stoner-Weiss, 1999: 87). The elected governor could thus obviously exert more leverage with the centre than his appointed predecessor. Partly due to the governors' aspirations for increased powers, partly as a result of the centre's benign neglect or even outright inability to defend its rights and interests, the governors therefore continued to expand their regional power base – also beyond what had been foreseen in federal legislation (governors were for instance regularly accused of seizing control over federal property and of flouting federal laws).

The introduction of the elected governor in 1996 thus proved to be a somewhat mixed blessing. On the one hand, it completed the transition to democratically elected executive and legislative state organs. Moreover, the elections undoubtedly strengthened the governors' legitimacy and contributed to consolidating the goal of decentralizing the Russian state. On the other hand, the fact that the Kremlin gave up its presumably most effective control mechanism made it more difficult to strike down on incidents of nepotism and abuse of power within the executive vertical.

The governor as a politician of federal importance – and his fall

By the latter half of Yeltsin's second period in office, most governors had not only successfully consolidated power within their own constituencies; they also appeared to belong to one of the most influential political forces at the federal level (Withmore, 1999). The image of the governors as politicians 'of federal importance' was boosted by their strategic partnership with the President: in order to obstruct legislative initiatives from the Communist-dominated State Duma, Yeltsin actively sought to enlist the governors' support in the Federation Council. In return for their loyalty, governors expected concessions from the centre in the form of active support (e.g. increased federal transfers or the establishment of federal programmes) or also non-interference in regional affairs.

In connection with previous federal elections it had been claimed that some regional leaders controlled the political life in their territories to the extent that they were able to 'deliver' results (cf. the 1996 presidential elections). From this, the thought that they would be able to make or break a president was not far removed. In the run-up to the 1999–2000 federal election cycle the combination of more self-confident 'clients' and an ailing 'patron' thus led to an upheaval within the established patron/client relations. Instead of rallying around a presidentially sponsored 'Party of Power' (at this point in the incarnation of Our Home is Russia) the governors in the run-up to the 1999 parliamentary elections chose to present their own alternatives. They already controlled the Federation Council, now they sought to take control of the State Duma, and eventually, to influence the election of Yeltsin's successor (Malyakin, 1999). Various initiatives were launched, and in the spring of 1999, the two most important – 'Fatherland' (*Otechestvo*) and 'All Russia' (*Vsya Rossiya*) – decided to run together. The new bloc seemed to be the vehicle for attaining power and the governors started to flock around this new alliance.

Seemingly on track to the pinnacle of power, however, the governors came under attack. They had apparently underestimated Yeltsin's instinct for power and his ability to mobilize when under threat. Yeltsin did not intend to let the governors interfere in the succession question. By late summer 1999 Yeltsin had launched a counterattack on the Fatherland/All Russia bloc. From his still formidable arsenal Yeltsin pulled out both a new heir-designate, Vladimir Putin, and a new, supposedly regionally based 'Party of Power', 'Unity' (*Yedinstvo*). The combination of an effective *apparat*, the use of 'administrative resources' and the seemingly successful military campaign in Chechnya forced the challengers onto the defensive. Already before the State Duma elections in December the governors started to defect from the Fatherland/All Russia camp, and after the bloc's poor performance in the elections (13.3 per cent of the votes cast for party lists as compared to Unity's 23.3 per cent), it soon lost momentum.

The governors had hardly come to terms with the failure of the Fatherland/All Russia bloc before they received yet another blow. Yeltsin's surprise withdrawal from power on 31 December 1999 paved the way for Putin to become Russia's next president. The disarray in the ranks of governors provided a golden opportunity for Putin to reintroduce federal control over the regions, and as soon as he was formally elected, this was what he set about to undertake.

Putin did not, however, attack the governors head-on. The first strike was presented merely as a 'realization of the centre's prerogatives' in the form of a reorganization of the presidential apparatus. Only a week after his official inauguration, Putin on 13 May 2000 reorganized the structure of presidential representatives. Arguing the need for a 'strong vertical', Putin slashed the number of representatives by introducing a new administrative layer consisting of seven federal okrugs, each of which was to be headed by a presidential representative. The representatives were given broad powers, including coordination of the work of federal agencies in the regions and personnel policy. As a result, the regional leaders lost much of the control they had amassed over federal agencies operating on their regions.

But there was more to come. On 17 May, in a televised address to the Russian people, Putin announced he would present a package of federal reforms. This turned out to include two draft laws entailing provisions that potentially could seriously undermine the position of the governors. The first, on the formation of the Federation Council, recommended abolishing the ex officio representation in this body, which, if adopted, would effectively spell an end to the governors' role as federal politicians. Moreover, the second draft, on the general principles for organizing legislative and executive organs of state power (or more precisely, on amendments to the existing law), would empower the President to sack popularly elected heads of executive power.

The December 1999 State Duma elections had led to a situation in which for the first time since 1993 the President could rely on having the support of the lower house. Putin's reform package thus sailed through the State Duma, whereas the Federation Council, as widely expected, voted down the part of the legislation the governors perceived to be detrimental to their powers. On 19 July, however, the State Duma in a show of strength overrode the Federation Council's veto (362 votes to 35, with 8 abstentions) on the second of the above-mentioned drafts and passed it on to the President to be signed into law.[9] The same day the Duma adopted the revised version of the law on the formation of the Federation Council and forwarded it to the Upper House.[10] By now the governors had realized they were fighting an already lost cause and caved in: On 26 July an overwhelming majority of the members of the Federation Council (119 to 18) voted in favour of stripping themselves of their ex officio representation and immunity.

Parallel to adoption of the reform package, Putin under the slogan of 'the Dictatorship of Law' launched a campaign to bring regional legislation into accordance with federal norms. The presidential representatives were tasked with reviewing all regional legislation within their okrugs and the federal subjects were given until October 2001 to adopt the necessary amendments. The governors and the republican presidents were thus pushed from barricade to barricade: they were ousted from the Federation Council, they had to give up their immunity and would once again have to live with the presidential sword dangling over their heads, and now they were told to get rid of the legislative idiosyncrasies that had arisen under their rule.

All in all, taking into account the potential power the governors were perceived to wield, their opposition to the federal reforms turned out to be surprisingly meek. The introduction of the federal okrugs seemed to have taken most by surprise, and in any case the way the reform was presented made it difficult for the governors to produce convincing counterarguments. But even when Putin turned against the governors themselves, they did not put up a very impressive resistance. After some initial posturing and noisy protests, most governors (and republican presidents) fell into line, grudgingly admitting defeat. The governors seemed, at least on the face of it, to have resigned themselves to the regions. With hindsight, how could we have been so wrong in our assessment of the strength of the governors?

An efficient institutional design?

As pointed out above, one may seek an explanation for the governors' fall within the institutional framework. The 1990s saw an unprecedented process of devolution of power in Russia. In a few years, the hitherto hyper-centralized state gave way to a decentralized structure which even included elements of confederalism. At the same time, the institutional design has undergone several fundamental changes over the last decade and has therefore had little time to get established. Moreover, the long Russian/Soviet tradition of centralized solutions could be expected to wield considerable residual power. The question is therefore whether the governors' fall could be ascribed to their position being insufficiently entrenched within the new institutional set-up. Could remaining legislative lacunae, inherent flaws in the devolution process and/or the very lack of any established form of institutional design help to explain why the governors so easily succumbed in the face of a reinvigorated centre?

As regards legislative lacunae, a federal framework should ideally clearly delineate the division of power and responsibilities between the executive branches at the federal, regional and local level as well as between the executive and legislative branch. If not, the different levels may easily get bogged down in conflicts of authority (Duchacek, 1987). The need for clearly delineated spheres of power and responsibilities is particularly great in a state like the Russian Federation, where separation and devolution of power do not have a long history, and where one thus cannot rely on customary law and tradition as additional sources of legitimacy. Without a firm legislative basis defining the governors' position within the executive vertical, the governors could therefore easily be vulnerable to pressure from the traditionally all-powerful federal centre.

For obvious reasons, the new institutional design came into being only gradually: no blueprint existed for how to restructure a Soviet type of state with a legacy of single-party rule and a planned economy. This was also the case for the new institution of governors: it was established without a commonly agreed notion of what its role should be. Hence, the process of defining its powers and responsibilities and of codifying this in law continued throughout the decade.

The development commenced with the above-mentioned presidential decree of 22 August 1991, which paved the way for the introduction of heads of administration/governors, although their precise status and rights were left unclear. Over the next couple of years, the President and the Congress of People's Deputies/the Supreme Soviet both tried to clarify the governors' position within the new institutional set-up while simultaneously imposing their own vision of the future distribution of power. In March 1992, the Supreme Soviet thus adopted a law introducing dual accountability for the governor. Yeltsin, on the other hand, issued a number of presidential decrees in which he attempted to further strengthen his control over the executive vertical.[11]

As a result of the lack of consensus, the signals from Moscow with respect to the role of the governor were often contradictory. In the absence of a commonly accepted grand design for the administrative-institutional system, governors, presidential representatives and regional Soviets were left to fight out their own turf battles, reminiscent of the one being fought at the federal level between the President and the Supreme Soviet. The first years after the dissolution of the Soviet Union could thus be seen as a period of institutional contest, trial and error.

The violent showdown in October 1993 put an end to the uneasy coexistence of presidential and parliamentarian elements in the institutional design. The governors were hence to be appointed by the President and be accountable to the same, while the legislatures were effectively sidelined. In addition, the governors received huge additional powers from Moscow, including the right to determine the structure of the new legislative assemblies and, in broader terms, the institutional make-up of the region (Zlotnik, 1996: 29). The governors were thus rewarded for their loyalty to the President during the conflict with the Supreme Soviet (whereas most regional Soviets had sided with the latter), but probably more important from Yeltsin's point of view, this led to a concentration of power within the executive vertical.

This strengthening of the executive vertical was carried out through presidential decrees rather than federal law (a procedure which underpinned the President's control over the executive). In the new Russian Constitution of 1993 specific references to the governors were conspicuously absent. It is symptomatic that whereas both the federal executive and the level of local self-government were given separate chapters in the Constitution, the scant reference to the regional executive is found in the chapter on the 'Federal Structure'. Article 77 simply states that the federal subjects themselves independently establish their 'bodies of state power', although these have to be structured in accordance with the basic principles of the Constitution and relevant federal law (*Konstitutsiya Rossiiskoi Federatsii*). Furthermore, the development of the general guidelines for the organization of the system of bodies of state power at regional level is listed as an area of joint federal and regional jurisdiction (ibid., Art. 72).

Only in October 1999 was a comprehensive law on the general principles regulating the executive organs of state power in the federal subjects finally adopted,[12] as an earlier attempt in 1995 to adopt similar legislation had been stopped by a presidential veto (Gel'man, 2000: 98). The new law incorporates basic principles such as the provision for equal and direct elections (unless regional legislation has introduced elections through an electoral college) and a limitation on the number of consecutive terms a governor can serve (two consecutive periods of maximum five years). Except for outlining some fundamental rights and responsibilities the governor holds *vis-à-vis* the federal centre and the regional legislature, the specific powers of the governor are not clearly defined in the federal framework legislation. It has thus been up to the federal subjects themselves to supplement the framework with regionally adjusted legislation.

The decentralization of the legislative process and the lack of comprehensive framework legislation in the interim between 1993 and 1999, a period which was formative for the new institutional design, facilitated regional variation. In most cases, however, the governors laid down the main principles of division of power and institutional set-up in the wake of the dissolution of the regional Soviets in October 1993. Hence, in spite of regional idiosyncrasies, the emerging pattern came to reproduce the relationship between the executive and legislative powers at the federal level: regional legislation usually provides for a powerful governor that overshadows a rather toothless legislature.[13] The governors were therefore frequently able to control the legislative processes at the regional level. Moreover, as a result of their ex officio representation in the Federation Council, they did also have the possibility to block unfavourable legislation at the federal level – as with their 1995 rejection of a bill on local self-government that would have forced regional governments to share financial responsibility with city governments (Stoner-Weiss, 1999: 100).

Consequently, the governors served as a 'veto group' in the process of elite bargaining and adoption of legislation defining their own position and powers. Although the relative ease with which the Kremlin deprived the governors of much of their former influence could have been an indication of insufficient legal protection of the governors' rights against federal infringements, the fact that the federal subjects themselves (read: the governors) had been entrusted with designing and delineating the powers of the regional executive makes this a less likely explanation. Such an interpretation is also supported by the fact that the Federation Council in October 2000 decided to refrain from passing Putin's new federal laws on to the Constitutional Court. This could imply that the governors did not interpret the new legislation as an infringement on their formal rights.

Another question is, of course, how relevant the letter of the law is in a post-Soviet context. Respect for the law and the formal rules of the game is crucial both for the development of elite politics and democratization in general. Soviet authorities paid scant attention to the extensive rights enshrined in Soviet law. At least on the face of it, the new Russian authorities appear to have chosen another approach. Although Putin's slogan about 'the Dictatorship of Law' should not necessarily be interpreted as the same as 'rule of law', the existing legal framework seems to have less of a declaratory character than its Soviet predecessor.[14] As such, the basics of the legal framework seem quite adequate.

A second factor to consider when examining the impact of the institutional design is whether there were inherent flaws in the way in which power was devolved to the regional level. A general characteristic of transition processes is that the legislative process usually lags behind the political ones. In the case of the Russian governor this problem of timing resulted in a situation in which their formal and actual power did not necessarily correspond: whereas some powers and responsibilities were granted to the regional executive in keeping with federal legislation, others were taken up by them as a result of a legislative vacuum and/or of federal inactiveness due to the decline of the centre's state capacities.

This problem was exacerbated at the intersection between federal and regional rights, the area defined as being under joint federal and regional jurisdiction.[15] As pointed out by Duchacek (1987), such grey areas can easily develop into battle zones between federal and regional interests. The later Yeltsin years were characterized by a benign neglect that spurred a tendency of areas of joint federal and regional (as well as some of undisputed federal) jurisdiction to slip in under the control of the regional executive. For instance, appointments to regional key posts in structures such as the Ministry of Internal Affairs and the Prosecutor's Office were presupposed to be a joint federal/regional matter. All the same, the governors were often able to circumvent the centre, and according to Sergei Filatov, former Head of the Presidential Administration (1993–1996), 'many of these key persons stopped working for the country and began working entirely for the governors' (as quoted in Tsukanova, 2000: 11). Likewise, the vast majority of presidential representatives ended up as allies of the governors or republican presidents, often having been put in power at their recommendation (Smirnyagin, 2000). As a result, most governors came to hold power portfolios that did not correspond well with their formal status and the legislative framework: almost invariably the governors ended up with an institutional strength that was stronger than what had been foreseen in the existing legislation and administrative reform.

At the same time, the flip side of this 'rise of the governor' could be said to be 'the fall of the state'. Without reducing the devolution process to a simple zero-sum game, the strengthening of the position of the governors within the process of elite bargaining was undoubtedly related to the decline of the federal state. The consequent weakening of the national elites and the governors' 'willingness to avail themselves of central weakness' (Stoner-Weiss, 1999: 100) further exacerbated this trend. The expansion of the governors' powers reduced the centre's ability to control the implementation of federal policies and laws. And as the governors in effect often came to control the regional branches of federal law enforcement agencies, the centre had limited possibilities to uphold its interests in the regions. The legal idiosyncrasies mentioned above as well as the further expansion of the governors' informal powers could therefore proceed largely unhindered. The result was a weakened state that seemed to be developing towards a confederal rather than a federal structure.

The leeway the governors were given in extending their control to include areas outside their formal jurisdiction was an important element underpinning their new status as politicians of federal importance. This was where they found their strength – and their weak spot: by reclaiming for the centre what undisputedly belonged to it, Putin could successfully challenge the governors. Whereas remaining lacunae in the legislative framework thus undoubtedly influenced the way in which governors delineated their powers, the initial passivity with which the governors met Putin's reform is probably better explained by the governors being caught red-handed when the new President drew up his inventory.

The third factor mentioned above was the short time span that has elapsed since the introduction of governors. The institution is still in formation. Even the fundamental question of a top-down appointed or bottom-up elected governor is not necessarily firmly settled. On the one hand, the Kremlin in the late 1990s seemed to accept that appointing and dismissing governors was now outside its direct administrative control. After 1996, the only time the Yeltsin administration openly contemplated ousting a popularly elected governor was in June 1997, when they threatened to sack the governor of Primore, Yevgenii Nazdratenko. Facing strong opposition in the Federation Council, the Kremlin chose to back down and the issue was never raised again. Even with the new emphasis on hierarchic subordination that permeated Putin's shake-up of the executive in spring 2000, the

Kremlin refrained from challenging the governors' popular mandate. Despite the tradition of a strong centre, the Kremlin thus seems to have endorsed a shift from a top-down to a somewhat more bottom-up-oriented executive.

On the other hand, the question of elected vs appointed governors has frequently resurfaced in the debate about the administrative/institutional design. The relative ease with which some governors have seemingly been ready to sacrifice their popular mandate and transfer control over the executive to the federal presidency, thereby effectively undermining their own independent power base, demonstrates that at least some governors see position as more important than abstract principles.[16] As the present institutional design – as almost all other designs for modernizing the Russian state throughout history – was initiated from above, the governors might have believed that the devolution of power could be reversed and their position put in jeopardy: what was extended from above could also be retracted from above. Nonetheless, the fact that governors themselves raised this issue indicates that the concept of the elected governor is still far from entrenched in Russian politics.

Despite these doubts about how deep-rooted some of the gubernatorial attributes are, it seems problematic to dismiss the gubernatorial structure as just another administrative Potemkin village. As pointed out above, the governors, filling the vacuum of a retreating state, had built up powerful institutional bases.[17] Putin's success in getting the federal reform adopted can therefore hardly be attributed to a lack of formal institutional strength on the side of the governor.

A breakdown of patron/client relations?

Another way to explain the rise and fall of the governors would be to look for answers outside the legislative/institutional framework and focus on informal politics instead. Can the manner in which the governors have been interacting with the federal centre and, more specifically, with the presidency, shed light on why the governors did not protest more loudly against their demotion?

The new institutional design outlined in the previous section came into being partly as a result of bargaining between national elites (1992), partly as a result of unilateral action by the President (1993). The regional elites thus initially found themselves largely on the periphery of these events. Moreover, the way in which power was devolved within the executive vertical made the regional executive dependent on the President. On the other hand, the President (and the Supreme Soviet) soon realized the need to enlist the regional elites as allies. The mutual dependence of national and regional elites thus became an important characteristic of the emerging political system (Slider, 1994: 259). Although patron/client networks and backroom politics were by no means new phenomena in Soviet/Russian politics, President Yeltsin's proclivity for cultivating personal ties/loyalties at the expense of formal institutions and bureaucratic procedures certainly further stimulated the tendency towards reliance on informal channels. The result was a general inclination towards disregarding the formal institutional set-up and an emphasis on personalized relations in the form of patron/client networks.

In relation to the regional leaders, the emergence of such networks was further facilitated by Yeltsin's political pragmatism. After his largely failed attempt to replace some of the regional party bosses in the wake of the August coup, he quickly shifted to a policy of cooptation: whenever the Kremlin could expect at least passive loyalty from the former leaders of the *obl-* and *kraiispolkomy*, Yeltsin was willing to let them slip into the role of governors. The Kremlin thus showed its readiness to prioritize pragmatism and stability over the potential appointee's democratic credentials. As a result, the new governors were often recirculated, although not necessarily completely reinvented former regional *apparatchiks*. The first set of governors appointed by Yeltsin in 1991 included no less than 29 former leaders of *obl-* and *kraiispolkomy* as well as a number of other representatives of the old elite (McFaul and Petrov, 1998).[18] Soon, however, the appointed governors, regardless of their ideological leanings, reached a mutual understanding with the President based on a common interest in strengthening the executive power. In return for the governors' loyalty in the power struggle with the Supreme Soviet and later the State Duma, Yeltsin would usually give them carte blanche to organize internal politics in their federal subjects at their own discretion. Non-interference in return for loyalty thus lay at the heart of Yeltsin's informal 'deal' with the governors and the republican presidents.

Short of a couple of instances (primarily the destructive Chechen wars), Russia's transition from authoritarian one-party rule to a decentralized federal structure has proceeded surprisingly smoothly. One explanation may of course be that this process was facilitated by the parallel decline of the federal state. It could also, however, probably be argued that this relative success was due partly to the Yeltsinite compromise: the federal presidency and the regional elites reached a *modus vivendi* which led to a lessening of the role of centre/periphery and/or ethnic cleavages in conflicts over elite change (Heinemann-Grüder, 1998: 2). Although Yeltsin's approach therefore can be seen to have eased transition, in many cases it also contributed to a distortion of the process towards democratization at the regional level. Due to the centre's non-interference, the process of devolving power frequently fizzled out after having reached the regional level. More often than not, the governors served as an effective clog in the system, thwarting the attempts at further decentralization. The gubernatorial administrations effectively absorbed the newly devolved authority, whereas only limited powers were passed on to the level of local self-government. Hence, the combination of non-interference and devolution paved the way for the emergence of seemingly omnipotent regional leaders. Rather than a transition to democracy, Yeltsin's compromise seemed to facilitate the emergence of what some observers characterized as 'regional authoritarianism' (Gel'man, 1996: 15).[19]

In Chapter 2, Higley *et al.* argue that the emergent elite configuration in Russia is best described as weakly integrated and widely differentiated. The regional elite, here represented by the governors, fits well into this description. While Yeltsin's reliance on patron/client networks fostered individually strong regional leaders, it simultaneously undermined the governors' opportunities for developing into a consolidated elite. As a rule, governors would prefer pursuing their own parochial concerns *vis-à-vis* the centre to building coalitions across the regions. This tendency was also manifest in the regionally based parties that emerged in 1999, as seen in the ease with which they disintegrated as soon as the Kremlin launched its counteroffensive. The patron/client structure meant that vertical relations almost invariably were given priority over horizontal integration and, as a result, the governors failed to coalesce into a unified group.

Another characteristic of the elite configuration was the lack of upward mobility for the governors (especially in comparison with Soviet times). Although they were able to build up powerful bases in their home regions, the governors' political capital was not easily converted into successful bids for a position at the federal level. Very few governors were promoted by the Yeltsin regime to positions in the federal government. As a rule, the governors were confined to their regions with little hope of making a future career in Moscow. This lack of vertical integration within the executive vertical further stimulated the growth of parochialism.

The vertical focus of patron/client relations had two important consequences: on the one hand, it contributed to defuse tensions between the governors and the federal presidency. It is self-evident that the imperative of maintaining good relations with the presidential administration served as a strong disciplinary factor as long as the governors were appointed. But even when the introduction of popularly elected governors strengthened the governors' formal independence, their reliance on federal transfers to prop up the regional budgets meant that cultivation of the relations with the federal executive, and first and foremost the President, remained important. An illustrative case in point is the behaviour of the governors elected with the backing of the opposition. The introduction of gubernatorial elections initially gave a high turnover of governors. Between 1995 and 1997, only 36 out of 70 governors/republican presidents were re-elected.[20] The newcomers included a number of so-called 'red' governors as well as representatives of other opposition groups. Although they had been supported, or even promoted, by organizations that defined themselves as being in opposition to the current regime, most governors became de-ideologized when first elected, preferring to cultivate an image as an able *khozyaistvennik* (economic manager), which basically implied ensuring good contacts in the centre (the presidential administration and the government). The combination of most federal subjects being net recipients of federal transfers and a redistributive process at the federal centre that was lacking in transparency stimulated lobbying, political horse-trading and the further development of patron/client networks.

On the other hand, the disregard of formal institutions and bureaucratic procedure made the governors very dependent upon the presidential patronage – and subsequently very vulnerable in the case of a change of presidency. Although they had a fall-back position in their gubernatorial seat, much of their informal power was vested in the informal deal with Yeltsin. And when Yeltsin stepped down, he simultaneously opened this arrangement to renegotiation.

The question of succession of power and patronage sparked a crisis in the relationship between the Kremlin and their governors. Moreover, the governors entered the 'negotiations' with the new potential patron with several disadvantages. First of all, the governors seemed to have miscalculated their own strength. Instead of waiting for the patron to appoint an heir (or maybe rather because of the rapid turnover of heirs apparent and the Kremlin's seemingly weakened position under the lack of presidential leadership), the governors ventured to find a new patron on their own. This resulted in a sort of gubernatorial overstretch in which not only the governors' electoral coalition disintegrated in the face of the Kremlin's counteroffensive, but the very system of patron/client relations was severely upset.

Second, the governors appeared to have underestimated the Kremlin's ability to reproduce itself. When Yeltsin pulled Putin out of his hat, most governors were taken by surprise. Few had any clear idea about what the former FSB director stood for. Due to Putin being a relative outsider in the Moscow power elite, even few governors among the 'loyalists' could exploit existing ties. The governors were thus facing the prospect of a new patron without strong vested interests in the existing network.

Third, the time aspect worked to the governors' disadvantage. The period between the appointment of Putin as Prime Minister and the scheduled presidential elections was relatively short. Putin was declared as Yeltsin's new candidate for Prime Minister on 9 August 1999, less than a year before the scheduled elections. Moreover, due to Yeltsin's early resignation, the presidential elections were moved up to March 2000. Hence, the governors had but a few months to position themselves before Putin was officially elected. Those who had openly sided with the Fatherland/All Russia bloc were thus in a hurry to realign themselves. All the same, valuable time and opportunities had already been lost. In order to minimize the damage and ensure the new patron of their loyalty, many governors were therefore willing to make sacrifices (cf. the above-mentioned proposals to reintroduce presidentially appointed governors). The hurried realignment caused disarray in the ranks of the governors as they were falling over each other to demonstrate their loyalty. The speed of the transition thus further undermined the bargaining position of the governors.

Finally, the negotiations were fundamentally asymmetrical. Not only were the governors by definition the weaker part in the power relationship, their stakes at risk were also considerably higher. As pointed out above, the governors ran the risk of losing important elements of their power base. Yeltsin's informal 'deal' with the governors had included the Kremlin turning a blind eye to the fact that the governors had amassed powers that far outstripped their formal competence. However, as these concessions were not reflected in federal legislation or formal procedures, they would have to be renegotiated when a new president entered the Kremlin. As a result, the governors had less to offer and more to lose.

Thus, it makes sense to explain the unravelling of the governors' position as mainly a result of a renegotiation process in which built-in asymmetries between the two parts were further exacerbated due to the specific circumstances leading up to the transition of power. During the Yeltsin years the governors (and to an even larger extent the republican presidents) had developed into what some have likened to the boyars of old, transforming their regions into personal fiefdoms (Sakwa, 2000). The renegotiation of the patron/client relationship in connection with the succession crisis did, however, include a redistribution of power and, as a result of their weakened bargaining position, the governors had to accept seeing their powers scaled back in return for retaining a privileged position.

In retrospect: but did the governors really fall?

Putin's federal reforms can hardly be said to represent innovations either in form, or in content. By pulling back from the periphery and regrouping at okrug level, Putin has embarked upon the same way of reforming the administrative structure as several of his predecessors. As to the substance of the reforms, all the chosen solutions had been discussed at length during Yeltsin's presidency.[21] What was new, however, was a President who was not bound by extensive patronage and dependence on the regional leaders. Backed by a pro-presidentially inclined State Duma, Putin was able to carry out his reform package with a force and a swiftness that seemingly dealt the governors a serious blow. But how deep did the governors fall? Are they back to square one? Or is it possible that, in the same way as some observers tended to exaggerate the strength of the governors, now we exaggerate the scope of their fall?

There can be no doubt that the power of the governors was severely circumscribed as a result of Putin's federal reform. The new procedure for forming the Federation Council clearly worked to the detriment of the governors. The fact that they had to give up their seats in the federal legislature implied a loss of prestige, not to mention that they were deprived of an important meeting place and a springboard for lobbying federal agencies and the presidential administration. Without membership in the Federation Council, the governors undoubtedly lost much of their former political clout in Moscow. And perhaps even more importantly, their removal from the Federation Council meant an end to their parliamentarian immunity. The governors thus not only lost their institutional footing in Moscow, but also became more vulnerable to accusations of abuse of power and malpractice.

Moreover, the President's new power to dismiss elected governors has fundamentally altered the formal power relations within the executive vertical. Although the right to select the governor still rests with the electorate, the Kremlin now has a new, although somewhat cumbersome, way of disciplining wayward governors. Certainly, a governor can only be forced to step down after a prior court ruling and the situation can thus hardly be equalled to the one before 1996, when the dismissal of governors was subject to Yeltsin's whims. So far, no governors have been formally dismissed. Nevertheless, it leaves the governors more exposed to federal attempts at reining in their powers.

Finally, the governors' regional power base has been undermined by the measures taken by the presidential administrations to restore the executive vertical through centralizing control over federal agencies. By removing the presidential representatives from the governors' immediate orbit and putting them in charge of the new federal okrugs, the centre has been able to reassert some of its lost influence. In addition, the new administrative layer has gradually been reinforced by federal agencies setting up their new regional main offices in the 'capitals' of the federal okrugs. Maybe most important here was the transfer of the oversight over law enforcement agencies to the okrugs. This step will potentially ensure better implementation of federal laws, as it restores some of the centre's capacity for control and coercion. As the governors' influence over the federal agencies slipped out of their hands, the governors lost one of their main sources for controlling their regions (Sakwa, 2000).[22]

Hence President Putin seemed to have succeeded in turning the tables on the governors: the former politicians of federal importance have been reduced to 'ordinary medium-rank officials' (Sakwa, 2000). The governors may thus be down, but they are nevertheless not necessarily out. Although weakened, they still wield considerable power at the regional level. An indication that the governors are allowed considerable leeway at the regional level came in January 2001, when the State Duma adopted amendments to the October 1999 law on the general principles for organizing executive organs of state power. As pointed out above, this law prevents the governors and republican presidents from seeking a third term in office. Accordingly, a number of Russia's most powerful regional leaders would have had to step down in the near future. However, in what has been interpreted as a major concession to the regional elite, the State Duma, with the consent of the presidential administration, decided to count the first term for a governor as the one starting after 16 October 1999. This allowed 69 of the existing regional leaders to run for a third term, with 17 of them having the option of running for a fourth.

Another example of the limits of the centre's control over regional politics is the outcome of recent regional elections. From May 2000 to May 2002, the incumbents secured re-election in 35 out of 50 gubernatorial elections. Likewise seven out of 14 republican presidents were re-elected. Although the success rate of the incumbents does not necessarily imply that the centre has little influence, it nevertheless shows that the governors have done quite well in defending their regional power bases. And for every Kursk where the centre is able to remove an unwanted governor, there is a St Petersburg where they do not succeed. The history of the centre's accomplishments when it comes to successfully promoting candidates at the regional level is at best chequered.

Midway through Putin's first term, it is probably fair to say the governors find themselves somewhere between the presidentially appointed bureaucrat of the early 1990s and the independent-minded boyar of the second half of the decade. It is still too early to say, however, whether the reforms actually represent a fundamental break with the Yeltsin legacy.

First, as noted above, the way in which Putin's institutional reform was carried out, presenting the regional elites with a fait accompli, harks back to a traditional Russian/Soviet approach to institutional reform. Putin's reorganization of the executive vertical was yet another example of a unilateral, top-down oriented reform. This way of managing centre/periphery relations could have negative bearings both on intra-elite relations and on the process of democratization as such, e.g. through marginalization and alienation of the regional elite as well as a feeling of increased democratic shortage in the sense that power is further removed from the subjects.

Second, as regards patron/client networks there is also the question of whether 'the fall of the governor' represented the fall of clientelism as such or just an unravelling of the existing ties. If the latter turns out to be the case, we may soon see the networks restored. The shift in the balance of power between the President and the governors does not change the latter's dependence on federal resources. The governors' incentives for seeking patronage are thus unchanged. A curbing of the excessive powers of the governors was probably necessary in order to prevent further federal decline as well as to proceed with the pronounced goal of strengthening the third administrative layer, the level of local self-government. Pending a second wave of federal reforms, however, these goals remain largely at the level of rhetoric. The risk is that they will remain there as long as Putin gets increasingly bogged down in vested interests and coalition building, having to draw on the support of the governors.

What is beyond doubt is that the role of the governor within the process of democratization in Russia is still in the making.

Notes

1. An earlier draft of this chapter was presented at the ASN Special Convention 'Nationalism, Identity and Regional Co-Operation', Forlí, Italy, 5–9 June 2002. I am grateful for comments and constructive criticism from Anton Steen, Vladimir Gel'man, Pål Kolstø and Dominique Arel.
2. Decree 75 'On Some Questions Concerning the Activity of Executive Power in the RSFSR'.
3. Resolution 'On the Organisation of Executive Power in the Period of Radical Reform', adopted 1 November 1991 (*Izvestiya*, 2 November 1991).
4. According to Gel'man (2000: 94), some 15 regions experienced conflicts between the Soviets and the governors-appointees, in most cases due to the appointment of the latter without the Soviet's agreement.
5. Besides the above-mentioned opposition, it soon turned out that Yeltsin in several cases had no choice but to rely on former leaders as there were no viable reformist alternatives.
6. Decree 1969 of 3 October 1994. A further prolongation of the moratorium (until the end of 1996) came with decree 951 of 17 September 1995.
7. The president of Karachaevo-Cherkessia successfully resisted elections until the spring of 1999. Today all subjects with the exception of Chechnya have elected heads (although not necessarily elected directly in popular elections).
8. In 1993, as a transitional measure, the members of the Federation Council had been elected. From January 1996, however, the Upper House was to be formed in accordance with the newly adopted law 'On the Order of Formation of the Federation Council of the Federal Assembly of the Russian Federation', which established the principle of ex officio representation of regional heads (governors or republican presidents) and chairs of regional legislatures.
9. For the full text of the law, see *Rossiiskaya gazeta*, 1 August 2000.
10. The revised version gave several concessions to the governors, including giving them the right to keep their seats in the Federation Council until their terms expired, or through the end of 2001, whichever came first. The governors were also granted the right to appoint their personal representatives to the Federation Council as long these candidates were not rejected by more than two-thirds of the votes cast in the regional legislature. For the full text of this law, see *Rossiiskaya gazeta*, 8 August 2000.
11. These included the 'Statute on Disciplinary Responsibilities of Heads of Administration' of August 1992, which gave the President broad powers with respect to dismissing governors, and the presidential decree 'On the Responsibility of Officials of Executive Authority in the Russian Federation' of March 1993, which was aimed at strengthening the executive vertical and implementation of federal policies.
12. 'On the General Principles for Organising Legislative (Representative) and Executive Organs of State Power in the Federal Subjects of the Russian Federation' (published in *Rossiiskaya gazeta*, 19 October 1999).
13. The picture was not uniform, however. There were notable exceptions in which the legislature was able to secure a more autonomous role.
14. For a discussion of the problems of implementing legal reform in Russia, see for instance Hendley (1997).
15. For a discussion of the problems that arise as result of joint jurisdiction between the federal centre and the regions, see Risnes (2001).
16. The willingness of some governors to give up their electivity may also be linked with the fact that they were serving their second term in office and therefore ran the risk of being legally barred from seeking re-election: in exchange for giving up their popular mandate, they hoped to retain power beyond their electoral period.

17 It is symptomatic that the re-election rate of incumbent governors peaked in the last year of Yeltsin's presidency at 71 per cent. And, although the State Duma elections did not turn out to be the parade some governors had envisaged (cf. the above-mentioned failure of the regional blocs), according to Robert Orttung (2000), governor-backed candidates won in about 75 per cent of the single-mandate constituencies. Today, however, the record is somewhat more mixed.
18 As discussed in the chapter by Higley *et al.*, there are widely differing opinions as to what extent the political elite in Russia represents continuity or change compared to its Soviet predecessor. Olga Khrystanovskaya and Stephen White (1996) have claimed that this elite is a recirculated nomenklatura elite, while David Lane and Cameron Ross (1998) have argued that there has been a circulation of elites. Without entering into this debate, it is clear from the above that at least a substantial number of the former *ispolkom* leaders made the transition into governors.
19 Gel'man defines the main features of 'regional authoritarianism' as the dominance of the executive power over legislative power, the existence of a 'contract' about mutual loyalty between the centre and the governor/president, the executive power's indirect control over mass media, the neutralization or suppression of regional centres of opposition and the executive power's patronage of public organizations (both NGOs and political).
20 Calculated from data in McFaul and Petrov (1998).
21 See for instance Busygina (1997: 554–555), Pain (2000) or SVOP (2000).
22 In the late Yeltsin period, some 380,000 out of total of 410,000 federal employees were working in the regions. In comparison, the 89 federal subjects taken together employed only 190,000 (Smirnyagin, 2000).

References

Busygina, I.M. (1997) Die Gouverneure im föderativen System Rußlands. *Osteuropa*, Vol. 47, No. 6, pp. 544–556.

Duchacek, I.D. (1987) *Comparative Federalism*. Lanham: University Press of America.

Gel'man, V. (1996) Regional'nye rezhimy: zavershenie transformatsii? *Svobodnaya mysl'*, No. 9, pp. 13–22.

Gel'man, V. (2000) Subnational Institutions in Contemporary Russia, in N. Robinson (ed.) *Institutions and Political Change in Russia*. New York: St Martin's Press.

Heinemann-Grüder, A. (1998) Why Did Russia Not Break Apart? Legacies, Actors and Institutions in Russia's Federalism. Paper presented at the Conference 'European Federalism between Integration and Separation', Department of Political Science, University of Pennsylvania, Philadelphia, 2–3 October.

Hendley, K. (1997) Legal Development in Post-Soviet Russia. *Post-Soviet Affairs*, Vol. 13, No. 3, pp. 228–251.

Khrystanovskaya, O. and White, S. (1996) From Soviet Nomenklatura to Russian Elite. *Europe-Asia Studies*, Vol. 48, No. 5, pp. 711–733.

Konstitutsiya Rossiiskoi Federatsii, in B.A. Strashun (1996) *Federal'noe konstitutsionnoe pravo Rossii. Osnovnye istochniki*. Moscow: Izdatel'stvo Norma.

Lane, D. and Ross, C. (1998) The Russian Political Elites, 1991–95, in J. Higley, J. Pakulski and W. Wesolowski (eds) *Postcommunist Elites and Democracy in Eastern Europe*. New York: St Martin's Press.

Malyakin, I. (1999) Gubernatorial Election Blocs: Russia without Moscow or Moscow without Russia? *The Jamestown Foundation Prism*, Vol. 5, No. 15 (Part 3).

McFaul, M. and Petrov, N. (eds) (1998) *Politicheskii almanakh Rossii 1997*. Moscow: Moskovskii Tsentr Karnegi.
Orttung, R. (2000) Resourceful Governors Able to Counter Kremlin. *EWI Russian Regional Report*, 15 March.
Pain, E. (2000) Institution of President's Regional Representatives Changed. *New Times*, June: 11.
Petrov, N. (1999) The 1996 Gubernatorial Elections in Russia, in B. Risnes and H. Blakkisrud (eds) *Perspectives on the Development of Russia as a Federation*, NUPI Report No. 243. Oslo: NUPI.
Risnes, B. (2001) Relations Between Moscow and the Regions of Northwestern Russia – The Legal Aspect, in G. Hønneland and H. Blakkisrud (eds) *Centre–Periphery Relations in Russia. The Case of the Northwestern Regions*. Aldershot: Ashgate.
Sakwa, R. (2000) Putin's New Federalism. *EWI Russian Regional Report*, 30 May.
Slider, D. (1994) Federalism, Discord, and Accommodation: Intergovernmental Relations in Post-Soviet Russia, in T.H. Friedgut and J.W. Hahn (eds) *Local Power and Post-Soviet Politics*. Armonk: M.E. Sharpe.
Smirnyagin, L. (2000) The Great Seven. *EWI Russian Regional Report*, 24 May.
Stoner-Weiss, K. (1999) Central Weakness and Provincial Autonomy: Observations on the Devolution Process in Russia. *Post-Soviet Affairs*, Vol. 15, No. 1, pp. 87–106.
SVOP (2000) *Strategiya dlya Rosii. Povestka dnya dlya prezidenta – 2000*. Moscow: Vagrius.
Tsukanova, L. (2000) Sergei Filatov: 'We Raised Reaction with Our Own Hands'. *New Times*, October: pp. 10–12.
Withmore, B. (1999) All Power to the Provinces? *The Jamestown Foundation Prism*, Vol. 5, No. 11 (Part 3).
Zlotnik, M. (1996) Russia's Governors: All the President's Men? *Problems of Post-Communism*, Vol. 43, No. 6, pp. 24–34.

6 Between centre and regions
The State Duma deputies and Russian federalism

Anton Steen and Vsevolod Timofeev

Introduction[1]

Federalism may be regarded as a bargained institutional outcome where the basic purpose is to reconcile unity and diversity. However, the balance between centralization and decentralization may stem from different sources. Power sharing between governmental levels may be spelt out in the letter of the Constitution, or continuously haggled by the elites where the locus of power may oscillate over time. Smith (1995) suggests that 'federalism' may be about formal guarantees for regional autonomy or an instrument for promoting democratic values and redistribution. Here we suggest a political culture approach arguing that the elite's orientations to federal institutions constitute what type of federation Russia is and actually determine the balance between centralization and decentralization. Since the Russian Constitution is not very precise on the issue of power sharing between centre and regions, the equilibrium becomes largely an issue of how politicians define the relationship between ruling levels and are able to establish compromises about governing responsibilities.

The purpose of this chapter is to contribute to a better understanding of the bargained Russian Federation by analysing the Russian political elite's confidence in central and regional government, their preferences about federal power relations and how policy responsibilities should be organized. We argue that the elite's norms on these issues reflect a specific Russian type of 'bargained federalism' where the contradictory principles of 'unity' and 'diversity' not only rest on general constitutional guarantees but more importantly are legitimated by the norms of the political elite.

Since elite norms have important consequences for political stability the main question is to what extent the political elite is conflicting on how the federation should be organized. According to democratic theory the very fundament for stable democracy is if political institutions are regarded as legitimate among the elites (Dahl, 1971; Higley and Burton, 1989). It is crucial for a 'civilized' elite competition for power that the political elite accept the basic conventions regulating the political games. In particular in a loose federation like Russia, central/regional controversies have long traditions and may easily create political tensions when power is diffused. However, on one point the Russian Constitution is crystal clear, it allots a great deal of power to the Russian President. While a strong Kremlin leadership is not a new phenomenon in Russia and in the predecessor state, the Soviet Union, a democratically elected national assembly representing the population throughout the federation was a radical innovation. The abolition of authoritarian rule spurred harsh vertical elite conflicts during the 1990s with heated vertical confrontations between President Yeltsin and the State Duma. This has created a picture of fragmented Russian elites during the 1990s while the period after Putin became President has been surprisingly tranquil with considerable elite harmony.

The present Russian Constitution was adopted in 1993 and describes the Russian State as a federation consisting of 89 subjects. The Constitution prescribes in general terms the distribution of jurisdiction and responsibilities between the levels of government,[2] but how does the federation function in reality? The State Duma, as any legislature, has a double function: to represent regional interests as well as being responsible for national coordination. In the Russian federal context with a strong presidency and considerable regional autonomy, the State Duma deputies have important functions as intermediaries between the centre and the regions. It becomes crucial how the political elite in the State Duma perceive and want to shape the 'federal bargain'. After all, the Russian Federation survived and the Constitution is intact. Our thesis is that despite the many oral confrontations among the elites, there exists a rather stable consensus among the political elites as to what type of federation the elite prefers. In the following the task is to detect this consensual 'federal bargain' among the Duma members.

After describing the data material and reviewing some of the literature in the field, we investigate first how much confidence the deputies have in federal and regional governing institutions. Second, we analyse the deputies' perceptions of power sharing between governmental levels; and third, we look into their attitudes about governing and who shall control budget resources.

The data

The main data were collected from structured questionnaire interviews with representative samples of deputies of the second (1996–1999) and third Russian State Duma (2000–2003). The first round of interviews took place in spring/summer 1998 (deputies elected in 1995) and the second in summer 2000 (elected in 1999). The samples consist of 100 deputies from each year. The respondents were drawn from among persons with leading positions in the Duma and from ordinary deputies from political parties and fractions according to their strength in the State Duma. The respondents are a sub-group of the larger group of elites analysed in Chapter 4 of this book. The interviews lasted on average one hour.

The federal bargain

Numerous definitions exist of what 'federalism' is about. One may distinguish between federalism as a 'political ideology' and an 'institutional arrangement' (Smith, 1995). As an ideology, it holds that decentralization within a framework of unity is best for liberal values, civic rights, democracy and fair distribution of resources. Federalism combines authority and freedom. Another justification for federalism is a concern for preserving stability and peace inside and between territorial units. Federalism may be explicitly construed as an instrument for pre-empting conflicts emerging from ethnicity, language or religion.

As an institutional construction federalism may be seen as a special form of political institutionalization in which diversity is the main principle. Also unitary states may be decentralized. What distinguishes federalism from other state forms is that decentralization is based on a constitution guaranteeing autonomous territories basic self-rule as well as electoral influence at the central level. More fundamentally the central government does not have the right to interfere with the jurisdiction of the local territory on certain defined issues. In this sense a federation consists of regional states with considerable autonomy.

In comparative and historical perspectives federalism obviously varies broadly regarding the ideological base and institutional arrangements. Despite the variations, the common principle for these states is that neither the central nor the regional government should be subordinate to the other, either legally or politically (Watts, 1992). As Watts argues, the principle of 'separation of powers' varies between federal states. Two main forms of federalism may be distinguished: the presidential federative system (as in the USA) where the executive and the legislature are clearly separated, and 'parliamentary federations' (like Canada) in which the cabinet emanate from an elected assembly and play a more prominent role. The Russian form of federation is located somewhere between the two.

The rather broad formulations in the Russian Constitution about responsibilities of the various governing levels are conducive to a bargained type of federalism. The emerging balance between an efficient executive and regional autonomy is not only about how the federation should be organized, but raises crucial democratic questions of representation and influence. The State Duma deputies, as elected by the people and empowered with executive responsibilities, are a strategic part of the federal structure with implications for the actual functioning of democracy. However, the main focus here is on federal relations while consequences for democracy are more implicit.

The Russian Federation is characterized by strong regions and a strong presidency that to some extent is also dependent on parliament.[3] As Nathan (1993) indicates, one way of assessing the 'federal bargain' of reconciling unity and diversity, going beyond a formal constitutional approach, is to study confidence in central and regional levels of government and their power relations, and the fiscal role of regions and central authorities in levying taxes. Here, to a large extent, we are following this approach as seen from the perspective of the group of elites in a democracy that shape the 'federal bargain', the deputies of the national assembly.

Trusting central and regional government

It seems reasonable that a viable balance between central and regional levels should rest on a substantial support among Duma members to both federal and regional government. If the loyalty of the deputies is anchored solely in the Kremlin leadership or only in the regional authorities one would expect such a federation either to move towards a unitary state or tending to fragment. During Yeltsin's period there were continuous conflicts between him and the State Duma and in particular the Communist opposition were critical to the radical economic reforms. One pertinent question is to what extent did Putin's entering of office in 2000 influence attitudes towards the President? In Table 6.1 the Duma deputies were asked about their confidence in two central institutions, the President and his administration, and two institutions representing the regions, the Federation Council and regional government.

Confidence in the *President* increased dramatically from only 13 per cent in 1998 to, amazingly, 71 per cent in 2000. The low score for Yeltsin is due to his second period in 1996 starting with many problems such as his illness, losing the first Chechen war (1994–1996), corruption among top state officials and crises in the economy. The main impression in Russia was that Yeltsin was not able to rule the country and most people, in particular the political elite, understood that his period was moving towards its end and many waited for a new leader.

Vladimir Putin was elected on 26 March 2000 after Yeltsin had resigned on New Year's Eve 1999. It is quite surprising that a man with little political experience was to become President and shortly after scored very high among the State Duma deputies in popularity. There are several explanations why Putin became so popular. First, many Russians appreciated the

Table 6.1 Confidence in central and regional institutions (%)*

	1998	2000
The President	13	71
The President's administration	11	25
The Federation Council	70	62
Regional government	54	57

Average response rate: 1998, 97%; 2000, 95%.
*Per cent having 'full' or 'quite a lot of confidence'.

peaceful change of power compared to precious changes of leadership in contemporary Russian history. Putin was elected according to the Constitution and existing laws were not violated. It is the first example in Russia of a change of the executive power in a civic manner. Second, a main part of Putin's programme was to re-establish Russia's status as a great power. Many were attracted by his promises of a more powerful state, recentralization and winning the Chechen war. Third, the new President was young, and few of his close people were connected with the rather scandalized Yeltsin staff. Fourth, his background from the KGB and good relations with the armed forces were regarded as positive for more stable rule. Fifth, many 'conservative' deputies in the State Duma now saw new career possibilities and a chance of gaining access to the new power circle.

The increase of confidence in the *President's administration* was more modest and indicated that the deputies first of all trusted the President personally although they had less confidence in the new administration he introduced. Second, this increase may be explained by the possibilities for influencing the new administration by the members of Putin's Unity Party. Third, the rather modest increase in support may be explained by the lack of change of the head of the presidential administration, Alexander Voloshin.[4] In general, the deputies were critical of the presidential administration during both the Yeltsin and the Putin periods.

The deputies were positively oriented towards the *Federation Council* in 1998 and 2000, with more than 60 per cent stating confidence in this institution. One explanation is the professional cooperation between the State Duma and the Federation Council since all are members of the legislature. The deputies want to have good relations with the upper chamber so that laws may be passed more easily. Further, a high level of confidence shows that the legislative system is stable. The minor decrease in confidence may be related to the discussion about the future status of the Federation Council and position of the governors. The deputies obviously tend to have less confidence in an institution that was attacked by the new President. The interviews of the deputies took place during this turbulent period and were possibly influenced by the rather heated debate on the future of the Federation Council.

A majority of the Duma representatives have confidence in *regional government* but it is not impressive. Since the deputies are representing regional interests one might have expected more positive orientations. One reason why the regional identification of the deputies is less developed is because of weak regional party structures and numerous examples of poor regional performance. This pattern is quite similar to that seen in Table 6.5 revealing that the deputies are not enthusiastic about strengthening the power of regional government, and where the attitudes remain quite stable throughout the two periods.

What implications have these patterns for the type of Russian federalism and political stability? There is no direct connection between the dramatic increasing support for the central power and subsequent lack of support to regional government. For the State Duma deputies, obviously, it is possible to be in favour of both a stronger executive and preserving a certain confidence in regional government. This pattern may be explained first by deputies who wish to influence development in the region they represent and who feel frustrated about obtaining access to regional decision-makers. Second, many of the deputies live permanently in Moscow,[5] of whom many are Moscovites. They are looking at regional problems from the level of federal policy-making and are becoming interested in strengthening central power at the expense of regional self-government. Third, the split along the middle among deputies may indicate a potentially unstable development for regional governors and the high level of 'no confidence' indicates support for future changes in the status of the regional government.

Why do the deputies have more trust in the Federation Council than in the regional government? First, the Federation Council is a federal organ that appeals to the more fundamental centralization attitudes of the deputies. Second, the deputies are interested in increasing the role of the legislative institutions[6] such that it may have greater influence on the executive power. One main channel is through the Federation Council, and such contacts are conducive to developing considerable confidence between the two institutions. However, as the data indicate this relationship seems to be less trustful than before. After Putin came into office the State Duma representatives are more oriented towards building good relations with the executive than with the Federation Council.

Obviously, the Russian type of federalism changed thoroughly from Yeltsin to Putin. The tremendous growth in support for the President among the political elite changed the balance between governmental levels and provided the legitimacy for Putin's programme of strengthening the vertical power structures of the federation. On the other hand, a denouncing of the regional institutions has not taken place and one may conclude that although the political elite has become more positive to power centralization and stronger leadership it does not imply that regional government has been renounced. The change towards supporting a centralized leadership is accompanying support for regional government. The tendencies towards eroding of legitimate central power have been substituted by a type of federalism where the political elite put confidence both in the President and in the regional government.

Power sharing

Federations may be organized in various ways along a centralization/ decentralization scale. The Russian Federation is an interesting case because it combines a powerful President and powerful regions. In this structure other institutions, like the State Duma, have been relatively weak. Although rather impotent it may also be seen as an strategic intermediary body where coordinating and collective considerations are competing with regional and special interests and as a democratically elected organ providing legitimacy to political decisions by sanctioning proposals from the executive. In the following we ask, first, how is the political elite's 'reality' of federal power sharing. Leaning to theories of political culture, and arguing that perceptions of the world that constitute stable patterns of orientations should be regarded as a factor that shapes political processes, we argue that it matters how politicians define their environment. Analysing how 'the world is' perceived by the deputies should be supplemented by their opinions on how the world 'should look'. Therefore, the second question is how do the political elite want the power relations between central and regional government to be organized.

How, then, does the political elite assess the power relations after the system has been operating for some years? Tables 6.2 to 6.5 show how the deputies of the State Duma on a scale from 1 to 5 evaluate the political strength of the federal and regional governments.

In 1998 very few of the State Duma deputies regarded federal government as strong, and a clear majority assessed it to be weak. In 2000, the proportion of 'strong' had increased from 8 per cent to 19 per cent, while the proportion of 'weak' had decreased from 64 per cent to 42 per cent. Thus, in both years the power of federal government is regarded as quite weak but there is a clear tendency towards perceiving the federal government as more powerful.

A weak federal government may imply strong regions. But, as the preceding section on confidence in central and regional government shows, this is not a corollary. Are the deputies estimating that the power of the regions has been increasing in parallel with growing centralization?

Table 6.2 The power of the federal government (%)[7]

	Very strong				Very weak	Mean	N
	1	2	3	4	5		
1998	2	6	28	22	42	4.0	98
2000	4	15	37	32	10	3.3	98

Table 6.3 The power of the regional government (%)[8]

	Very strong				Very weak	Mean	N
	1	2	3	4	5		
1998	1	9	59	15	15	3.3	97
2000	2	23	41	25	8	3.1	99

In the second State Duma, 10 per cent regarded the power of regional government as strong and 30 per cent as weak. Many deputies chose the middle position. In the third Duma, the percentage of 'strong regional power' is increasing considerably to 24 per cent. Obviously, in tandem with describing central/regional relations as more centralized after Putin came into office, the deputies also regard the regional level as stronger than before.

By summer 2000 Putin's policies of recentralization, as seen from the perspective of the political elites, evidently had consequences for federal government while the power position of the regions also became strengthened. The reason for this apparent anomaly may be that institutions had got a real foothold among the political elite and the Constitution, laws and special agreements protected the status of the regions. Thus, the main task for Putin in controlling the regions is to change the relationship between the centre and regions regulated by Russian law.

One thing is how the political elite define their environment, quite another is the question how they *prefer* the distribution of power to be in the future. The distance between how the political elite assess power relations and how they would like it to be is an indicator of cognitive dissonance. If the dissonance is considerable it signals dissatisfaction and may easily have effects on the legitimacy of federal institutions regulating central/regional relations. Tables 6.4 and 6.5 show the deputies' preferences for central/regional relations.

There are increasingly strong preferences for a more powerful central government, which shows that Duma members have been and are becoming more positive to centralization. This is not only a response to the more popular centralizing policies of Putin but is the very fundament for such policies. Those who are in favour of more centralization are likely to come from the Unity Party and also the Communist Party. One explanation of the strong support from the Unity Part may be that its members were overwhelmingly elected on party lists. Their connections to the regions are therefore weaker and they have a closer dependency on the administration of the President.

We also observe that while only 19 per cent say that central government is stronger after Putin became President (see Table 6.2) as many as 64 per cent want more power to central government (see Table 6.4). There seems

Table 6.4 Preferences for future power of central government (%)

	More power				Less power	Mean	N
	1	*2*	*3*	*4*	*5*		
1998	29	24	24	18	4	2.4	95
2000	22	42	28	6	2	2.2	100

Table 6.5 Preferences for future power of regional government (%)

	More power				Less power	Mean	N
	1	2	3	4	5		
1998	6	20	47	20	6	3.0	95
2000	6	24	44	23	3	2.9	100

to be a large potential for political support for more power centralization after Putin came to power. This tendency is even more articulated than during the Yeltsin reign.

How then does the wish for central rule match with regional autonomy? Do we find the same tendency to 'normative cognitive dissonance' as was found for the political elite's description of power relations?

The representatives of both State Dumas exhibit fairly stable attitudes to powerful regions. The proportion of the elite who want the regions to be stronger is about the same as those who want them to enjoy less autonomy. The large number of deputies (almost half) who adopt the middle position may be interpreted as 'sitting on the fence' and being rather indeterminate about the future of regional autonomy but may also reflect a moderate position. Whatever the interpretation of the concentration on the middle of the scale, there exists a clear-cut wish for more power to the central government under Yeltsin and Putin that is not reciprocated by desiring weaker regional government. It is also obvious that the 'cognitive dissonance' is rather modest when comparing the deputies' *description* of the power of regional government with their *preferences* for regional power.

Scrutinizing Tables 6.1–6.5 on the political elites' attitudes to federal power sharing illuminates a wide range of orientations towards how the federation *is* and *should be* organized. In sum what do the data reveal about *elite integration* on the issues of federal centralization and decentralization? There are two rather obvious tendencies. First, the political elites were under Yeltsin and are under Putin very concerned about the eroding of central power and want to strengthen it but not to an extreme extent. It is fair to conclude that the political elites are quite integrated and express considerable consensus to support for more centralized power in the Russian Federation. Second, the political elite's manifest support for regional autonomy reveals a more composite picture. In fact a majority among the political elite is combining preferences for strengthened central rule with keeping regional power relatively strong. This paradox is rather easy to explain: the political elite could not just passively watch the fragmentation of the Russian Federation under Yeltsin, and consequently has opted for stronger central leadership. However, the entire democratic and economic reform project was intimately connected with decentralization of state power and autonomous local business decisions (Aron, 2001). Apparently, the political elite does not want to jeopardize the decentralizing reform project. They want to protect the newly won autonomy and consequently see no contradiction between a more efficient central ruler and regional power.

Organizing central/regional relations

Principally, there are two main ways to organize the relations between the centre and the regions: by special agreements and by federal law. The centre can deal with the subnational actors as a collective or individually (Solnick, 1998). But, in reality there is no clear-cut division between the two. According to Solnick, universal agreements do not exclude bargaining but are likely to ensure greater transparency in the bargaining process and more equal treatment in distribution of resources. The latest special agreement between the centre and the regions was signed in 1997. Our questions to Duma deputies were posed in 1998 and 2000. The deputies have since had time to assess how the system of special agreements is functioning. Since special agreements and federal law obviously may have very different consequences for the Russian Federation one important issue is how the central political elite assess these alternatives.

During Yeltsin's time the real power was in the hands of the President and the governors. Yeltsin's policies at the beginning of the 1990s were aimed at strengthening his own power position and the struggle with the State Duma was only possible with the support of the governors. In return Yeltsin promised to give the governors virtually as much power as they wanted. By special presidential decrees he delegated power to the regional level. Later, the relationship between the centre and the regions was regulated by special agreements. The agreements created a rather unclear situation about the actual power sharing between the centre and the regions since these varied from region to region. Special agreements were established between the President and the governors that were not ratified by the legislature. In other words other political institutions were excluded from bargaining the new central/regional agreements that became a main element in the new federation but not regulated in the Constitution.

The treaties form a complex system of relations (Stoner-Weiss, 1999; Solnick, 2000; Stepan, 2000). In all, agreements were signed with 46 regions, commencing with Tatarstan in 1994 and St Petersburg in 1996. The contents of the agreements differ widely between the various republics and regions. The agreements with Tatarstan and Bashkortostan were comprehensive including a considerable autonomy. In Vladimir Oblast and others the agreement was fairly restricted and formal, and in some regions such as Yakutia the agreements regulated the use of natural resources. The agreement between Moscow city and the federal government was quite special because of the capital status of the city. It gave the Moscow city government a certain degree of autonomy. A decree from Yeltsin secured special rights in the privatization of city property, and gave special tax and budget privileges that aroused envy in other regions.

A more universal way of regulating relations between the centre and the regions is through federal law. The most important are the Constitution and constitutional laws, including special laws for the Supreme Court and Constitutional Court. Various federal laws also exist, regulating taxation, education, labour, health, police as well as public relations and the mass media. Table 6.6 shows the attitudes of the deputies towards these two main forms of regulating the federation.

A large majority of the deputies are in favour of federal law as a regulating mechanism. In 1998, 75 per cent supported federal law, increasing to 84 per cent in 2000. Very few respondents buttress the widespread special agreements that were implemented during the 1990s. The overwhelming sympathy for federal regulations is substantial evidence of an integrated political elite with much concern for strengthening the central state institutions. How might the overwhelming sympathy for federal law be explained?

First, the special agreements served specific functions. After the last agreement was signed the deputies acquired experience in how this system of special treatment worked. A widespread opinion in Russia is that this kind of agreement is good only for some ethnic republics because it contributes to preserve their culture and language. During the very turbulent period in national relations of 1993–1995 the agreements were a compromise between the centre and these particular regions. In the absence of federal law serious ethnic tensions were alleviated by these special agreements that contributed to preventing further fragmentation of the Russian Federation and were useful for both the centre and the republics. Later, federal laws were adopted filling the vacuum between the centre and regions. As Treisman (1999) argues, the centre 'bought' loyalty from rebellious regions through the special agreements.

Second, the special agreements caused concern in other regions and the governors of the Oblasts and krais complained about the special status given to the ethnic republics and its leaders. According to the Constitution all regions are equal and the governors wished to obtain the same favourable treatment as granted to the ethnic republics and tried to persuade President Yeltsin to sign such agreements with them. But they were not successful in having the same kind of agreement as with Tatarstan and Bashkortostan.

Table 6.6 Support to special agreement and federal law (%)[9]

	Agreement				Law	Mean	N
	1	2	3	4	5		
1998	3	7	15	12	63	4.3	99
2000	2	6	8	21	63	4.4	100

During the period 1995–1997 federal law was introduced on a broader basis and the necessity for the special agreements disappeared. Except for the special agreements with some of the ethnic republics, the agreements with other regions became rather formal and often ineffective.

Third, the institutional setting influences the interests of deputies. A strong sympathy for federal law is simply explained by the fact that the State Duma deputies are responsible for passing federal laws but were not able to exert influence over the special agreements made directly between the President and the governors. Thus, elites outside the State Duma, e.g. members of the Federation Council and among leaders of ethnic republics, are much more positive to special agreements.[10]

One may conclude that the State Duma members constitute a strong basis for federal law, while special agreements still enjoy much popularity in the regions. As Solnick (1998) argues, universal agreements appeal to collective instincts but do not exclude bargaining. Dealing with separate regions obviously fosters selective mechanisms for problem solving. Clearly, the Russian executive is backed by strong support in the State Duma for instituting federal law.

Controlling resources

The main instrument for a viable state is to collect sufficient tax incomes to meet the expectations of the population. Federative states meet specific problems compared to unitary states since the regional level is both authorized to collect taxes and also required to hand over a certain proportion of the taxes to the centre. The present-day tax organization in Russia is centralized in the Ministry of Finance and the Ministry of Taxation and every region also has its separate taxation authority. The purpose is not to investigate the formal tax system, which is not an easy task in Russia where the whole state fiscal system was reorganized following the decentralization of the state and the capitalist economy. Here we ask what is the political fundament for the new taxation system of the Russian Federation?

As Nathan (1993) argues, in addition to studying the trust in federal institutions and centre/regional power relations, going behind the formal institutions also includes uncovering the role of the regions and central government in levying taxes. Placing the responsibility for tax collection is important but equally crucial is which governmental level shall decide how to distribute these resources? One may broadly differ between four tax regimes: (1) the federal government controls and distributes all taxes; (2) the federal government controls a major part of the tax revenues and the rest is distributed by the regions; (3) the federal government controls only a minor part and the regions are the main responsible for collecting and distributing tax revenues; (4) all taxes, except for certain basic expenditures to certain collective tasks like defence and infrastructure, are the responsibility of regional authorities.

The division of tax revenues during the 1990s was as follows: in 1998, 53 per cent of the tax revenue was retained in the regions, and 47 per cent was transferred to the federal agency. A main part of federal tax was used for defence, energy, railways etc. Some was redistributed back to the regions. At the end of the 1990s one main issue of discussion concerned changing the proportions between the levels. The federal government wanted to increase its tax revenues and by 2000 the share for the federal government increased to 57 per cent and in 2002 63 per cent. One major priority was to make tax collection more effective. After Putin came to power a new law on taxation, simplifying the complicated system of varying tax rates, was adopted in spring 2000. However, the idea of reorganizing the tax collection was not something new. During his second presidential period Yeltsin continually advanced plans to change the taxation system, but these were not carried out because of his loosening grip on power.

A common responsibility for taxation between centre and regions involves cooperation between government levels. In May 2000 Vladimir Putin introduced a new level of governance between Moscow and the regions, and appointed leaders of seven 'federal districts'.[11] The purpose of these presidential representatives is to coordinate the work of the central and regional levels, of which taxation is one of the main challenges. The tax regime that has been formed during the 1990s with a rather equal sharing of tax incomes may be seen as a bargained outcome between central and regional authorities. In Table 6.7 the question is to what extent does the political elite support this type of tax regime?

Rather few of the political elite are in favour of only federal or regional control of taxation. Generally speaking the majority support the policy that federal government should control a major part of the tax revenues; and about one-third prefer a more prominent position for regional authorities without allowing full decentralization. The bargained Russian tax regime is clearly reflected among the political elite's consensual attitudes to shared responsibilities, with a tendency to prefer a more prominent position for the central government.

Somewhat surprising is the considerable sympathy for federal tax control during Yeltsin's decentralization period. One explanation is that in 1998 many deputies were concerned about the increasing power of the governors and fragmentation of the Russian Federation, and one instrument for

Table 6.7 Controlling tax-incomes (%)[12]

	Federal control			Regional control	Mean	N
	1	2	3	4		
1998	18	46	27	8	2.3	95
2000	9	49	36	5	2.4	96

reducing their influence was to acquire more central control of tax revenues. Further, many of the deputies elected on party lists felt they had a special responsibility for the federal budget. After Putin came to power and the new law on taxation was adopted in the summer of 2000, the deputies still support considerable central control over taxation and that the federal government should be in charge of coordinating the distribution of financial resources between the regions. But there is also a smaller tendency towards sympathy for more regional control.

Because of the rather centralist attitudes both in the second and third State Dumas it was not particularly difficult for Vladimir Putin to introduce the new tax law and to increase the centre's share of the tax incomes. Also, he has a firm political basis for this type of bargained and 'shared' tax regime. However, as the elite's attitudes demonstrate, the tax bargain could not very easily be moved towards a full centralized state control without raising considerable negative sentiments among the political elite. As shown in previous sections the State Duma members' confidence in the President and positive attitudes to a stronger central authority do not imply a wish for centralization of state resources. The sympathy for decentralized authority is not only rhetoric. Not only is a considerable proportion of the tax incomes actually distributed to the regions, the political elite substantiate this type of tax regime.

Conclusion

Graham Smith (1995) distinguished between federalism as 'ideology', that is promoting certain democratic and egalitarian values, and as an 'arrangement' specifying how power should be shared. The purpose here has not been to consider the Russian Federation as a political programme or a formal institution but as a continuously bargained outcome determined by the orientations of the political elites.

To understand how the Russian Federation works one has to know the political culture and values underpinning the institutional forms, which are not guided by clear prescriptions in the Constitution. It is of particular concern to analyse the orientations of the State Duma representatives who operate on the interface between a powerful President and a decentralized regional structure. Our argument is that the 'federal form' is an amorphous structure that is continuously being reshaped by the elites' conceptions of power relations, their confidence in central and regional government and perceptions of how the responsibilities of the various levels are to be apportioned.

Several observers claim that under Putin there are clear tendencies towards more centralization and a reduction in the responsibilities of the regions, and some even suggest a return to more authoritarian rule. In our opinion the situation is more complex than that. In order to comprehend the functioning of the Russian Federation it is necessary take into consideration the attitudes of those who are involved in the political processes, such as members of the State Duma. How they orient themselves towards the federation constitutes the real centralization puzzle. The members of the Duma are especially interesting when considering the Russian Federation since the legislature is institutionalizing a parliamentary principle that might have the potential to act as a counterweight to the President. In this structure the deputies' orientations vary between centralization and regional autonomy and in a democracy such attitudes must be taken into consideration by the President.

The main finding is that the political elite's orientations are quite integrated as to how they perceive sharing of responsibilities between governing levels. The State Duma representatives are in favour of a powerful executive and effective central government, but at the same time they want to preserve at least parts of the independent status of the regions established during Yeltsin's period. But the deputies do not generally support special agreements between the centre and regions; a clear majority considers that federal law should regulate relations between governmental levels. However, while federal law gives power to the centre it also provides legal guarantees to the regions. The attitudes of the deputies are still considerably influenced by egalitarian thinking, which explains the importance of the centre in taxation but very few want the federal government to control all tax revenues.

As a political ideology, one could argue, decentralized institutions and regional autonomy are the best instrument to sustain democratic values and redistribution. Ross (2000) maintains that decentralization is fine for Western democracies while in Russia far from encouraging civic values federalism has allowed authoritarian tendencies to prosper in many of the regions. On the other hand, after Putin came to power and commenced the process of recentralization, a much-discussed question is whether Russia is now moving away from democracy. Vladimir Putin soon expanded his control over the regions by introducing the 'federal districts', the heads of which are appointed by the President himself. Quite unexpectedly, Putin also changed the procedures for the Federation Council, reducing the power of the governors. These moves towards centralization and strengthening of presidential power have received widespread support among the deputies, especially from members of the Communist Party and the Unity Party. Some may argue that when a major part of the people's representatives support centralization the implications for democracy may be a cause for concern. But as Cameron Ross argues, decentralization may also have negative effects on democracy.

After Putin introduced the policy of recentralization, representatives of liberal political parties openly expressed fear of the violation of democratic principles and they were especially concerned with suggestions about changing the federal system. On the other hand, Putin raised the question about giving local government more power at the expense of regional government so that problems may be solved as close as possible to those who are directly affected. Does this only illustrate a rhetorical attitude, or does it indicate a special type of 'hierarchical decentralism' with roots in Russian history and traditions? Here Putin is in accord with the politicians' sympathy for the idea of combining strong leadership not only with regional but also with local autonomy.

The main conclusion is that the success of Vladimir Putin's policies of centralization depends on his ability to build alliances with the Duma members. Thus, the future development of the Russian Federation obviously will be influenced by the orientations of the legislators. The rather integrated attitudes of the Russian political elite investigated here show signs of strengthening the Kremlin leadership which will be combined with considerable scope for regional autonomy within the framework of the present Constitution. The Russian type of federal bargain has been legitimated by broad elite support for a strong centre allowing considerable decentralization to the regions.

Notes

1 We are grateful for comments from Helge Blakkisrud and Jon Erik Fossum, and to Knut-Andreas Christophersen for computer assistance.
2 We are here referring to Articles 5, 71 and 72, in Sakwa's (1996) translation of the Russian Constitution.
3 As shown under Yeltsin's period the State Duma is capable of making serious obstacles to laws and budgets proposed by the President.
4 Alexander Voloshin is a special figure in Russian politics who was previously adviser to Boris Beresovsky, who recommended that Yeltsin engage Voloshin as the leader of the Presidential administration.
5 In 1998, 87 per cent of the respondents were living in Moscow. In 2000 the proportion was 82 per cent.
6 By 'legislative institutions' we mean the Federal Assembly of the Russian Federation consisting of the State Duma and the Federation Council.
7 The term 'federal government' is the English translation of the Russian term 'federal power' (*federal'naya vlast'*).
8 The term 'regional government' is translated from 'regional power' (*regional'naya vlast'*).
9 The question was introduced with a short statement of some advantages and disadvantages with the use of special agreements. Then the respondent was asked to mark the attitude on a scale from 1 to 5 with the extremes: 1 'Support special agreements for the regions/federal law is less important', and 5 'Do not support special agreements/federal law should be superior'.
10 The study also included other elite groups like a selection of members of the Federation Council and regional leaders. Figures are not shown here.
11 Each 'federal district' consists of six to 18 regions. See also Chapter 5 in this volume.
12 The question alternatives:
  1: 'All tax revenues should be controlled by the federal government, and the federal government should decide how to distribute them between centre and the regions, and among the regions'.
  2: 'A major portion of the tax revenues should be controlled by the federal government, and the rest should be distributed directly by the regional governments'.

3: 'A small portion of the tax revenue should go to the federal government, and the regions should themselves be responsible for allocating the major portion of the revenues'.

4: 'All tax revenues, with the exception of certain basic expenditures on national infrastructure and defence, should be controlled by the regional governments'.

References

Aron, L. (2001) *Boris Yeltsin. A Revolutionary Life*. London: HarperCollins Publishers.
Dahl, R. (1971) *Polyarchy: Participations and Opposition*. New Haven: Yale University Press.
Higley, J., and Burton, M.G. (1989) The Elite Variable in Democratic Transitions and Breakdowns. *American Sociological Review*, Vol. 54, No. 1, pp. 17–32.
Nathan, R.P. (1993) Federalism, in J. Krieger (ed.) *The Oxford Companion to Politics of the World*. New York: Oxford University Press.
Ross, C. (2000) Federalism and Democratization in Russia. *Communist and Post-Communist Studies*, Vol. 33, No. 4, pp. 403–420.
Sakwa, R. (1996) *Russian Politics and Society*, second edition. London: Routledge.
Smith, G. (1995) Mapping the Federal Condition: Ideology, Political Practice and Social Justice, in G. Smith (ed.) *Federalism: The Multiethnic Challenge*. London: Longman.
Solnick, S. (1998) Will Russia Survive? Center and Periphery in the Russian Federation, in B.R. Rubin, and J. Snyder (eds) *Post-Soviet Political Order. Conflict and State Building*. London: Routledge.
Stepan, A. (2000) Russian Federalism in Comparative Perspective. *Post-Soviet Affairs*, Vol. 16, No. 2, pp. 133–176.
Stoner-Weiss, K. (1999) Central Weakness and Provincial Autonomy: Observations on the Devolution Process in Russia. *Post-Soviet Affairs*, Vol. 15, No. 1, pp. 87–106.
Treisman, D. (1999) *After the Deluge: Regional Crises and Political Consolidation in Russia*. Ann Arbor, MI: University of Michigan Press.
Watts, R.L. (1992) Federalism, in V. Bogdanor (ed.) *The Blackwell Encyclopaedia of Political Science*. Cambridge: Blackwell Publishers.

7 Party extinction in Russia, 1993–2002
An elite connection

Grigorii V. Golosov

Introduction

Since the early 1940s it has been almost universally assumed that the study of political parties is virtually a prerequisite to a realistic understanding of the problems of democracy, both in theory and in action (Leiserson, 1967). As Richard Katz (1980: 1) has put it, 'modern democracy is party democracy'. Hence it is only natural to view the lack of party development as a systematic impediment for the ongoing process of regime change in Russia (Fish, 1995; Golosov, 1998). An important aspect of party underdevelopment in the country is the fact that political parties have failed to emerge as important actors in the vast majority of Russia's regions. This fact has been empirically established in a number of recent studies, including a comprehensive analysis of party representation in the regional legislative assemblies in 1995–1998 (Golosov, 1999). So far, however, the dynamics of the process have not attracted much scholarly attention.

The major reasons for this gap in our knowledge about party development in Russia are, first, the lack of reliable information about regional elections held in 1993–1994, and second, the lack of empirical evidence on the elections held after 1998. One of the goals of this analysis is to provide an empirically oriented overview of party development in the regions of Russia in the course of the whole period when the 1993 constitution was in effect. The lower chronological limit of the study is thus December 1993, and the upper limit is May 2002. This goal will be achieved in the first section of this chapter. Then I will discuss the reported findings by proposing and evaluating several explanations of the observed lack of party development in the regions. Most of these explanations refer to elite-level politics in contemporary Russia. In my conclusion, I will summarize the elite component of party extinction in Russia and briefly discuss the prospects for the revitalization of political parties.

The data and findings

While the results of the 1995–2000 elections were officially published in two volumes produced by the Central Electoral Commission of Russia (Vybory, 1998, 2001), and elections held in 2001–2002 continued to be covered in a variety of publications of the named agency, the results of less recent elections remained dispersed in the regional sources. This made me undertake a comprehensive search for relevant information in the available sources, primarily in the official newspapers of the regions. The Central Electoral Commission publications, while being an extremely valuable source of information, contain a lot of minor mistakes and inconsistencies. Thus even for the 1995–2000 elections, and especially for the 2001–2002 elections, local official sources, when available, were widely employed for the purpose of cross-checking the data.

By regions, I understand constitutionally defined subnational units of the Russian Federation. One region systematically excluded from this analysis is Chechnya. This north Caucasian republic did hold two legislative elections in 1996–1997, but one of these elections was unfair due to political limitations imposed by the Russian military authority, and another took place in an effectively independent state. Thus the set of theoretically available cases includes 88 regions. The framework for my empirical analysis has been provided by the notion of 'electoral cycles', which warrants a brief comment on the notion itself. By an electoral cycle, I understand the whole set of elections held in the Russian Federation from any given national legislative elections to, but not including, the next national legislative elections. So understood, the first electoral cycle in Russia started on 12 December 1993, the second on 17 December 1995, and the third on 19 December 1999. Since Russia's institutional design obviously makes national legislative elections less important than presidential races, one may plausibly argue that such a delineation of electoral cycles is substantively inadequate and ought to be replaced with one based upon presidential elections. While readily recognizing that this may be useful for the study of many aspects of Russian politics, I would like to mention that due to the non-party nature of the country's presidential elections, their impact upon party formation is indirect. It is the legislative component of any national electoral cycle that defines the set of viable party alternatives. From this perspective, employing the Duma elections as starting points for electoral cycles is simply instrumental for achieving the goals of this study.

The first cycle of regional legislative elections in Russia, starting with 12 December 1993, comprised 85 elections. Two regions – the republics of Adygeya and Khakasiya – did not hold elections because they retained their Soviet-type legislatures in power, and one, Ul'yanovsk Oblast, managed to unconstitutionally postpone legislative elections up to the beginning of the next electoral cycle. The second electoral cycle comprised 88 elections held in 84 regions. Three regions, Sverdlovsk, Volgogradsk and Vologodskaya Oblast, held two elections each because of the system of 'deputy rotation', which means that they re-elected parts of their assemblies on a biannual basis. The legislative assembly of Kemerovo Oblast was elected twice because it had a two-year term. At the same time, three republics that elected their assemblies for five-year terms, Karachaevo-Cherkesiya, Mordoviya and Tatarstan, did not have to schedule fresh elections in the course of the second electoral cycle, and Taimyr autonomous district did not elect its new assembly until 19 December 1999. As of May 2002, the third electoral cycle remains incomplete. The number of regions that have already held their legislative elections, 70, as well as the number of elections themselves (72), is, however, large enough to allow for reporting preliminary conclusions on the basic trends under observation.

Overall, the first, second and third electoral cycles resulted in the election of 2,796, 3,382 and 2,499 deputies, respectively. This significant increase in the number of deputies between the first and second electoral cycles may be puzzling, but it can be explained with reference to two major circumstances. First, due to a number of political reasons that cannot be discussed here, some of the assemblies elected in 1993–1995 were smaller in size than their successors. Second, and more importantly, the 1993–1995 elections often failed to return deputies because of low voter turnout. This led to a marathon series of by-elections that would last throughout the whole assembly term.

With very few exceptions, calculations reported in this analysis are based on the results of initial elections (or, in case of majority electoral systems, in the two rounds of initial elections) without taking these by-elections into account. By the end of 1995, most regions either lifted or significantly softened turnout requirements for the validation of electoral returns, which naturally increased the numbers of deputies elected in the initial elections. To achieve the goal of this study, I have divided deputies elected in the three electoral cycles into three categories, 'party deputies', 'quasi-political organization deputies', and 'independent deputies'. By party deputies I understand those who were nominated by officially recognized organizational entities contesting elections under their own names, locally referred to as 'electoral associations and blocs'. Alternative forms of party affiliation are disregarded for reasons explicated elsewhere (Golosov, 1999: 1335–1336). All deputies not nominated by electoral associations and blocs comprise the category of independents, which does not necessarily imply the complete lack of political engagement. The principal empirical indicator employed in this study is the average share of party deputies elected to the regional legislative assemblies in the given electoral cycle. In order to avoid double counting, each of the regions is entered into my calculations only once, which means that I also averaged the figures for those regions that held two elections in the course of a single electoral cycle.

The most visible result of my empirical inquiry to be reported here apparently differs from my general conclusion reflected in the title of this chapter. The role of political parties does seem continuously insignificant, yet the overall pattern seems to be curvilinear rather than decaying. While in the first cycle of regional legislative races the average share of elected party nominees was as low as 12.5 percent, the second cycle brought their share to a higher level, 20.2 percent, and it was only in the third electoral cycle that the indicator fell to the all time low of 11.2 percent. A closer look at the data, however, results in an important refinement of these findings. To achieve this, I divided the category of party deputies into two subcategories, 'Communist deputies' and 'non-Communist deputies'. By Communist deputies, I understand those nominated by the principal Russia's Communist successor party, the Communist Party of the Russian Federation (KPRF), by officially registered electoral blocs that included the KPRF, by local Communist-oriented coalitions and movements, by organizationally autonomous Communist parties in the ethnic republics and by a number of satellite organizations such as the Communist youth union. Since politically independent from the KPRF left-wing parties such as the Russian Communist Workers' Party and the Agrarian Party of Russia were not included in this category, it would be fair to say that by and large, the 'Communist deputies' are those within the organizational reach of the KPRF. In 1993–1995, the respective levels of representation of the Communist deputies and other party deputies were 4.6 and 7.9 percent; in 1995–1999, 13.4 and 7.7 percent; and in 1999–2002, 5.6 and 5.6 percent. Hence the observed dynamics between the first and second electoral cycles point not to what can be plausibly described as party system development, but to an upward trend in the electoral success of one particular party that, however, drastically decayed later on.

Other parties did not score in terms of regional assembly representation even as dubiously well as the KPRF. In order to substantiate this claim, I will employ a set of additional, party-specific indicators of strength. These are the number of regions where the given party managed to win legislative seats during the given electoral cycle and the average size of thus created legislative delegations expressed as the average share of the given party's nominees in those legislatures where it held or holds seats. In the three electoral cycles, the KPRF (not the whole conglomerate of Communist deputies as defined above) achieved representation in 22, 34 and 28 regions, and average delegation sizes were 7.5, 22.0 and 11.0 percent, respectively.

Overall, the short-living 'parties of power' of the first and second electoral cycles fared worse: Russia's Choice (1993–1995) won seats in 15 assemblies with average delegation size 11.1 percent, while Our Home is Russia (1995–1999) created only 11 delegations, the average size of which was merely 4.3 percent. The most recent 'parties of power', Unity and Fatherland, have so far replicated this pattern by winning seats in nine assemblies with the average delegation size of 8.9 percent, and in just five assemblies with the average delegation size of 4.0 percent, respectively. The principal party of 'democratic opposition', Yabloko, entered the electoral arenas of the regions in the second electoral cycle by winning seats in ten regions (7.1 percent average delegation size), but similarly to the KPRF, and even more visibly, it failed to maintain the once achieved level of success: in the third electoral cycle, it won representation in only two assemblies. Of all other parties only the Agrarian Party of Russia (APR) has ever won seats in more than five regions in the course of a single electoral cycle, the respective indicators for the three electoral cycles being 9 and 14.0 percent in 1993–1995, 6 and 13.5 percent in 1995–1999, and 5 and 10.5 percent in 1999–2002.

Discussion

Hence the empirical data convincingly prove that there is no progress in the development of Russia's party system. One way to explain this situation is to refer to a particularly unfavorable constellation of political and institutional factors in the country as a whole. In addition to a number of useful theories that normally refer to the deteriorating impact of the Soviet legacies upon party formation (Sakwa, 1993), such an explanation involves identifying three distinct, albeit interrelated, factors: the mode of regime change, the timing of founding elections, and institutional design chosen by the 'engineers' of Russia's nascent democracy. The mode of regime change conditions the emergence of new competitive actors. If the old regime passes through a phase of semi-competitive elections, the emerging political parties tend to be weaker than under the conditions of more abrupt regime change (Shugart, 1998: 13–14).

In particular, semi-competitive elections conducted before the advent of party politics enable individual politicians to build personal political resources and reputations that suffice for electoral success. This renders political parties irrelevant (Aldrich, 1995). Indeed, the electoral strength of administrative and economic managers has been identified as a factor impeding party development in a number of descriptive and analytical studies of Russian politics (Slider, 1996; Golosov, 1997; Moser, 1999). The timing of founding elections is crucial in the sense that if regime change temporarily coincides with convoking them, both collective and selective incentives for party activism resist the pressures of transition from mass anti-Communist political mobilization to the political demobilization of the masses (Golosov, 1998). In Russia, a two-year gap between the event of regime change and the 1993 national legislative elections exerted a heavy negative impact upon party development. Finally, presidential systems are often said to create unfavorable environments for the development of political parties (Linz, 1994). Indeed, the role of political parties in the 1996 and 2000 presidential campaigns was negligible. Not only the winning candidates thoroughly rejected any party affiliation, but even the second-runner, the leader of the Communist Party, downplayed his party affiliation by building loose coalitions of 'popular patriotic forces'. In fact, his affiliation with KPRF was actively – and not inefficiently – exploited in his rivals' campaign rhetoric.

Below, it will be demonstrated that despite all these negative influences, it is the national political arena that provides the most important – even though weak – stimuli for party development in the country. But, prior to making this argument, it is important to discuss why regions cannot produce political parties on their own. One reason for that is presidential institutional design currently employed in all but one of Russia's regions, which drastically reduces incentives for party activism and party vote. Of course, there is vast cross-national evidence that presidential systems do not necessarily exclude party development. Hence it is important to specify conditions under which regional party systems in Russia are likely to emerge. In an analysis of a 'deviant case' region with a relatively high level of party development, Sverdlovsk Oblast, it has been shown that the situation giving rise to political parties is that of an 'intra-elite conflict ... that emerges in (1) electoral competition among the elite participants where (2) political parties, and not the alternative forms of mass electoral mobilization, are meaningfully employed in the competition by some competitors, and (3) the conflict's outcome does not result in one set of elites possessing all or virtually all the political rewards' (Gel'man and Golosov, 1998: 31). The first of these conditions holds in many – even though by no means in all – of Russia's regions. It is the second condition that filters out most regional political arenas as potential sites for party development. To become an important tool in electoral competition held by plurality or especially by majority rules, a party must win the support of a very significant portion of the given region's population. Otherwise, party affiliation becomes a liability within the context of electoral competition, and a gubernatorial hopeful should rely primarily upon his personal political resources and reputation for building winning coalitions.

A comprehensive descriptive study demonstrates that this is what happens in the majority of regions (Solnick, 1998). The 'winner-takes-all' nature of presidential elections completes this picture by making the third of the conditions identified above rarely achievable. A statistical analysis of factors facilitating party development in the regions of Russia has proven that while intra-elite conflicts do indeed emerge as the most direct determinant of the process, their contribution does not suffice for a decisive breakthrough in its flow (Golosov, 1999).

The patterns of presidentialism in Russia's regions vary, and judging from their constitutions and statutes, some of them employ president-parliamentary systems with quite sizeable assembly appointment powers. Even in purely presidential systems that seem to be more common, the legislative assemblies still have important powers confined to the budgetary process and subnational taxation. Yet irrespective of formally specified institutional arrangements, the modes of policy-making employed in many regions are associated with political arenas strongly dominated by the heads of administrations. Sometimes, such arenas are referred to as 'consolidated regional regimes' or even stronger, 'regional authoritarian regimes'. One of the most widely cited characteristics of such regimes is the complete domination of the executives over the legislatures (Gel'man et al., 2000). Consolidated regional regimes appear to be very widespread in the regions of Russia, and especially (but by no means exclusively) in the republics, where the domination of the executive elites seems to be reinforced by the widespread use of unfair electoral practices (Löwenhardt and Verheul, 2000). As a result, politically influential regional assemblies seem to be exceptional. The dominant executives have little if any incentives to support party nominees in legislative elections. Their institutionally defined interest is to enhance their control over the legislatures. One way to achieve this would be to create political parties controlled by the executive and capable of winning legislative majorities. But such a strategy, partly because of the non-party nature of the executives themselves and partly because of the excessive political fragmentation in the electorate, is rarely realistic.

Indeed, regionally dominant political coalitions are rather rare and unusual, even though they gradually develop in a number of regions, such as Krasnodar krai and Kemerovo Oblast. The regional strongmen (Nikolai Kondratenko and Aman Tuleev, respectively) fought protracted struggles against highly unpopular Yeltsin appointees who were continuously supported by the federal authorities. Both strongmen had left-wing and nationalist inclinations, which partly explains the federal authorities' aversion to them. Even though Kondratenko and Tuleev maintained non-party standings for themselves, they found it instrumental to enhance their electoral chances by creating coalitions of left-wing and nationalist groups active in the regions. This is how the Fatherland movement in Krasnodar krai and 'People's Power – The Bloc of Aman Tuleev' in Kemerovo Oblast came into existence. Both movements outlived their founders' eventual triumphs. I would explain these unusual outcomes with reference to the initial compositions of the winning coalitions. Even upon taking power in their regions, Kondratenko and Tuleev, well aware of the electoral appeal of the KPRF that constituted the core of both coalitions, preferred to keep this party's regional leaderships under control by caging them into the movement's organizational frameworks. Thus 'Fatherland' and 'People's Power' can be viewed not as regional political parties properly, but rather as means of the organizational capture of a national political party by the regions' political executives.

Normally, regional executive authorities simply do not need such a means of translating their influence into assembly seats. Non-Communist governors prefer to support independent candidates – or anybody who is willing to cooperate. For instance, the list of Vladimir Yakovlev in St Petersburg (1998) included, in addition to many independents, both 'democrats' and Communist nominees. In Rostov Oblast (1998), the pro-gubernatorial political movement, For Socio-Economic Progress and Civil Accord, did not nominate its own candidates but supported independents and Yabloko members. The cases of Krasnodar and Kemerovo are unusual primarily because in these regions, charismatic chief executives were able to build reputations strong enough to be shared with their movements. For an individual candidate, affiliation with such a movement becomes an important political asset, which definitely facilitates the movements' political survival, but also makes it politically dependent on the executive.

The second way, maneuvering among and bargaining with parties represented in a fragmented legislature, is feasible yet hardly optimal from the point of view of the regional executives. Average assembly sizes in 1993–1995 and 1995–1999 were 37.8 and 41.4 representatives, respectively. The most feasible way to enhance control over small-size legislatures is to create conditions under which bargaining with individual deputies allows the executive to entirely avoid compromises on substantive policy issues. From this perspective, party-structured legislatures are undesirable (Shugart, 1998).

Precisely for the reason that the institutional locus of elite consolidation is the non-party executive, political insiders, that is those candidates who belong to the consolidated elites of the regions, can be logically expected to run and win as independents. A winning candidate is most often a 'boss' belonging to the region's administrative or economic managerial elite who not only avoids party affiliation but also quite vocally emphasizes his non-party status. If elected, such a candidate is strongly motivated to retain this status throughout his legislative term. Moreover, those deputies who actually run under party labels become motivated to skip them upon winning legislative seats. This happens because maintaining a specific programmatic stance and external loyalty decreases the deputy's bargaining power *vis-à-vis* the political executive on the assembly floor, while the chances for reelection without employing a party label become greatly enhanced with the arrival of incumbency advantage.

Elsewhere, I identify another factor that is potentially important for party development in the regions of Russia, rules for electing regional legislative assemblies (Golosov, 1999). In particular, under list proportional systems, parties, and not individual candidates, are those who contest elections. Then proportional systems naturally encourage politicians to invest in party reputations and make them turn to parties in their search for electoral success. Not surprisingly, the factor to which the difference between plurality/majority and proportional formulae can be reduced, the weighted average district magnitude, appears to exert a strong impact upon party development in the regions of Russia. In fact, however, electoral systems with the elements of proportionality remained rare and unusual throughout the three electoral cycles under discussion.

In the first electoral cycle, mixed electoral systems were employed in Marii El, Tyva and Saratov Oblast; in the second cycle and third cycles, such systems were continuously in use Sverdlovsk and Kaliningrad Oblast, and Krasnoyarsk krai; they were also tried and rejected in two autonomous districts (1995–1999) and recently introduced in Pskov Oblast. The second important moment is that the numbers of deputies elected by the PR components of the mixed systems, with the exception of Sverdlovsk Oblast and Krasnoyarsk krai, were usually very small. Saratov Oblast used PR to allocate ten of 35 seats; Pskov Oblast – 11 of 33; Marii El – eight of 30; and Tyva and Kaliningrad Oblast – five of 32 each. The consequences of using PR in small magnitude districts are well known. First, this yields rather disproportional results; second, unless formulae like D'Hondt divisors further impeding proportionality are employed (which is not the case in the regions of Russia where the mode of seat allocation is invariably Hare quota[1] and largest remainders), this yields unreasonably high levels of fragmentation. For instance, in the 1993 elections in Marii El, eight PR seats were distributed among seven parties, while of 22 deputies elected in single-member districts, only one was a party nominee. It is quite symptomatic that of those nine regions which ever elected parts of their assemblies by proportional formulae, as many as five rejected them by May 2002.

Why so little experimentation with PR? On the one hand, the acting deputies of the legislative assemblies are precisely those people who have benefited from plurality/majority systems. They have little interest in changing the rules of the game. On the other hand, the most important regional political actors – the governors – are directly disinterested in introducing proportional systems. Under presidentialism, a multiparty parliament is too often a parliament in opposition (Mainwaring, 1992–1993). One of a few regions where the local legislators have dared to introduce a mixed electoral system with a significant share of proportional seats is Omsk Oblast. As long ago as in December 1995, the region's legislators adopted a statute stipulating that a third of them, that is ten, should be elected by a proportional formula. Changing regional statutes is often no less difficult than changing the 1993 federal constitution, so the provision remained intact thereafter. Yet proportional elections never took place.

As of May 2001, they were delayed twice: officially, for a variety of technical reasons such as the lack of funding, and effectively, because the governor's analysts have calculated that this provision, if implemented, would have brought the number of Communists in the assembly to fifteen. Clearly, yielding a near majority in the assembly to the opposition was not very advantageous for the governor. But it was equally disadvantageous for those loyal deputies who, being in a legislative majority, were entitled to make the decision. The presence of a meaningful opposition would have made their lives a lot more complicated. This appears to be the case in those regions where statute-drafters were never as adventurous as their Omsk colleagues used to be. In other words, region-level incentives for introducing PR are normally absent. It is not the evil most often associated with PR, excessive political fragmentation (Rae, 1967), that makes it unacceptable for regional elites. After all, an assembly that consists of truly independent representatives is as fragmented as it is allowed by its size. The genuine reason is that a deputy's independence of political parties is most often his dependence upon the regional executive. Under such conditions, inviting political parties – and that is what PR actually does – is less than desirable for regional authorities.

Therefore the dominant preference for plurality/majority formulae is quite well motivated. They prevail because they are advantageous for the executive elites. The risk-aversion properties of the plurality system can be explicated with reference to its well-established ability to produce binary formats of electoral competition. Under the specific conditions of party underdevelopment in Russia, the two competitors effectively supported by the plurality formula are the pro-executive independent and the nominee of a major opposition party, if not a non-party oppositionist. Overall, it can be concluded that most regions elect their assemblies by plurality/majority formulae because they fit well into their current political regime configurations.

One more factor that has been identified as a determinant of party development in the regions is the development of national political parties, understood as a downward flow of influence from the national party headquarters to the regions. In other words, even though political parties do not emerge on the local level, they can penetrate the localities by mobilizing local voters in national elections, prima facie in the State Duma elections, and utilizing the results of such a mobilization in regional elections. An obvious alternative explanation is, of course, that it is the given party's grassroots activity that facilitates its success in national elections. While the current state of party research in Russia scarcely allows for an empirical verification of the stated theory and its alternative, an indirect test can be provided by comparing the shares of party nominees elected at the different layers of Russia's state-administrative structure – national, regional and municipal. If the major impetus for party development comes from the grassroots, than we may expect that more party deputies will be found on the municipal level; if the notion of downward flow holds, there will be more party nominees elected on the national level.

To make the data comparable, I disregard the proportional part of the State Duma elections. Then it can be calculated that the shares of party nominees elected in single-member constituencies in 1993 and 1995 were 40.6 percent and 65.8 percent, respectively (Gel'man and Golosov, 1999). As we have seen, the shares of party nominees in the regional legislative assemblies were 13.6 percent in 1993–1995 and 20.5 percent in 1995–1999. Dynamic data on municipal elections are not available, but, judging from an official publication covering the period 1995–1998, the share of party nominees among them is as small as 3.0 percent (Formirovanie, 1999). This piece of evidence is especially striking given that the overall number of municipal councilors amounted to 111,446. Political parties were apparently unable to explore this field of opportunities.

From this perspective, it is interesting to look again at the data on party representation in regional legislative assemblies. The sets of parties that secured at least some levels of success in the three cycles of elections were very different. Now it can be observed that, while being only slightly reminiscent of each other, these sets practically replicated the lists of front-runners in the State Duma elections that started each of the respective electoral cycles. A closer look reveals that in order to survive for participation in the regional elections, a party had to satisfy two conditions on the national electoral arena: first, to cross a 5 percent barrier in the proportional part of the Duma elections, and second, to get a significant number of its nominees in single-member constituencies elected. In 1993, both conditions were met by Russia's Choice, the KPRF and the Agrarians. As we have seen, they fared relatively well in the regional assembly elections too. In 1995, three parties, KPRF, Our Home is Russia and Yabloko, met the conditions. All of them were also visible on the regional electoral arenas. The Agrarians failed to cross the 5 percent barrier, but their single-member constituency delegation was the second largest in the Duma. This was immediately reflected in the results of regional legislative elections. While obviously decaying, the party continued to enjoy some limited success. In the third electoral cycle, the overall representation of political parties in regional legislative assemblies decreased, yet those parties that do survive on this electoral arena are still the same as those who won the 1999 national legislative elections, the KPRF, Unity, Fatherland and the Agrarians who allied themselves with the latter in the 1999 campaign.

What made KPRF especially successful in the course of the 1995–1999 electoral cycle, thus blurring the picture of 'party extinction'? The results of the 1995 State Duma elections suggest a simple answer to this question. In these elections, KPRF emerged not only as the largest national party, with its share of the proportional-system vote almost twice as large as the second-runner's, but also as a credible alternative to the ruling group. Moreover, under the conditions of extreme political fragmentation the share of the votes cast for KPRF was almost doubled when translated into the Duma seats. Of course, the credibility of the Communists' claims for power suffered a heavy blow after Yeltsin won the 1996 presidential election. But at the same time, the role of the major opposition party remained fully at the Communists' disposal. Hence in this case, presidentialism did not work against party development. But, needless to argue at length, the development of a single party cannot be equaled to party system development. Turning to more recent events in Russia, it is worth mentioning that no party emerged as a clear winner in the 1999 State Duma elections. The credibility of KPRF appears to be undermined by its inability to further capitalize on the idiosyncratic nature of votes to seats conversion, and even more by its candidate's poor performance in the presidential race. Hence it is only natural that the final phase of party extinction in Russia is on its way: party representation plummets, primarily because the KPRF fails to secure its already gained positions and nobody can effectively replace it.

Conclusion

Are elite-related factors important for party development in Russia, or rather for the lack of such development? In my conclusion, I will argue that they are. To substantiate this point, it is useful to present the possible explanations of party extinction in Russia as a causal chain of events occurring on the elite level. First, the Russian elites, national and regional alike, were exposed to the experience of competitive elections before parties were formed. This equipped them for further political survival without party assistance. Second, the survival of old administrative and managerial elites was not endangered by the necessity to fight their way through founding elections. Third, presidential institutional design both in the Centre and in the periphery rendered political parties largely irrelevant. This, in combination with the winner-takes-all outcomes of intra-elite conflicts on the regional level, explains why the cure for the illnesses of Russia's party system cannot be found in the regions. The vast majority of regional elites in Russia are simply disinterested in political parties and even view them as an impediment to their political domination, as testified by their unwillingness to accept proportional representation systems on the regional level. Jointly, these factors produced the phenomenon of elite non-partisanship in the regions of Russia.

Administrative incumbency, economic power, and insider status within the executive elite have superior electoral utility, while party labels are attractive for relatively weak non-elite candidates who seek to supplement their limited individual resources. Many of such candidates fail anyway, thus reinforcing the image of low party utility. Then in the next electoral cycle, candidates have no reason to affiliate themselves with the same parties. Quite the reverse, national legislative elections produce more attractive options. Weak candidates still have incentives to affiliate themselves with parties – that is, with new parties. As they fail, the story happens again. True, some of them win. But even within the category of winners, party utility becomes reduced for three reasons: first, because delegation sizes are often too small to allow for setting party agendas on the assembly floor, which makes party affiliation meaningless; second, because the winning party nominees' personal incentives for party affiliation decline with the arrival of the incumbency advantage; third, because even if party affiliation meaningfully supplemented those candidates' resources, those parties often do not survive into the next electoral cycle.

The latter applies primarily to the 'parties of power'. Being limited to a relatively narrow circle of relatively weak candidates, the existing set of incentives for party affiliation keeps political parties in their current niche of regionally marginal actors. This picture remains adequate even when applied to the only party that is relatively successful in escaping the trap, the KPRF. Throughout the second electoral cycle, this was the only party capable of crossing the effective thresholds of representation set by plurality electoral systems. Occasionally, this made the party viable either as a minority opposition party or as the executive's 'transmission belt' in the legislature, depending on the political orientation of the executive. The causal logic of the KPRF's survival in the second electoral cycle is therefore quite consistent with the logic of other parties' extinction.

The national political arena in the form of the Duma elections places parties under pressure too. The 1993–1999 campaigns resulted in notoriously high levels of systemic fragmentation and voter volatility. But it appears that at the moment, national political elites become more interested in party development than ever before. The leaders of parliamentary parties are naturally motivated to support party development. But what is more important within the current political context is that even for the national political executive, strengthening the country's party system appears to have its attractive sides. On the one hand, the centralizing efforts of Vladimir Putin's administration may be assisted by the increased salience of national political parties. On the other hand, it may be instrumental to create a viable presidential party capable of successful participation in legislative elections, something that was not affordable for Boris Yeltsin but could be done by Putin who explicitly stated such a goal on a number of occasions. So far, however, the Unity party has not been very active in preparing itself for such a role.

Since regional political turf is less than fertile in terms of party development, a feasible way to induce it is by means of institutional engineering. From this perspective, the most important component of the new law on political parties that will be fully in effect as of July 2003 and is currently in the process of partial implementation is that it legally eliminates the multiplicity of 'public political associations' that are entitled to run their candidates. The law stipulates a number of criteria (primarily, large membership and wide territorial spread) that have to be met by an association to become a party, and introduces state funding of thus recognized parties. It is expected that such a provision will contribute to party development by creating additional incentives for party building. While that may be true, it must be remembered that the major alternative to political parties within the context of Russia's electoral politics are not quasi-parties lacking organizational structures in the regions (not to say regional parties that are bluntly eliminated by the new law) and not the lack of state funds that are doomed to fall far short for efficient campaigning anyway, but rather elite non-partisanship on the regional level. The law did not address this problem, thus leaving ample space for non-party politics in the future.

Hence the second move undertaken by the national legislature with the support of the executive in May 2002: according to the new law on the basic guarantees of citizen electoral rights, starting with July 2003, all regional legislatures will be elected by mixed electoral formulae, with no less than a half of deputies in the legislature, or in one of its chambers, being elected by proportional system. Not surprisingly, this radical move has met resistance in the regions, and there is little doubt that the regional elites will wage a war against it by all means available. It remains to be seen whether the party-building drive of the early Putin period is strong enough to make him neglect and/or boldly confront such a resistance. If not, then the process of party extinction in Russia is likely to proceed.

Note

1 'Hare quota' is a special term for an electoral system using a special method of distribution of seats under proportional representation.

References

Aldrich, J.H. (1995) *Why Parties? The Origin and Transformation of Political Parties in America*. Chicago and London: University of Chicago Press.
Fish, M.S. (1995) The Advent of Multipartism in Russia. *Post-Soviet Affairs*, Vol. 11, No. 4, pp. 340–383.
Formirovanie (1999) *Formirovanie organov mestnogo samoupravleniia v Rossiiskoi Federatsii, 1995–98: elektoral'naya statistika*. Moscow: Ves' Mir.
Gel'man, V. and Golosov, G.V. (1998) Regional Party System Formation in Russia: The Deviant Case of Sverdlovsk Oblast. *Journal of Communist Studies and Transition Politics*, Vol. 14, Nos. 1–2, pp. 31–53.
Gel'man, V. and Golosov, G.V. (eds) (1999) *Elections in Russia, 1993–1996: Analyses, Documents and Data*. Berlin: Edition Sigma.
Gel'man, V., Ryzhenkov, S. and Brie, M. (eds) (2000) *Rossiia regionov: Transformatsiia politicheskikh rezhimov*. Moscow: Ves' Mir.
Golosov, G.V. (1997) Russian Political Parties and the 'Bosses': Evidence from the 1994 Provincial Elections in Western Siberia. *Party Politics*, Vol. 3, No. 1, pp. 5–21.
Golosov, G.V. (1998) Who Survives? Party Origins, Organisational Development, and Electoral Performance in Post-Communist Russia. *Political Studies*, Vol. 46, No. 3, pp. 511–543.
Golosov, G.V. (1999) From Adygeya to Yaroslavl: Factors of Party Development in the Regions of Russia, 1995–1998. *Europe-Asia Studies*, Vol. 51, No. 8, pp. 1333–1365.
Katz, R. (1980) *A Theory of Parties and Electoral Systems*. Baltimore: Johns Hopkins University Press.
Leiserson, A. (1967) The Place of Parties in the Study of Politics, in R.C. Macridis (ed.) *Political Parties: Contemporary Trends and Ideas*. New York: Harper and Row.
Linz, J. (1994) Presidential or Parliamentary Democracy: Does it Make a Difference?, in J. Linz and A. Valenzuela (eds) *The Failure of Presidential Democracy: Comparative Perspectives*. Baltimore: Johns Hopkins University Press.
Löwenhardt, J. and Verhuel, R. (2000) The Village Votes: The December 1999 Elections in Tatarstan's Pestretsy District. *Journal of Communist Studies and Transition Politics*, Vol. 16, No. 2, pp. 113–122.
Mainwaring, S. (1992–1993) Brazilian Party Underdevelopment in Comparative Perspective. *Political Science Quarterly*, Vol. 107, No. 4, pp. 677–707.

Moser, R.G. (1999) Independents and Party Formation. Elite Partisanship as an Intervening Variable in Russian Politics. *Comparative Politics*, Vol. 31, No. 2, pp. 147–165.

Rae, D. (1967) *The Political Consequences of Electoral Laws*. New Haven: Yale University Press.

Sakwa, R. (1993) Parties and the Multiparty System in Russia, *RFE/RL Research Report*, Vol. 2, No. 31, pp. 7–15.

Shugart, M.S. (1998) The Inverse Relationship Between Party Strength and Executive Strength: A Theory of Politicians' Constitutional Choices. *British Journal of Political Science*, Vol. 28, Part 1, pp. 1–29.

Slider, D. (1996) Elections to Russia's Regional Assemblies. *Post-Soviet Affairs*, Vol. 12, No. 3, pp. 243–264.

Solnick, S.L. (1998) Gubernatorial Elections in Russia, 1996–1997. *Post-Soviet Affairs*, Vol. 14, No. 1, pp. 48–80.

Vybory (1998) *Vybory v zakonodatel'nye (predstavitel'nye) organy gosudarstvennoi vlasti sub"ektov Rossiiskoi Federatsii, 1995–97: elektoral'naya statistika*. Moscow: Ves' Mir.

Vybory (2001) *Vybory v organy gosudarstvennoi vlasti sub"ektov Rossiiskoi Federatsii, 1997–2000: elektoral'naya statistika*. Moscow: Ves' Mir.

8 Local elites in Russia's transition

Generation effects on adaptation and competition

James Hughes and Peter John

Introduction

Scholars consider that democratic consolidation in post-Communist states is *path dependent* because of the persistence of particular institutional and attitudinal legacies inherited from the Communist era (Linz and Stepan, 1996; Offe, 1996). By path dependent, we do not just mean that history is important, but that elites and policy-makers are locked into an equilibrium which they find hard to break out of (Pierson, 2000). The concern of political scientists and reformers is that the 'democratic consolidation' of transitional regimes is hindered by the presence of Communist era elites who have retained their core values and have recirculated into positions of power. Indeed, it would be extraordinary if the longevity of the institutions, organizations and modes of rule of 70 years of Communist monism did not leave an imprint on the values and behaviour of the Russian elites. Nevertheless, while the Communist system disintegrated with surprising rapidity in the late 1980s and early 1990s, it is not clear whether the norms internalized by elites operating under the 'command-administrative' system have changed along with the political system or whether the values and assumptions of the old pattern of government have continued to be influential.

This research analyses data from a large-scale systematic elite interview project conducted in 1997 and 1998 in the key Russian city of Novosibirsk, which investigated patterns of elite recruitment, attitudes and behaviour. Two main trends are revealed by this study. First, elite continuity is concentrated in the administrative sector. It is not that the administrative structures of post-Communist Russia have been captured by elites from the CPSU apparatus, it is simply that they were never dislodged in the first place. Second, elite change is most apparent in the economic sector, where the move to a market economy has seen the emergence of a completely new innovator elite, largely recruited from the cultural/professional intelligentsia with relevant social capital. While the framework of institutional structures of the CPSU monist regime collapsed rapidly in 1990–1991, the values and operational culture of this regime have persisted and their residues are compressed in the administrative elite, which has been largely inherited intact from the CPSU apparatus. The adaptation of this old elite segment was eased by Yeltsin's concentration of state power in a vertically structured administrative hierarchy that operated on a patrimonial principle. A younger, more dynamic and skilled innovator elite that has emerged in the new world of privatized business could over time increasingly challenge the existing elite structures and networks since they do not share similar values on the transition. Post-Communist transition in this Russian city has, therefore, been processed largely within pre-existing power dependencies, though these are not immune to change as new values are filtering through into the elite system by gradual adaptation.

Why elites matter

Russia is an exceptional case for the investigation of elites in post-Communist transition for many reasons. The most important factor is that as the Communist system endured there for the longest it effected a deeper socialization of elites with Communist values. Other reasons are history, size, location and former superpower status which all contribute to Russia being a special case. Moreover, in contrast to East-Central Europe, there was no de-communization process and pressures from external agencies, such as the EU, NATO and the IMF, played a marginal or no role in the reconfiguration of the elites. If democratic consolidation is heavily dependent on elite attitudes, the fact that Russia has largely been untouched by a revolutionary systematic purging of Communist elites from positions of power as in the DDR, or even the ritualistic expiatory 'lustration' that characterized most other East European transitions to a greater or lesser degree, makes it even more likely that the imprint of the Communist legacy on elite values and behaviour has survived the regime transition. Thus it would be a fair assumption that elite adaptation during post-Communist transition is one of the principal vehicles by which the values and practices of Communist monism are sustained over time.

The role of elites and trends in recruitment to elite positions tend to reflect the available power resources in a state. Modern studies of how elites interact can be broadly placed into two categories, each of which are concerned with decision-making, and each with its own central hypothesis. The first to develop was the *power elite* paradigm, which assumes that power is monopolized by an amorphous, informally organized but integrated elite. This elite is composed of a socially homogeneous conglomeration of leadership cohorts drawn from political, business and military bureaucracies. The centralizing effects of modern capitalism, it is argued, led to the emergence of 'interlocking' and 'multiple directorates' in business that 'blended' with governmental and military elites to give rise to a 'power elite' (Mills, 1956). The power elite is motivated primarily by mutual economic self-interest, while its capacity to sustain itself in power is determined by the degree of flexibility that it exercises in coopting and controlling constituents from alternative structures in emergent, and potentially destabilizing, new social forces. The second is the *pluralist* approach, which holds that while there is a 'governing' elite located in the political sphere, there is always a fragmentation of power among a broad strata of influential elites (Dahl, 1961). Political equilibrium is maintained, it is argued, by a government which acts according to the norms of reciprocity and obligations, and this maintains the proper functions of elites. Typically, there is no overarching, dominant elite as power and authority is dispersed among many constituencies (political and economic groups, military, bureaucracies, churches, professional groups). Following Pareto's ideal type, there is a permanent risk to elite power as a natural circulation and competition results in the replacement of old stagnated elites by innovator new ones.

Contemporary debates on the nature of elites have elaborated and re-engaged with Dahl's conundrum of 'who governs?' Dahl's bottom-up approach to the study of democracy led to important research into agenda-setting, informal networks and the issue-dimensions of organizational networks in states. The modern conception of elites, consequently, is grounded on the existence of networks of elite 'actors' and 'groups', often informally integrated, who are defined by their dominance of decision-making processes due to their functional or occupational status and influence (Giddens, 1974). This understanding of the nature of elites is central to the work of sociologists engaged in the study of elites in democracies (Higley *et al.*, 1991). The analysis of elite groups is also used as a tool for broader investigations of the boundaries of policy-making, recruitment patterns, shared ideologies, attitudes, images and lifestyles, as well as of the constraints on the ways that a system functions (Moyser and Wagstaffe, 1987). The role of specifically urban decision-making elites has generated a comparative research focus in recent years that has examined long-term coalitions between the public and private sectors that try to solve common policy problems which have emerged due to greater economic competition in the global economy. These alliances are often informal and are not attached to the formal mechanisms of local government and are, inevitably, extremely difficult for researchers to penetrate (DiGaetano and Klemanski, 1999). Comparative studies of Western elites suggest that there are two key predictors of elite behaviour and values. The first is the spatial dimension 'country' (Putnam, 1973). The second is 'generational' or age-based. It is generally accepted that elites are not only socially and spatially integrated but tend to have a common set of values across functional categories with distinctions generated by the socialization and maturation of generational cohorts (Eldersveld *et al.*, 1995). The main conclusion is that country-specific conditions shape political generations and determine the conflicts that emerge in most Western urban political settings.

This literature offers many useful perspectives for analysing the elites of post-Communist transition states, yet so far it has been barely applied to these cases. One of the most important ways in which this comparative literature can illuminate the study of post-Communist elites is by focusing on how elites use their existing power resources to reproduce their structures and attitudes over time. An 'elite adaptation' thesis would assert that if Communist era elites have been reproduced on a wide scale and if they have preserved their spatial organization, social integration and moral solidarity or binding 'creed', then the role of these elites for achieving the consolidation of democracy and a market economy is highly questionable.[1] Equally, an 'elite decomposition' thesis would suggest that the collapse of the Communist power monopoly has been followed by processes of democratization and marketization that have been important sources of fragmentation and disaggregation of old Communist elites. Thus transition undermines the moral solidarity of old elites while the emergence of new dynamic and entrepreneurial elites creates a more differentiated, and potentially pluralistic, elite structure. This recasting of the elite in a pluralist orientation, it is suggested, promotes democratic consolidation. The principal objective of this case study is to test which of the above-mentioned propositions are most valid. We begin, however, by highlighting some of the weaknesses in the conventional transitological and area studies approaches to the study of elites in transition.

Elites in transition studies

The assumption that the 'elite variable' is of central importance to the causation of regime transitions originated with Rustow and is now one of the key pillars of transitology (Rustow, 1970). It reflects a shift away from the structuralist determinism of modernization theory, specifically Lipset's correlation of socio-economic development, the decrease of social differentiation and the rise of a wealthy middle class with democracy (Lipset, 1960 and 1983). In transition states, it is argued, the role of elites is vastly magnified, since the process itself necessarily fractures the old elite consensus, creates new elite cleavages primarily along ideological lines, thus requiring a negotiated transaction between old elites and new social forces. Alliances forged in an 'elite settlement' or 'elite pact' between old and new elites, often referred to as *reforma pactada* after the Hispanic model, are seen as the crucial factor in the development of new democratic institutions and the embedding of democratic values. An elite pact, it is argued, will 'largely determine whether or not an opening will occur at all', and constitutes 'an explicit, but not always publicly explicated or justified, agreement among a selected set of actors which seek to define (or, better to redefine) rules governing the exercise of power on the basis of mutual guarantees for the 'vital interests' of those entering into it' (O'Donnell and Schmitter, 1986: 37). Democratic consolidation, according to the classic statement of the position by Higley and Burton, requires a 'consensually unified elite' (Higley and Burton, 1989).

In much the same metaphorical way that Lenin's revolutionary omelette required broken eggs, so students of transition propose that an end to authoritarianism necessitates the cracking open of the old national ruling elite and some combination of the resulting fractures with newly emergent elites in the making of a grand alliance for reform. To understand better the nature of the alliances forged between old and new elites recent work on transitions has applied game theory models, and consequently the focus has shifted to nebulous categorizations of 'actors' rather than elites *per se*. The leading exponent is Przeworski who views transitions as a four-player game between 'Hardliners', 'Reformers', 'Moderates' and 'Radicals' (Przeworski, 1992).

Studies of the role of elites in post-Communist states follow the conventional focus of transitology on state-level elite configurations. A recent cross-country comparative study of elites in Eastern Europe by Higley *et al.*, revealed a trend for a radical break with the past legacies of Communist 'ideocratic unity',[2] comparatively narrow differentiation and centralism, and a more pluralist power structure and greater autonomy of elites acting within a consensus about the new democratic rules of the game. Admittedly some countries have advanced further than others while the trend in a few is less certain. Higley *et al.* identify four patterns of elite change: (1) a negotiated settlement creating consensual elites (Poland, Hungary and the Czech Republic after 1992); (2) a regime implosion, displacement of Communist leaderships and territorial reconstitution (Czechoslovakia, DDR, Yugoslavia); (3) liberalization followed by elite fragmentation (Bulgaria, Albania and Slovakia after 1992); (4) a 'pre-emptive coup' that divides the elites (Romania, Ukraine and Belarus). Russia, it is argued, combines elements of all the above. This conceptual framework, however, is largely disassociated from empirical research (Higley *et al.*, 1998).

Oddly, despite their role being considered of central importance by transitologists, elites are weakly investigated whether as regards their composition or values. Linz and Stepan, for example, suggest three dimensions of consolidation: behavioural, attitudinal and constitutional. However, they view the 'attitudinal' variable as a problem that concerns only the remoulding of 'public opinion', and indeed, they make no specific reference to the role of 'elites' in their discussion of the three dimensions of consolidation (Linz and Stepan, 1996: 6). Rustow, on the other hand, recognized that the difficulty of what he termed the 'habituation' phase of democratization lies in the embedding of a particular set of attitudinal reformist values and processes of dissension, conciliation and realignment, specifically among the elites. The essence of democracy for Rustow is an elitist Schumpeterian one, for it required national elites to adhere to 'the habit of dissension and conciliation over ever-changing issues and amidst ever-changing alignments' (Rustow, 1970: 363). This is the essence of Linz's oft-repeated maxim that democracy must be the 'only game in town'.

The proposition that state-level elite 'settlements' and 'pacts' are a crucial precondition for the evolution of stable democracies and the avoidance of a descent into the anarchy of warring factions, rests on the assumption that transition is predominantly, and is best understood as, a state-led process. Thus, the transitologists take the 'state' as their fundamental unit of analysis: the state being broadly understood as including national governments, parliaments, parties and other national elite sectors. The evidence for such propositions is fragile, as the study of elites in transition is strong on assumption and conceptualization, but weak on empirical foundation. We aim to demonstrate that the concentration on the macrovariable 'state' does not fully capture the reality of transition. The process by which democracy and the market is consolidated in a transitional society is multidimensional even among elites, and should be analysed accordingly. Transition is as much a local process as it is a national one. We believe that the most fundamental basis for a consolidated transition is the extent to which democratic values and the operating codes of a market economy have permeated down to and are embedded at the substate level. How quickly and in what ways this percolation of transition occurs will largely be determined by the response of substate elites. To paraphrase another well-known maxim: *all transitions are local*.

Adaptation versus competition

Has transition in Russia generated a major cleavage in its elite structure and, if so, what is its nature? The collapse of Communist rule in the Soviet Union has removed many of the obstacles to the study of elites. Two main approaches can be differentiated: studies of state-level elites, which tend to be quantitative, and studies of substate regional and local elites, which have tended thus far to be qualitative in nature. The most empirically rich work has been on the process of elite formation, and the values and behaviour of post-Soviet state-level elites during the transition. Although these studies broadly accept that there is a pattern of continuity between the old Soviet nomenklatura and post-Communist ruling elites, there is wide disagreement over the scale of turnover and recirculation. Studies of elites in Russia generally analyse how continuity, circulation or turnover of ruling elites affect the prospects for transition by drawing a major distinction between the *reproduction of old elites*, which maintain values, promote stability and continuity and, perhaps, stagnation, and the *circulation of new elites* into power, which can be carriers of democratic and market values, so diffusing these values into elite behaviour and society at large. This bifurcation into what we may term an *inherited old versus innovator new* elite cleavage rests on two widely employed conceptions of the role of elites in the Russian transition.

First, and perhaps naturally given the absence of decommunization, an *elite adaptation thesis* has obtained the widest currency among analysts.

So comprehensive, it is claimed, was the reproduction of the CPSU elites into the new political and economic arenas that the process amounted to the 'privatization of the nomenklatura' (Wollman, 1993). The old nomenklatura, it is argued, adapted to the transition and reasserted itself as the new 'party of power' (Badovsky, 1994). It is important to note that the use of the term 'nomenklatura' to categorize the governing elites of the Communist era is not without controversy, as Sovietologists in the 1960s and 1970s spent many years debating the parameters and meaning of this term. What is less excusable is the way in which studies of post-Soviet elites often loosely employ the terms 'elite' and 'nomenklatura' interchangeably (see, for example, Kryshtanovskaya and White, 1996). It is misleading to use the catch-all term 'nomenklatura' in determining elite reproduction in the post-Communist transition precisely because the category does not sufficiently differentiate between former elites and lower-level functionaries appointed by the party. The elite adaptation thesis suggests that power at the national level is exercised by an 'interlocking directorate' of the administrative and business elites who have largely been recirculated from the nomenklatura. It is surmised that the informal networks of power of the Communist era adapted during the transition by a process described by one commentator as 'the politicisation of industrialists, and of the 'industrialisation' of politicians' (Kliamkin, 1993).

Second, there is what we may call an *elite competition thesis*. One of the most systematic studies of Russia's post-Communist elites is by Lane and Ross who analyse the social configurations and value systems of the Gorbachev-era and Yeltsin-era national elites to demonstrate that the Russian transition has been marked by a fragmentation of elite values and a lack of recirculation of the old elite. The competitive struggle which has ensued, they argue, is partly generational between older and younger elite cohorts, but is mainly driven by 'class' dynamics: a 'political class' of senior administrators is confronted by an ascendant 'acquisition class' of members of the intelligentsia with the relevant skills to take best advantage of the new conditions of transition (Lane and Ross, 1999). Similarly, Kryshtanovskaya and White have used national elite sociobiographical data to propose that the simple dichotomy between 'old' and 'new' is better understood as a functional bifurcation between 'old' political/administrative elites who are in competition with 'new' economic elites (Kryshtanovskaya and White, 1996). Lane and Ross, however, challenge the transition model assumption of an elite consensus for a stable transition, and confirm the notion of a bipolarized conflict along an old/new cleavage and around the key issue dimensions of democratic governance and privatization. Most commonly this notion of a dichotomous conflict between 'old' and 'new' elites is viewed as a simple *ideological* one, whether in Western or Russian, national or local studies (Kullberg, 1994; Melville, 1999).

How appropriate is this old/new cleavage, conceptually and analytically, for understanding the role of elites in Russia's transition? Empirical research on regional elites suggests that there is not a rigid old/new elite bifurcation along functional or class lines, but rather that the governing elite at the substate level is an amalgam of the elites in two key sectors: administration and business. The old versus new elite distinction does not, therefore, capture the complex nature of the 'interlocked' elite. The governing elite at the substate level is overwhelmingly recruited from administrative and economic managerial elites from the Communist era that colonized the newly democratized elected assemblies from 1994 in order to preserve their grip on local power (Hughes, 1997).[3]

There is much evidence for the view that the struggles among Russia's local elites have mirrored those at the centre, turning on economic issues and the protection of existing power structures and patronage networks through the privatization of state assets. The struggle over privatization was a key, if not the most important, mobilizing factor for Communist-era local elites, who used their administrative control of the local economy to 'regroup' and consolidate their authority during the transition. This type of centre/regional territorial-based issue cleavage is a product of the decomposition of the CPSU integrated elite. The fragmentation of the elite in a disintegrating economy has led to the mobilization of regional and local elites around distributive issues of economic control and privatization and the localization of a countermetropolis culture that cross-cuts ideological identities. The relative unimportance of elite ideological cleavages goes some way to explaining why political party formation in Russia has been so underdeveloped. Party formation requires elites to exhibit ideological commitment, whereas for the Russian elites the major concern is self-preservation, political flexibility and pragmatism, combined with *enrichissez-vous* practices.

Evidence for the kind of elite ideological cleavage, as envisaged in the transition models of Higley and Burton or Przeworski, is sparse. Qualitative studies of elites have suggested that ideological cleavages have been salient in the more modernized metropolitan regions such as St Petersburg, but confirmed the continuity of the old elite in power in Russia's provincial cities and regions (McAuley, 1997). The failure of Russia's transition to a market economy is frequently attributed to the 'rent-seeking' practices of its elites to control privatization and to ensure that old networks and power relationships are preserved (Aaslund, 1996; Stiglitz, 1999). The patrimonial nature of Russia's political system under Yeltsin, with power concentrated vertically in the administrative sector (at the state level in the presidency, at the substate level in governors and mayors) meant that elites tended to take the risk-avoidance option not to be drawn into the kind of overt ideological stance that transitologists expected. This is not to say that ideological cleavages have not been significant among national and local elites in Russia, but that they have not been institutionalized in political party development, which is seen by transitologists, and political scientists more widely, as the key mechanism for the stabilization of democratic institutions.

Transition and local elite autonomy

Understanding who the elites are during a transition is just one dimension of the 'elite variable'. We also need to explore elite values, behaviour and networks. Lane and Ross have provided evidence for national elite configurations and values, but there is no systematic study of local elites. One of the aims of this article is to investigate the prospects of post-Communist transition in Russia by re-evaluating the old/new elite cleavage and the nature of 'interlocked' elites through a systematic study of local elites in one Russian city. The focus on one city is informed by a desire to make a conceptual break from the national-level fixation of transitology, and much of the existing literature on Russian elites. Moreover, the work of Dahl and urban theory demonstrates just how much we can learn about inherent power structures in a society from the case study of one city.

There are also strong contextual grounds for paying more attention to the local political arena in Russia. The overbearing hand of Sovietology continues to be evident in many Western studies of Russian politics. Even political scientists focus on 'high politics' and Kremlin personalities. This approach overlooks the most significant reality of post-Soviet Russian politics – the fragmentation of power during the 1990s following the disintegration of the CPSU and the resulting greater spread of power resources in Russian politics. State-level regulation of elites and their recruitment patterns was previously one of the primary functions of the CPSU, performed by the Central Committee apparatus in Moscow since the Eighth Party Congress in 1918. To counter 'localism' (*mestnichestvo*) the party periodically rotated its leading personnel around the country. The practice gradually spread to other elite sectors so that by the 1980s elite mobility was established practice in the political, economic and cultural/professional domains. Rotation of elites ended with the collapse of the CPSU. The weakness of the post-Communist central state authorities in Russia and the weak development of integrative institutions, notably political parties, means that local elites have become highly territorialized and more autonomous, particularly in their recruitment.

The dramatic rise in localism in Russian politics is largely a result not only of the immobility of local elites, but also of the pressures of democratization as elites are compelled to respond to the demands of their local constituencies. Elite self-interest and pressures from below largely explain why conflicts over economic distributive issues have been accentuated in centre/regional political struggle in contemporary Russia. Certain Russian republics and regions have been fertile ground for the mobilization of local elites around political economy issues of decentralization of political and economic power that have often been cloaked in a language of competing identities. Regional mobilizations have been most evident in the Urals, Siberia and the Far East, where there are strong territorial identities grounded in the particularistic 'frontier' experience of settlement in a harsh environment, a political tradition of regionalism dating from the late nineteenth century, and a deeply ingrained historical resentment against corrupt Moscow-based elites who plunder the wealth of natural resources in these regions (Hughes, 1994). The fact that the local elites are now more localist and self-regulating of itself does not lead to a more pluralistic elite structure, and indeed it may have quite the contrary effect in reinforcing a stagnant closed undemocratic and anti-market elite. The trend for self-regulation does, however, accentuate the importance of analysing post-Communist transition at the substate level.

The focus on local elites and local transition is justified by several other factors. First, the power of the local and regional elites over the transition process has been strengthened by the breakdown of financial and economic norms of control in Russia with the shift to a demonetarized economy in the aftermath of 'shock therapy'. As a weak state Russia's transition has been characterized by problems with an overarching cohesion and identity, and basic functional ineffectiveness, with poor tax collection and remission of receipts from local authorities being universally accepted as one of the major obstacles for the transformation of Russia. The questionable capacity of the federal government in Moscow to exert control over regional governments and elites is one of the recurring dilemmas of post-Soviet transition. In practice regional and city government are the key conduits for financial and economic regulation and elites at this level have a profound influence on the local economy through a plethora of administrative, financial and economic levers: policing, planning consent and waivers and rollovers in tax collection and enterprise debt management being perhaps the most important.

An ideal type of marketization assumes that Russian cities would develop a governing and elite structure which resembles that of Western counterparts with their balance between public bureaucratic politics and private economic power. Just as Western elites are characterized by interlocking membership between these segments and recruitment from the higher social strata, so too the trend in post-Communist Russia may be to replicate this structural configuration. Likewise, one would expect Russian elites to exhibit a similar pattern to Western elites in sharing the same values across functional categories, with distinctions primarily by age cohort (Eldersveld *et al.*, 1995). We recognize that the exposure of former Soviet cities to the global economy and the emergence of a private sector closely involved with former local administrative elites makes for a strong likelihood that coalitions of public and private elites will be important aspects of the behaviour of post-Soviet elites and their adaptation strategies over the longer term.

A case study of elites in Novosibirsk

Our case study of local elites in transition investigates Novosibirsk, capital of Novosibirsk Region and the acknowledged territorial capital of Siberia,

Russia's main resource periphery. We selected Novosibirsk because of its status as one of the most important regional cities of Russia, for not only is it the administrative, industrial, financial and cultural capital of Siberia, and as such the traditional base of the Siberian elite, but also it is generally regarded as Russia's 'third' city in terms of status (after Moscow and St Petersburg).

An important regional city such as Novosibirsk provides insights into the process of substate elite change in a key region. To minimize the issue of identities in analysing the structure and attitudes of post-Communist elites we selected an overwhelmingly Russian populated city where there is no significant ethnic factor. As noted earlier, Siberia does, however, have a tradition of regionalism dating back to the late nineteenth century, and the region views its relationship with Moscow as one of colonial exploitation from the centre. The governor of Novosibirsk Region during the research period (1996–1998) was Vitaly Mukha, the former CPSU Obkom Secretary until 1990. Mukha acted as a proactive regionalist and a strong advocate of decentralization to the interregional association Siberian Agreement, based in Novosibirsk, which attempted and failed in the early 1990s to establish itself as a meso-level government for all Siberia. A structural legacy of Soviet central planning left the city economy dominated by once prestigious but now bankrupt and severely downsized military/industrial industries, though the city is a major communications hub linking European Russia with the Pacific. In close proximity to Novosibirsk is a major skills asset in Akademgorodok, one of the greatest concentrations of academic institutes outside of Moscow and St Petersburg, including the prestigious Institute of Economics which provided some of the leading intellectual advisers for Gorbachev's reforms (for example, the economist Abel Aganbegyan and the sociologist Tatyana Zaslavskaya). Novosibirsk, consequently, is an exceptional regional city that exhibits some of the best potential and worst legacies of a Soviet regional capital in transition.

Defining the post-Soviet elite

We defined the elite as those persons exercising power and influence as a result of their functional or occupational status at the top of a range of socially significant hierarchies. We selected the elite by a *positional analysis* of occupants of leading positions and by an appraisal of the *networks* within which they operate. In this way we aimed to uncover the layers of the elite stratum. A selection based purely on the formal institutions of power would ignore the key individuals and networks that operate outside the formal decision-making process. Networks, commonly termed 'clans' in Russia, and usually interlocked with organized crime, play a significant role in politics and business. These informal elites are virtually immune to direct investigation and we did not approach them, calculating that had we done so we would have disrupted our fieldwork. Instead we constructed our research in such a way that these informally influential persons would emerge if they were in regular contact with the rest of the elite.

Using positional analysis we identified four key segments of the elite: (1) *Administrative*: senior administrative officials (governor and deputy governors, mayor and deputy mayors, raion administration heads, senior federal officials based locally); (2) *Elected*: politicians and heads of political organizations (national and local); (3) *Economic*: directors and senior managers of state and privatized enterprises, important entrepreneurs, directors of banks and financial institutions; (4) *Cultural*: leading cultural figures and professional intelligentsia. We consolidated the positional membership of the elite by a reputational analysis performed with the assistance of a panel of local experts (academics and journalists) to a group of over 100 elite members. Once this core elite was identified, we selected others and added them to the list by ascertaining from the core members during interviews who else was important. This self-identification of the elite was then verified by a continual triangulation of responses. The research is based on 97 interviews (53 of which were completed by British researchers and 44 by local journalists acting as paid assistants) using a standard questionnaire and conducted over two periods of time, April and August–September 1997. In cases when core members of the elite refused to be interviewed we replaced them by someone else from the list. This membership of the segments was a follows: administrative: 24.7 per cent, political: 10.3 per cent, economic: 46.4 per cent and cultural/professional: 18.6 per cent. The key questions that we asked of respondents concerned their relationships with other elite members, who they have most dealings with in problem-solving, the regularity and quality of these contacts, and their estimations of their own influence and of others. We decided the cut-off point for the sample on the basis of the rapidly diminishing importance of elite members. This method helped us to extract information from elites which confirmed anecdotal evidence regarding some key members who were positioned in the informal structures.

Interviewers filled in the questionnaire during the interview and extracted key information necessary for the sociological and attitudinal profile of the elite: current status and responsibilities of subject, career background, personal data, personal identification of their networks and how these are changing, attitudes to democratization, marketization and privatization, relations with Moscow, and patterns of local economic policy-making. These last questions were open-ended: respondents were asked to state their views on the subject which would be summarized by the interviewer and post-coded according to the most common words or phrases used by respondents to describe their attitudes. These codes represented a simple scale of extent to which respondents favoured or did not favour these issues.

The research measured the scale of elite continuity and survival in Novosibirsk between the Soviet and post-Soviet periods. We took the 19 August 1991 coup as a historical marker for the end of the Soviet regime and the birth of an independent Russian state. This date was used as the point demarcating 'old' and 'new' elites, with anyone in an elite position prior to this being classified as 'old' elite. We recognize that this demarcating point between old and new elites is problematic, but we consider that is on balance preferable to other demarcating points such as the regional elections in 1990, the USSR elections in 1989, or even the Nineteenth Party Conference in 1988, as less viable since they did not result in any significant influx of new non-Communist elites. We examined the nature and scale of any turnover in the elites by cooption, renewal and adaptation, and the emergence into influential positions of new elites, especially in the economic sector. Then we investigated the sources of power and channels of influence available to elites during the transition. We asked questions about the background and career trajectories of elite members. We report the means and standard deviations of the main variables in Table 8.1.

In general, our research provides an empirical foundation to test theories about the composition and values of elites in the post-Soviet political context. We can also reveal how the old elite has fragmented and where its residues are concentrated. In the interviews we asked all elites to comment

Table 8.1 Selected descriptive statistics

A. Categorical variables Variable	N	Per cent	
Sex (male = 1)	97	88.7	
Member of CPSU apparatus = 1	97	46.4	
Old elite = 1	97	55.7	
B. Interval variables Variable	N	Mean	Standard deviation
Age	97	3.04	.934
Education	97	2.12	.388
Own influence	97	3.13	1.187
Attitudes to municipal privatization	97	1.92	.9519
Attitudes to federal privatization	97	1.82	.9243
Attitudes to political change	97	1.72	.8629
Attitudes to decentralization	97	1.46	.791

Old elite – calculated from a question about respondents' roles before and after the August 1991 Coup; new = 0, old = 1.
Age – coded as 1 = <30, 2 = 30–39, 3 = 40–49, 4 = 50–59, 5 = 60–69, 6 = >70 years.
Member of CPSU apparatus and Komsomol – coded as 1 = members of the CPSU apparatus, plus members of the Komsomol apparatus; 0 = members and candidate members of the CPSU.
Attitudes to privatization – we asked respondents whether they thought that the privatization of state or local assets had been a good or bad thing for the city. The variable takes the values of 1 = good, 2 = neither good/bad and 3 = bad.
Attitudes to political change and decentralization – we asked respondents about their attitudes to political changes in Russia since 1991. It takes the values of 1 = positive, 2 = neither positive or negative and 3 = negative.

on changes in economic policy decision-making in the city both over the previous year and since 1991, and interpreted the results as a self-assessment by the elite of its political capacity and economic performance. We also noted the general comments elites made about their networks to understand how decision-making operates and how it has changed during the transition.

Our research was informed by five sets of questions that were framed to test the extent to which the structure and attitudes of the Novosibirsk elite follow a particular account of the post-Communist transition. We expected that new elites would be concentrated in the private sector; old elites would occupy administrative and political offices; and new elites would be more positive toward change and privatization than old elites. We also expected age and education to affect elite values: older people and the less educated would be more conservative. We anticipated that different types of elite would be reputed to be powerful, thus confirming a pluralist open elite structure. Finally, we expected informal elites would be prominent, having high reputed influence.

Beyond the old versus new elite cleavage

We tested the hypotheses by running two-way tables. Following Goodman we treated snowball samples in the same manner as randomly drawn ones (Goodman, 1961). Thus we tested for the significance of the associations with chi-square statistics. Because of the small size of some of the cells we also used Fisher's exact test, though the probabilities were not much different from those from the chi-squares. Cross-tabulation with the attitudinal variables reveals how the values of new and old elites differ on the processes of democratization, marketization and economic performance in addition to the standard sociological variables. In this way, we were able to determine the extent to which progressive innovator new elites act as a driving force for regime transition and the importance of the inherited old elites, embued with outdated Soviet values.

Old and new elites: continuity or change?

The relative size of the segments of the elites provides some initial clues about the character of post-Communist government. The political and administrative elites take up 35 per cent of the total and indicate the importance of bureaucrats and political leaders in the pattern of governance. Their prominence may be both a feature of the legacy of the Communist system with its overlarge bureaucracy and a normal feature of urban governance as these elites tend to be prominent in any governing system. More interesting is the size of the economic segment at 46.4 per cent, by far the largest group, which indicates the extent to which the new private sector elite has been incorporated into the governing elite. These proportions need to be interpreted with some caution. Traditionally economic managerial elites were a key element of the old Soviet elite. Although some of this new private elite are drawn from the newly privatized industries and are former bureaucrats, most of these new private sector actors are new entrants into the elite. Analysis of the current and prior employment types of the elite reveals that of the 45 economic elite members only 8.9 per cent and 6.7 per cent were respectively politicians or bureaucrats in their previous employment, whereas 76.9 per cent had economic jobs in their previous role, a much higher stability in employment type than the other sectors investigated. More strikingly, only two members of the economic elite were members of the administrative and political segment before 1991, while 28 of them are completely new elite members. By implication, just as the new elite is concentrated in the economic segment the elite inherited from the pre-1991 Soviet era saturates the senior administrative positions of power. We found that 62.8 per cent of the new elite were in the economic segment, whereas 40.8 per cent of the old elite were in the administration. This suggests that old elite adaptation strategies have depended on their hegemony over administrative power, which has remained largely undisturbed by democratization.

At first sight this would tend to support the idea that new elites are concentrated in the private sector and old elites occupy administrative and political offices sectors. If so, this would confirm the standard assumption about post-Soviet elites in Russia that an inherited pre-1991 Communist-era elite remains entrenched in senior administrative positions as the 'party of power' and that elite turnover has been most marked in the economic sector of society which has been infused with a new dynamic innovator segment.

This analysis appears to be reinforced when we analyse the attitudes of the elite to post-1991 changes – democratization, decentralization and privatization (federal and municipal). Those who held elite positions prior to 1991 tended to be much more negative towards change than the post-1991 new elite (Table 8.2). This seems to be a weak confirmation of the idea that new innovator elites are more positive toward change and decentralization than old inherited elites. However, the associations do not reach the conventional significance levels, both for chi-square and exact tests, which suggests that the difference is not that strong. Even if the values of indifferent and negative are collapsed into one value and cross-tabulated with positive attitudes, the probability level only improves to 0.117 for the chi-square, which is still outside the 95 per cent confidence limit. There is a similar set of relationships over attitudes to decentralization, where there is almost no difference between the new and old elites (Table 8.3). The area where there is a major difference is over attitudes to federal and municipal privatizations, where the associations are strong and highly significant (Tables 8.4 and 8.5). The new elite is much more positive toward privatization whereas the old elite tends to be negative. These attitudes are equally different for both municipal and federal processes. The explanation of why the elite differs in these attitudes may result from the different composition of the old and new elites. As the new elite is largely composed of the private sector, it follows that it would be more positive to greater freedom and support rights of private ownership.

A much more complicated picture of elite change emerges, however, when we analyse the relationship between attitudes to change and respondents' personal characteristics. We found that level of education had no marked influence on attitudes (Table 8.6). The place of education (whether

Table 8.2 Attitudes to change by new/old elite (%)

	New elite (n = 43)	Old elite (n = 54)	Total (n = 97)
Positive	60.4	44.4	51.5
Neither for nor against	16.3	25.9	21.6
Negative	23.3	27.8	25.8
No response	0	1.9	1.0
Total	100	100	100

Chi-square = 3.2, p = 0.361; Fisher's exact test (two-sided) = 3.095, p = 0.303.

Table 8.3 Attitudes to decentralization by new/old elite (%)

	New elite (n = 43)	Old elite (n = 54)	Total (n = 97)
Positive	67.4	70.4	69.1
Neither for nor against	14.0	11.1	12.4
Negative	18.6	16.6	17.5
No response	0	1.9	1.0
Total	100	100	100

Chi-square = 1.03, p = 0.79; Fisher's exact test (two-sided) = 1.06, p = 0.919.

Table 8.4 Attitudes to privatization of federal property by new/old elite (%)

	New elite (n = 43)	Old elite (n = 54)	Total (n = 97)
Positive	53.5	27.8	39.2
Neither for nor against	11.6	20.4	16.5
Negative	30.2	51.9	42.5
No response	4.7	0	2.1
Total	100	100	100

Chi-square = 10.3, p = 0.016; Fisher's exact test (two-sided) = 9.77, p = 0.013.

Table 8.5 Attitudes to privatization of municipal property by new/old elite (%)

	New elite (n = 43)	Old elite (n = 54)	Total (n = 97)
Positive	65.1	37.0	49.5
Neither for nor against	7.0	22.2	15.5
Negative	25.6	40.7	34.0
No response	2.3	0	1.0
Total	100	100	100

Chi-square = 10.285, p = 0.016; Fisher's exact test (two-sided) = 10.08, p = 0.01.

Table 8.6 Attitudes to change by educational background (%)

	Middle/high (n = 83)	Post-graduate (n = 14)	Total (n = 97)
Positive	49.4	64.3	51.5
Neither for nor against	21.4	7.1	21.6
Negative	25.3	28.6	25.8
No response	1.2	0	1.0
Total	100	100	100

Chi-square = 2.324, p = 0.508; Fisher's exact test (two sided) = 2.6, p = 0.494.

the elite was educated in Novosibirsk, Moscow or another region) was also not important in explaining attitudes to change. Local socialization, however, did have an impact on attitudes to decentralization with local elites educated in Novosibirsk and Moscow being more sympathetic to greater local autonomy while those educated in other regions tended to oppose it. Neither was there a significant relationship with respect to gender. In contrast, there are more marked differences in attitudes to change between the generation cohorts as younger elites are much more positive and older elites are much more negative irrespective of elite segment, with relationships that are just about significant at about the 0.05 level (Table 8.7). It is important to note that old/new elite is not synonymous with old/young in terms of the generation cohorts, thus, a young person in the elite prior to 1991 is classified as old elite. In ordered probits reported elsewhere (Hughes and John, 2001), we are able to show, when controlling for other variables, that the new/old distinction does not explain the values of the elites while position in the former *apparatchiki* and age are the important factors.

Of course, expressed attitudes to change are not always reflected in behaviour. This becomes evident if one accepts the counterintuitive

Table 8.7 Attitudes to change by age (%)

	<39 yrs (n = 24)	40–49 yrs (n = 45)	>49 yrs (n = 27)	Total (n = 96)
Positive	66.7	53.3	33.3	51.0
Negative	33.3	47.7	66.7	49.0
Total	100	100	100	100

Chi-square = 5.82, $p = 0.054$; Fisher's exact test (two-sided) = 5.74, $p = 0.051$.

estimations of some business elite respondents that the generationally younger and more overtly 'democratic' in political rhetoric and market-oriented Mayor of Novosibirsk, Viktor Tolokonsky and his team in the city administration were much more corrupt than the more overtly pro-Communist and generationally older administrative elite which surrounded the governor in the regional administration (located in an adjacent building). The regional administration under Governor Mukha was generally regarded by business people as also being less corrupt and more business-friendly than the preceding administration of Governor Indinok, who was a vigorous supporter of Yeltsin and a member of the 'pro-reform' Our Home is Russia Party. Indinok was also a pre-1991 mayor-equivalent of Novosibirsk. Although a nomenklatura old elite member, Indinok was acutely aware of the significance of age in the struggle to transform Russia, acknowledging to interviewers: 'We, the older generation of leaders do not understand the changes in society, it is time for us to make way for new younger people.'

Segmented or power elite?: local administrative hegemons

After initial uncertainty in the immediate post-collapse period, the power of the old administrative elite was underpinned by the institutional design of the Yeltsin presidential system, with its pyramidal concentration of power in the vertically organized administrative hierarchy. The structure of the elite in Novosibirsk by 1997–1998 indicated that parallel, but interlocked and well-defined political and economic network systems dominated the city. The authority of the formal institutions of political power (regional and city soviets) varied: the regional Soviet (and regional politics) was more powerful largely because local administrative and business elites colonized this assembly in the 1994 elections and thereby enhanced its reputed power. Elite networks were dominated by the senior administrative elite, however, which was only accountable to the electorate though its two leaders: Governor Mukha and Mayor Tolokonsky. The governor and mayor acted the roles of two local hegemons, presiding over their respective administrative branches, and regulating local power.

The defining feature of the local transition in Russia is the conflict between these two levels of power and their respective hegemonic leaders. Outwardly a clear division of power was apparent in Novosibirsk between a specific element of the pre-1991 old elite, namely the inherited administrative elite from the CPSU apparatus (*apparatchiki*) which was dispersed in both regional and city administrations and the new post-1991 innovator economic elite which was concentrated in the privatized business sector. By this stage the economic elites of the old Soviet MIC enterprises were marginalized.

The self-preservation adaptation strategy of the *apparatchiki* was to abandon the party and colonize the post-1991 democratizing state institutions, and thereby continue to dominate, if not hold a near-monopoly, of administrative power at the regional and city substate levels. Of 24 administrative elite interviewees, the apparatchiki accounted for 14, and two others were inherited from the pre-1991 state bureaucracy. The inflow of the Soviet-era economic managerial elite (*khozyaistvenniki*) into the post-Communist administrative elite was minimal, as only four members of the current administrative elite originated from this segment. The marginal scale of the turnover of administrative elite is clear from the finding that only two members of the elite interviewed held non-elite positions prior to 1991. Emblematic of the trend in administrative elite recruitment are the careers of the two local hegemons. Governor Mukha was the pre-1991 Novosibirsk Region party secretary, while Mayor Tolokonsky was deputy chairman of the Planning Commission of the city party committee.

The impact of the infusion of innovators into the elite has been most acute in the economic sector. The view that the privatized business elite in post-Communist Russia is saturated with former Komsomol *apparatchiki* who extracted 'seed capital' from their administrative positional power in the late 1980s to fund the 'first generation of post-Soviet entrepreneurial activity' is not confirmed by our research (Solnick, 1998: 124). In Novosibirsk we interviewed 45 current economic elite members, none of whom were recruited from the pre-1991 Komsomol apparatus, and only 2 of whom had formerly been part of the administrative elite. There was some continuity as 13 of the economic elite interviewees had held a position in the economic elite prior to 1991 and 1 was in the political elite and 4 in the administrative elite. The majority (30 of 45) of our economic elite interviewees had assumed their positions post-1991, and most of these (27 of 30) had emerged from non-elite positions in the pre-1991 period. We identify this group as the core of the innovator elite. A significant number of them (16) were drawn from the cultural/professional intelligentsia. Local social capital is an important explanatory factor here, since Novosibirsk has a substantial resource of academic institutions in Akademgorodok, together with the third most important university outside of Moscow and St Petersburg, and economists trained at these institutions have a domestic and international reputation. Significantly, a cluster of the innovator economic elite was recruited from the economics faculty of the university and the Institute of Economics at Akademgorodok. This relevant skills capacity may well be unusual, since while most regional capitals have their own universities they do not match the concentration and prestige of Akademgorodok. Furthermore, Akademgorodok was closely integrated with local enterprises in the economic planning for Siberia in the Soviet period, thus, creating a ready-made corridor for the transference of intellectual capacity into entrepreneurial capacity once the economic transition and privatization developed. How locally specific and exceptional this trend is can only be tested by further cross-regional comparisons.

The administrative hegemons are reluctant to concede their enormous power. One deputy-governor claimed that there is very little administrative control of the local economy since some 80 per cent of products on the Russian market are now from the non-state sector. On the other hand, the reach of administrative power in post-Soviet society is still very pervasive, even over the private economic sector. Observation by the researchers in Novosibirsk revealed how local entrepreneurs and managers congregated *en masse* in a daily routine as supplicants outside the offices of senior regional and city administrators. This is a classic case of lobbying as these buildings are the key forums for elite networking. The superiority of administrative power is also evident in the following illustration provided by the head of a city district (raion) administration. A privatized water utility cut off the supply of water to an educational institute for non-payment of bills during the examinations period. In response the raion head ordered the traffic police to go to the water company headquarters and blockade transport movement in and out of the company by levying fines for traffic offences. Through the regular use of this tactic, which he termed an 'informal racket', he is able to overcome market forces and maintain basic services in his area.

Reputed power: a pluralist trend?

By asking elites to identify and rank the most important persons/groups in the city, this study has revealed an open structure to the elites, at least as regards elite perception of influence in the city (Table 8.8). As one would expect, given the levers of power at the disposal of the administrative hegemons, almost without exception the governor, the mayor, and their deputies were named as occupying the top three positions of influence in the city. At the same time, when respondents identified the fourth and fifth positions of influence they nominated a wide range of actors, such as key business leaders and influential pseudo-entrepreneurs from the criminal sector. Few actors outside these top five could attract more than five other elites who mentioned them as influential. Local power is what generally counts as regards perceived influence, as local politicians operating at the national level in the Duma were widely seen as not influential. The results

Table 8.8 Persons cited as being the most influential in the city (%)

	1st	2nd	3rd	4th	5th
Mukha[1]	63.9	15.5	5.2	2.1	1.0
Tolokonsky[2]	25.8	51.5	8.2	3.1	1.0
Kiselev[3]	0.0	9.3	23.7	6.2	1.0
Gorodetksy[4]	0.0	8.2	1.0	0.0	2.1
Sychev[5]	0.0	0.0	5.2	9.3	3.1
Others	5.1	9.3	46.4	54.4	49.5
No response	5.2	6.2	10.3	24.9	42.3
Total	100.0	100.0	100.0	100.0	100.0
N	97	97	97	97	97

Others = those with fewer than five respondents citing them as influential.
[1]Governor Novosibirsk Region.
[2]Mayor Novosibirsk City.
[3]First Deputy Governor Novosibirsk Region.
[4]First Deputy Mayor Novosibirsk City.
[5]Chairman of Novosibirsk Region Legislative Assembly.

show that the balance of power among elites is changing as innovative new economic elites have emerged and we can expect that given time they will challenge the hegemonic power of the inherited elites of the administrative sector.

Conclusion

This study confirms that just as Russia lacks a 'consensually unified elite' at the national level, likewise, as far as our case study shows, there is no evidence of a widespread ideological consensus at the local level. This suggests that the key requisite for stable democratic transition proposed by transitologists is missing at both key levels of the state. The conventional focus on the political/economic bifurcation, and the old/new monochrome elite cleavage in previous studies of Russian elites disguises important sociological factors shaping attitudes to political change in its transition. This study has identified the difference of values between age cohorts as a key determinant of the pace of change in one of Russia's most important regional cities. The significance of the age factor in determining elite attitudes suggests that the challenge of building a post-Communist Russia is being reflected in a generational conflict as much as it is a struggle between inherited and innovator elites. This is not unlike the kind of elite conflict between 'establishment' and 'newcomer' that one would encounter in any modernized urban setting.

After a decade of Russia's post-Communist transition, the problem of consolidation of a democratic state and market economy is fully comprehensible only if we shift the focus from the state to the substate. It is here that the residues of Soviet values have been concentrated by the successful elite adaptation strategies of former party *apparatchiki*, who dominate local administrative power and are a major obstacle to change. It is in generational change among economic elites that we see the most powerful system-undermining dynamic, as a new, younger, more innovatory cohort has come to the fore. Our research demonstrates that its values are, on the whole, better adjusted and more receptive to the demands of democratizating change and the market. Whether this young innovator entrepreneurial elite can erode the reform-resisting corps of Communist-era elites that continue to dominate the powerful administrative segment of the elite will have a crucial bearing on the transformation of Russia.

Acknowledgement

The authors would like to thank Dr Gwendolyn Sasse, the London School of Economics and Political Science, for her work as research assistant. This chapter is based on research conducted with the financial support of ESRC Grant No. 3850XG4.

Notes

1 Here we follow Giddens' definition of 'moral' integration as 'the degree to which those in elite positions share common ideas and a common moral ethos; and to how far they are conscious of an overall solidarity', see Giddens, 'Elites in the British class structure', 5. The notion of a 'creed' binding elites is from Dahl's, *Who Governs?*, Chapter 28.
2 It is not clear what, if any, the distinction is between 'ideocratic unity' and 'consensually unified elite'.
3 This study compared the results of regional elections in 1990 and 1994 in seven of Russia's eighty-nine regions.

References

Aaslund, A. (1996) Reform vs 'Rent-Seeking' in Russia's Economic Transformation. *Transition*, Vol. 2, No. 2, pp. 12–21.
Badovsky, D.V. (1994) Transformatsiya politicheskoi elity v rossii – ot 'organizatsii professional'nykh revoliutsionerov' k 'partii vlasti'. *Polis*, No. 6, pp. 42–58.
Dahl, R.A. (1961) *Who Governs? Democracy and Power in an American City*. New Haven and London: Yale University Press.
DiGaetano, A. and Klemanski, J.S. (1999) *Power and City Governance: Comparative Perspectives on Urban Development*. Minneapolis, MN: University of Minnesota Press.
Eldersveld, E.J., Stromberg, L. and Derksen, W. (1995) *Local Elites in Western Democracies*. Boulder: Westview.
Giddens, A. (1974) Elites in the British Class Structure, in Philip Stanworth and Anthony Giddens (eds), *Elites and Power in British Society*. Cambridge: Cambridge University Press, pp. 4–9.
Goodman, L.A. (1961) Snowball Sampling. *Annals of Mathematical Statistics*, Vol. 32, pp. 148–170.

Greene, W.H. (1993) *Econometric Analysis*, third edition. London: Prentice Hall.
Higley, J. and Burton, M.G. (1989) The Elite Variable in Democratic Transitions and Breakdowns. *American Sociological Review*, Vol. 54, No. 1, pp. 17–32.
Higley, J., Hoffmann-Lange, U., Kadushin, C. and Moore, G. (1991) Elite Integration in Stable Democracies: A Reconsideration. *European Sociological Review*, Vol. 7, No. 1, pp. 35–53.
Higley, J., Pakulski, J. and Wesolowski, W. (1998) Introduction: Elite Change and Democratic Regimes in Eastern Europe in John Higley, Jan Pakulski and Wlodzimierz Wesolowski (eds) *Postcommunist Elites and Democracy in Eastern Europe*. Basingstoke: Macmillan Press Ltd, pp. 1–33.
Hughes, J. (1994) Regionalism in Russia: The Rise and Fall of Siberian Agreement. *Europe-Asia Studies*, Vol. 46, No. 7, pp. 1133–1161.
Hughes, J. (1997) Sub-national Elites and Political Transformation in Russia: A Reply to Kryshtanovskaya and White. *Europe-Asia Studies*, Vol. 49, No. 6, pp. 1017–1036.
Hughes, J. and John, P. (2001) Local Elites and Transition in Russia: Adaptation or Competition? *British Journal of Political Science*, Vol. 31, Part 4, pp. 673–692.
Kliamkin, I.M. (1993) Politicheskaia sotsiologiia perekhodnogo obshchestva. *Polis*, No. 4, pp. 41–63.
Kryshtanovskaya, O. and White, S. (1996) From Soviet Nomenklatura to Russian Elite. *Europe-Asia Studies*, Vol. 48, No. 5, pp. 711–733.
Kullberg, J.S. (1994) The Ideological Roots of Elite Political Conflict in Post-Soviet Russia. *Europe-Asia Studies*, Vol. 46, No. 6, pp. 929–953.
Lane, D. and Ross, C. (1999) *The Transition from Communism to Capitalism, Ruling Elites from Gorbachev to Yeltsin*. New York: St Martin's Press.
Linz, J.J. and Stepan, A. (1996) *Problems of Democratic Transition and Consolidation: Southern Europe, South America and Post-Communist Europe*. Baltimore and London: Johns Hopkins University Press.
Lipset, S.M. (1983) *Political Man: The Social Bases of Politics*, New York: Doubleday, 1960, and *Political Man: The Social Bases of Politics*, expanded and updated edition. Baltimore: Johns Hopkins University Press.
McAuley, M. (1997) *Russia's Politics of Uncertainty*. Cambridge: Cambridge University Press.
Melville, A. (ed.) (1999) *Tranformatsiya rossiiskikh regional'nykh elit v sravnitel'noi perspektive*. Moscow: Moskovskii obshchestvennyi nauchnyi fond.
Mills, C.W. (1956) *The Power Elite*. Oxford: Oxford University Press.
Moyser, G. and Wagstaffe, M. (1987) *Studying Elites*. London: Unwin Hyman.
O'Donnell, G. and Schmitter, P.C. (1986) *Transitions from Authoritarian Rule: Tentative Conclusions About Uncertain Democracies*. Baltimore and London: Johns Hopkins University Press.
Offe, C. (1996) *Varieties of Transition: The East European and East German Experience*. Cambridge: Polity Press.
Pierson, P. (2000) Increasing Returns, Path Dependence, and the Study of Politics. *American Political Science Review*, Vol. 94, No. 2, pp. 251–267.
Przeworski, A. (1992) The Games of Transition, in Scott Mainwaring, Guillermo O'Donnell and J. Samuel Valenzuela (eds) *Issues in Democratic Consolidation: The New South American Democracies in Comparative Perspective*. Notre Dame: University of Notre Dame Press, pp. 105–152.
Putnam, R. (1973) *The Beliefs of Politicians. Ideology, Conflict and Democracy in Britain and Italy*. New Haven: Yale University Press.

Rustow, D.A. (1970), Transitions to Democracy: Toward a Dynamic Model. *Comparative Politics*, Vol. 2, No. 3, pp. 337–363.

Solnick, S.L. (1998) *Stealing the State: Control and Collapse in Soviet Institutions.* Cambridge: Harvard University Press.

Stiglitz, J. (1999) Whither Reform? Ten Years of the Transition. *Keynote Address World Bank Annual Bank Conference on Development Economics*, 28–30 April.

Wollman, H. (1993) Change and Continuity of Political and Administrative Elites in Post-Communist Russia. *Governance*, Vol. 6, No. 3, pp. 325–340.

9 Reforms and orientations of regional elites
The case of St Petersburg

Alexandr Duka

Introduction

Changes that occur in Russia have certain limits that correlate with attitudes of the population and elite towards new values and their willingness to follow the process of reform. First of all this relates to elites. Implementation of any policies (not to mention institutions) by the central elite is defined by institutional contexts, interests, actors' capabilities and so on (see Calista, 1994). There is a 'breaking point' of any political system connected with the strength of opposition and counteraction. That is why the Kremlin leadership needs political backing. The problem of elite (dis)unity and consensus on basic values is closely connected in this way with the problem of regime stability, reform realization and leading group survival. Support by the population at large and that of the elite for democratic institutions and market economy is a current area of research interest. Studies undertaken in recent years have enabled us to say with confidence that contemporary reforms in Russia have been losing the support of the majority of the population (Burmykina and Nechaeva, 1998; Kapustin and Klyamkin, 1994; Maiminas, 1996; Safronov *et al.*, 1999; Whitefield and Evans, 1994). This is partly due to the fact that neither liberal nor democratic ideas have had deep foundations in traditional Russian culture (Bahry, 1993). In spite of this, mass and elite surveys in Russia, Ukraine and Lithuania conducted in 1992 and 1995 have shown quite a high orientation towards democracy and market economy among national elites (Miller *et al.*, 1995, 1997; Miller *et al.*, 1998; see also Golovachev and Kosova, 1995).

Surveys have shown that a higher level of education increases the likelihood of acceptance of democratic and market values (Gerber, 2000). If we keep in mind that the elites are more educated than most of the population, so these findings would confirm previous results. The survey of local deputies in five Russian provinces conducted in 1992 showed support for reforms aimed at the development of a market economy and a more democratic political system (Hahn, 1993). The observed differences between mass and elite attitudes are not surprising; this phenomenon had been recorded in a number of comparative studies (Stein, 1998; Stouffer, 1992;

Sullivan et al., 1993). Scholars in former socialist countries achieved similar results where, for example, liberal and democratic attitudes were found in the Czech and Slovak elites (Matějů, 1997). Polish researchers have found that the political elite in Poland is democratic and pluralistic, but non-integrated (Wasilewski, 1997). Bulgarian students have observed orientations towards new liberal economic and democratic political values among elites (Toneva, 1997). Nevertheless in a modern, industrial, very diversified society that is heavily burdened with transformational problems there naturally exist differences of opinion about the way a country should develop. And it is possible to suppose that there is disagreement among various elite groups on some problems, especially groups with different life experiences. In this sense distinct generations could represent different cultures (Inglehart, 1990).

In this chapter I will be using the St Petersburg elite as a case and discuss the following aspects of elite orientations:

1   The regional elite's attitudes towards Russia's identity. This is one of the principal points in dispute about the country's past, present and future. Discussions about civilization choice and whether Russia belongs to European, Western, Oriental, Slavic or specific Eurasian civilization are now in their third century. The questions concern the way that Russia ought to go. The country's destiny or its destinations are not academic or rhetorical; they are actually important for politicians, intellectuals and scholars. Conceptions about the country's identity are significant elements of universality of meaning: they create a common framework for explanation, interpretation of reality and motivation in the public sphere.
2   Attitudes towards institutions of democracy and market economy.
3   The problem of legitimacy in the political sphere bearing in mind that there is a correlation among institutional changes in political, economic, social and other spheres of life.
4   Associations between elite's attitudes, value orientations and socialization of elite members.

Elites and institutions

Attitudes of the elite groups towards the transformation processes are of great importance for changes in Russian society. Research literature stresses the role of the elite in Russian transformation processes (Devlin, 1995; Kryshtanovskaya and White, 1996; Lane, 1996; Pakulski, 1999; Wesolowski, 1992). It is typical that the role of elites increases in times of rapid and cardinal institutional transformation. They act as the principal goal determinants. Ruling groups proclaim reforms, define their destinations and attempt to control the process of alteration. Russia is no exception.

In all countries the dominating social groups control the main resources of the society and determine the nature of relations between social agents and institutions. Thus their activity contributes to reducing the societal uncertainty and to the search for optimal forms of social interaction. At the same time they operate as social integrators (Mannheim, 1940; Keller, 1968; Toffler, 1981: Chapter 5). It is important to understand that elite activity not only stabilizes a society as a whole or its subsystems, but also that such activity may destabilize a society.

The leading groups are not actors that make decisions at will. The activity of the elites has strong limitations. Moreover, they create a framework for elites' existence. Historical and social background, customs and traditions are very important. Thorstein Veblen argued that institutions are results of processes that have occurred in the past and are adapted to circumstances of the past and thus not fully applicable to circumstances and demands of the present. Current institutions are not entirely suited to the current situation given the accepted contemporary social structure (Veblen, 1984: 202).

The delay in institutional development in meeting the 'demands of the time' enables us to say something about the influence of context, and the embeddedness of certain formal and informal institutions. It is difficult to change the trajectory of a societal development over time. Thus path-dependency becomes a main factor of activity of elites. This may indeed lead to a society characterized by institutional dichotomy and institutional imbalance. Thus we may experience the coexistence of two or more norms of main actors' activities with various interpretations of the social reality and attitudes towards social change.

Coordination of its members is very important for the activity of the elite. This was emphasized by James Meisel in his 'three Cs' – group consciousness, coherence and conspiracy (in the sense of common intentions) (Meisel, 1962: 4).

At the same time it is necessary to emphasize that any social and political circumstances may influence the real existence of elites and their 'sub-universes of meaning' (Berger and Luckmann, 1967). Thus, there are states and types of elites that are characterized by open conflict between factions, absence of consensus on basic social, political and economic values (see, for example, Burton and Higley, 1987; Burton *et al.*, 1992; Field and Higley, 1980; Higley *et al.*, 1976). That is to say conflict exists between contradictory sub-universes of meaning. In a situation of social change this means a confrontation between the old institutional order and the new.

Moreover, it is possible to assume that there is a difference in the conception of future institutional design between the various elite sectors. In particular, a rivalry exists between representative and administrative elites for the spheres of competence and for resources in conditions of unfinished new political and social system institutionalization. Furthermore, differences in the recruitment of new members create some possible distinctions in value-orientations among members of elite sectors.

Further, any social group and society in general consists of persons belonging to different generations. Various generations are characterized by distinctive features of socialization and which are shaped by the different formative experiences. It is natural that variations are to be found in the generation's sub-universes of meaning (Berger and Luckmann, 1967). These temporal transformations of sub-universes of meaning could also be represented as culture shifts, including enduring differences in basic attitudes, values and skills (Inglehart, 1990). Any speculation about elites as agents of reform has to include internal distinctions that are associated with different value orientations. Reverting to the problem of the elites' role in Russian transformation, it is necessary to note the significance of the regional elites. An autonomization of regional power structures, a reinforcement of regional elite's positions as a result of central federal power instability and economic crisis establish the possibility for relatively independent formation of political, economic and social priorities in regional development. It would not be an exaggeration to say that the future of Russian reforms largely depends on regional elites. Regional leaders correct dominant institutional reformers' design of the planned future, thereby creating *institutional limits of reforms*. According to Douglass North,

> even discontinuous changes (such as revolution and conquest) are never completely discontinuous [as] a result of the embeddedness of informal constraints in societies. Although formal rules may change overnight as the result of political or judicial decisions, informal constraints embodied in customs, traditions and codes of conduct are much more impervious to deliberative policies. These cultural constraints not only connect the past with the present and future, but also provide us with a key to explaining the path of historical change. They also assist us in explaining divergent paths of historical change across societies.
> (North, 1990: 6)

In this sense elites (and a society as a whole) do and think as they like. The Russian Prime Minister Victor Chernomyrdin, after the usual government failure in 1993, stressed: 'We wished to do better, but results are as ever.'

On the one hand, one can assume that institutional limits of reforms correlate with basic value orientations of regional elites' members, their universe of meaning. On the other, they correlate with notions about legitimacy of the new institutional order spread among regional power groups. This is linked to the problem of the stability of democratic transformations (sometimes regional elites support them and sometimes not), as well as to problems of a character and a type of a political regime and elite group. Thus, an estimation of limits of possible social change turns out to be linked to an exploration of an actor who moves transformations forward. This can be more important for prognoses than revealing 'objective obstacles' to reform.

The elite sample

The empirical basis of this study consists of the results obtained in a survey of elite representatives in two constituent units of the Russian Federation (St Petersburg and Leningradskaya Oblast) conducted in 1998.[1] A *positional approach* was used for the identification of regional elite members.

The regional *political elite* consists of the State Duma members who are elected in the region, members of St Petersburg and Leningrad *Oblast* Legislative Assemblies, chairpersons of representative bodies in districts (*raions*) of Leningrad Oblast, heads of regional political parties and regional branches of national political parties.

The *administrative elite* includes chairpersons and vice-chairpersons of committees in the administration of St Petersburg and Leningrad Oblast, heads of *raion* administrations in St Petersburg and Leningrad Oblast as well as their deputies, heads of structures that are subordinated directly to federal bodies and representatives of federal ministries in St Petersburg and Leningrad Oblast.

The *economic regional elite* incorporates heads of the largest state and private industrial and financial structures and their deputies in St Petersburg and Leningrad Oblast.

The regional elites in St Petersburg and Leningrad Oblast and participate in a decision-making process which influences political, economic, and social spheres in the region as a whole.

Using reference books, ratings of firms and expert interviews singled 780 elite positions in the political, economic and administrative spheres of life in St Petersburg and Leningrad Oblast (Appendix Tables 9.11 and 9.12). We took 171 formal interviews in the course of our survey of elite members. Our analysis included 163 of these interviews. A weighting procedure was used because a proportion of political, administrative and economic group of elite in our sample did not coincided with this proportion in the general elite sample. The sample included 23 per cent persons from 23 to 40 years old, 54 per cent respondents from 41 to 55 and 23 per cent were from 56 to 68 years old. The most part of the youngest group belonged to the economic sector of regional elite.

Our sample demonstrates a disproportion of middle-class descendants' representation. Both parents of 42 per cent of elite members are intellectuals or high-standing professionals. Twenty-nine per cent of our respondents are from workers' and peasant families, and the same proportion of the sample is of mixed parentage. Only 4 per cent did not graduate from university or college. One-fifth has two university or college degrees.

The major part of the interviewed elite had experience of Soviet, Communist Party or Komsomol (Young Communist League) activity. Only 39 per cent of regional leaders have not had such experience. Of those who have a background from the former regime, 29 per cent have an experience of professional work in the Soviet bodies, 32 per cent worked in Communist Party organizations and 40 per cent worked in Komsomol.

Identification of Russia: West or East?

For several years since 1991 the discussion about civilization identity of Russia among politicians and scholars has been very formidable (Rukavishnikov et al., 1998: 290; see also Gaidar, 1995). We asked two questions: 'There are discussions about Russia's place in the world. What do you think, Russia is . . .', and 'When crucial historical changes would happen in Russia, Russian people would seek for a way of Russia's progress. Which of the following alternatives is the best one for the country now?' (Table 9.1). Forty-seven per cent of our respondents believe that Russia has its own, specific and original way of development. Forty-two per cent suppose that Russia politically and economically belongs to Europe and Asia at the same time ('the Eurasian country'). Approximately 10 per cent of the respondents placed Russia among the European countries and 1 per cent thought that it belongs to Asia.[2] Politicians are the group that most closely identifies Russia with Europe (14 per cent). Ten per cent of administrators and 9 per cent of economic elite have the same opinion. The largest proportion of those who believe that Russia has a specific way of development is among economic elite (49 per cent). Members of political and administrative elite share this point of view with 48 per cent and 45 per cent correspondingly. Thus, membership in the political, administrative and economic subgroups does not influence the answers to this question very much.

Age of the respondents has much greater influence on this issue. Among those who are less than 40 years old, one-fifth places Russia among European countries, one-fifth speaks about her distinctive way of development, and about 60 per cent see Russia as a Eurasian country. Most of the respondents who are middle aged (41 to 55 years old) and the next higher age group (from 56 to 68 years old) are inclined to see Russia as a very specific

Table 9.1 Family background and identification of Russia, $N = 139$ (%)

Family background	Russia is first and foremost European country	Russia is first and foremost Asian country	Russia belongs equally to Europe and Asia ('the Eurasian country')	Russia is original country with a special role in the world
Low class (e.g. both parents are workers or peasants)	2	0	63	35
Mixed	7	0	30	63
Middle class (e.g. both parents are intellectuals or high professionals)	16	0	42	42
Total	10	1	42	47

country: 55 per cent and 52 per cent, correspondingly. Eight per cent of the middle-age respondents and 5 per cent of the highest age group link Russia with Europe.

Social origin of elite members influences their attitudes to an even greater extent. The data confirm the role of early socialization as one of the important factors for the formation of the basic orientations. Sixteen per cent of those whose parents belonged to intelligentsia see Russia as a European country. Seven per cent of respondents of mixed origin, but only 2 per cent of those whose parents were labourers or peasants take the same position.

Identification of Russia with a specific civilization (European, Asian, Eurasian) influences opinions about *possible ways of the country's development* (Table 9.2). Twenty-four per cent of respondents prefer the *original* way of development. Most of the respondents insist on the necessity of using both Western and Asian experience (70 per cent). Only 5 per cent of the respondents prefer solely the Western way of development. Members of the political elite are the most pro-Western (8 per cent). Most of those who prefer the original way of development also are concentrated within this subgroup (34 per cent). Within economic and administrative elite such an orientation consists of 18 per cent and 29 per cent respectively. Ten per cent of the younger age cohort are pro-Westerners (compared to 3 per cent in the other cohort).

In this case the difference based on the family type is not so significant, but one can see the tendency connected with socialization factor.

The state and the market

It is quite probable that besides certain myths, knowledge about real events of Russian history influences the respondents' ideas about Russian ways of development. A long dominance of etatist values and a significant role of the state in all spheres of life helped to form a point of view that has

Table 9.2 Family background and orientation towards the possible way of Russia's development, $N = 140$ (%)

	Western way of development	Using both Western and Asian experiences	Original way of development	Using 'Asian Tigers' experience
Low class (e.g. both parents are workers or peasants)	1	72	23	4
Mixed	4	63	33	0
Middle class (e.g. both parents are intellectuals or high professionals)	7	76	17	0
Total	5	70	24	1

moved towards state-oriented attitudes. Thus, though our respondents are oriented towards development of private property and market economy, they still are in favour of a dominant position of the state in heavy industry and a strong state influence on national credit and monetary policies (Table 9.3). Similar attitudes were found at the popular level in sociological studies before perestroika (Bahry, 1993) and one later (Safronov, 1996).

Though this model is oriented towards capitalism, it is not entirely liberal. The reformers' 'blueprint' capitalism conflicted with the regional elites' notion about required capitalism. It is quite possible that such attitudes are the results of the country's historical experience in 'the motivating dynamics of institutionalised conduct' (Berger and Luckmann, 1967: 65). Hence, predetermination by the past (path-dependency) becomes a main factor. Such a situation can lead to elite controversies. When the Kremlin leadership constantly try to change rules of the game and to use norms that are introduced without the agreement of the other main players, privatization policies will easily clash with the attitudes of a more conservative regional elite.

So when we talk about orientations of the regional elite towards the market economy we must keep in mind the specific content of this notion. At the same time it is possible to say that in general regional elite members are oriented towards supporting new economic institutions. But to what extent do the political, economic and administrative elites agree on such a development?

Two indices were constructed. The first one (Table 9.4) shows the quantity of the economic activity spheres shown in the previous table that should be developed 'mainly on the basis of private ownership' and 'only on the basis of private ownership'. 'Low support for private ownership' means that no or one sphere was chosen. 'Medium support for private ownership'

Table 9.3 Orientations towards development of the Russian economy (%)

We should develop our economy . . .	Heavy industry	Light industry	Agri-culture	Credit and monetary sphere(*)	Sphere of services and trade
Only on the basis of state ownership	30	2	1	8	0
Mainly on the basis of state ownership	32	6	7	26	0
Equally on the basis of state and private ownership	23	24	37	44	12
Mainly on the basis of private ownership	13	42	32	19	35
Only on the basis of private ownership	2	26	23	3	53
Total	100	100	100	100	100

For all cases $N = 163$; except (*) $N = 159$.

Table 9.4 Support for private ownership, $N = 162$ (%)

	Low	Medium	High
Political elite	43	36	21
Economic elite	20	56	24
Administrative elite	21	61	18
Total	25	53	22

means that two or three economic spheres were indicated. And 'high' means that four or five spheres were chosen.

One should expect that the economic elite ought to be more oriented towards private ownership, but there is no significant difference between this group of elite and average attitudes of elites who support private ownership. Why? Different groups comprise the economic elite and are reflected in our sample. This consists of four subgroups: heads of the financial structures, private industrialists, top managers of state-owned enterprises and 'monopolistic' enterprises in the sphere of public utilities, such as gas line maintenance services, heating, electricity supply companies, the telephone companies ('Lengaz', 'Lenenergo', 'Petersburg Telephone Network' etc.). However, the strongest support for private ownership was found among the leaders of private business and the weakest among top managers of the state-owned enterprises. Nevertheless the problem of economic leaders' insufficient support for private ownership exists.

I believe that at least two explanations are possible. The first is connected with the specificity of the Russian economic leaders, their rise and close ties with political and administrative authorities. Their experience (during the Soviet era and after) demonstrates to them that real control, management and disposal of a property are often more important than possession at law. Moreover, in some circumstances it is more comfortable and effective because the state or municipalities bear responsibility and amenability, and the managers get the benefits. Furthermore the status of state or public enterprise assists when the budget is being disposed. The second explanation is based on the assumption that an individual's attitudes are more important than their positions. Value orientations formed solely through the processes of socialization and life experiences turn out to be a more significant factor in the perception of private property than real social activity. These explanations do not contradict each other.

The second index (Table 9.5) measures the respondents' agreements with the judgements that characterize individual stimuli, efforts and individual responsibility in the economic sphere. 'Absent or very low economic individualism' means that the respondent agreed with no or one judgement. 'Moderate economic individualism' means that the elite member agreed with two or three judgements. 'Strong economic individualism' indicates agreements with four or five judgements.

Table 9.5 Orientations towards economic individualism, N = 162 (%)

	Absent or very low	Moderate	Strong
Political elite	28	32	40
Economic elite	7	37	56
Administrative elite	11	34	55
Total	12	35	53

Table 9.6 Age and orientations towards private ownership, N = 159 (%)

Age group	Low	Medium	High
23–40	9	47	44
41–55	21	60	19
56–68	51	46	3
Total	26	51	23

Independent economic activity in the market demands individualism as the essential business style of life. In contrast to top bureaucrats and politicians, economic leaders have to be oriented towards individual stimuli, efforts and individual responsibility for being successful in the economic sphere. In general the regional elite seems to be more liberal when it comes to the value of 'liberalism' than concerning 'ownership'.

What then about differences between generations? Table 9.6 shows that the youngest group is considerably more market-oriented. The future of economic reforms depends on the real influence of this elite layer.

These results are not surprising. Mass surveys in Russia demonstrated a distinction between generations in market economy orientations (Khakhulina, 2001; Levada, 1995, 1999b; Safronov *et al.*, 1999). This is a common tendency in Russia. In all likelihood it is connected with the change in the general context of socialization over time.

Significant differences were found in the orientations towards economic institutions among respondents with various family backgrounds. Only 6 per cent of low-class descendants (whose parents are either workers or peasants) have high orientation towards private ownership, and one-third of those whose parents belong to the middle class (intellectuals or professionals). Among mixed family posterity we discovered 25 per cent with a high orientation. A similar tendency is observed regarding orientations towards economic individualism.

One may argue that acceptance of the new economic institutions depends on the professional experience in the Communist Party as well. Table 9.7 shows those persons without such experience more often support private

158 A. Duka

Table 9.7 Communist Party official experience and orientation to economic individualism, $N = 159$ (%)

	Absent or very low	Moderate	Strong
Don't have experience	4	38	58
Have experience	30	27	43
Total	14	36	50

ownership (27 per cent with 'high support' in this group against 10 per cent among those who have experience). They are also more strongly oriented towards economic individualism.

The problem of legitimacy

Rejecting the past?

Institutional legitimacy relates to recognition of a 'new institutional order' that replaced the Soviet one. This new institutional order manifests itself first in negative attitudes towards the old institutional system (society) and in positive attitudes towards the new institutional system, and second in certain orientations towards the structuring of political institutions. As to negative attitudes towards the past, according to Montero and Morlino this correlates with individuals' preference for an alternative system rather than preference for an existing regime. Montero and Morlino see negative attitudes towards the past as one of the main features of legitimacy – 'legitimacy-by-reaction-against-the-past' (Montero and Morlino, 1996: 15–16).

A rejection of the old order by the new elite also fulfils important functions of identification and demarcation. The elite politically defines certain time and space, which belong to *us*. Thus, the elite defines the political circle of its supporters, creating demarcation between *them and us*. So, separation of *our* people from others (including foreigners) occurs, and this is defined as our heritage or as historical chance or as obsolescence, and so on. Besides, emotional-value features reinforce demarcations, create clarity for followers, and institutionalize the past.

The image of the past is closely connected with the perception of the present and possible (or desirable) future. Owing to these connections any institutional order can exist as a legitimate or illegitimate societal continuity. Institutional order in a symbolic totality constitutes a symbolic universe. 'The symbolic universe [. . .] orders history. It locates all collective events in a cohesive unity that includes past, present and future. With regard to the past, it establishes a 'memory' that is shared by all individuals socialized within the collectivity' (Berger and Luckmann, 1967: 103).

Different social and historical conditions of socialization form various symbolic sub-universes.

All these circumstances influence our special interest in the subjective perception of the recent past of Russia by members of the elite. The more so as results of the national mass survey conducted by the All-Russian Center for Public Opinion Studies in the beginning of 1999 demonstrate some nostalgia. More than half of the national sample (58 per cent) agreed with statement: 'It would be better if everything would remain the same as it was before 1985' (Levada, 1999a: 7). And the correlation of positive and negative perceptions of the Brezhnev period is 51:10 (Levada, 1999a: 11; see also Gorshkov *et al.*, 1998: 63–64).

We asked our respondents to evaluate certain specific features of Russia before perestroika according to four grade scales that had evidently positive and negative extreme points. Our statistical analysis shows that eight of nine indicators correlate with each other. This helped us to construct an integral index of negative attitudes towards the Soviet system. This measures a quantity of negative judgements selected by the respondents. Twenty-four per cent of the respondents have low negative attitudes towards the Soviet system (they chose one or two negative positions). Twenty-nine per cent of the respondents chose from three to five negative characteristics of the Soviet system. The others who have very negative attitudes to the former system selected from six to eight negative aspects of that system. Members of the economic elite have the most negative attitudes to the Soviet past. The administrators are in the middle position, and the politicians have the less negative attitudes. But the differences among the groups are very small. Different age cohorts show very distinctive attitudes towards the Soviet system (Table 9.8).

One should bear in mind that the answers reflect not only attitudes, but also stereotypes of the country's past. Different age cohorts had a different past, and personal histories and history of the country are interconnected. Primary socialization has a decisive impact on many personal preferences. The childhood of the elder age cohort occurred at the time of World War II and post-war restoration of the country. The Soviet power demonstrated its

Table 9.8 Age of the respondents and negative attitudes towards the Soviet system, $N = 159$ (%)

Age group	Negative attitudes towards the Soviet system		
	Low	Medium	Strong
23–40	7	33	60
41–55	22	30	48
56–68	46	22	32
Total	24	29	47

effectiveness in the struggle against external enemies. It also successfully overcame the devastation. Every year brought improvements of life to the major part of the population. It is not surprising that 58 per cent of the elder respondents see Soviet society as humane (38 per cent in the youngest cohort and 39 per cent in the middle cohort).

More than half of the respondents agree that the Soviet state was for the entire people. Only one-tenth of the youngest cohort agrees with such a characteristic of the Soviet Union. At the same time, three-fifths of the respondents agree that the USSR had a totalitarian regime before perestroika.

Childhood and youth of the youngest age cohort coincided with the period of late stagnation and perestroika. Aggravation of ethnic relations, ethnic violence, attempts of the Union centre to prevent the splitting up of the USSR with the help of the military, and many saw a link between democratization processes and the problem of the survival of the USSR. All this created a specific background for primary and secondary political socialization. Almost two-thirds of the younger respondents agree that the Soviet state pursued an imperial policy. Almost the same proportion among the elder generation believes that the USSR was a united family of peoples.

The middle class family descendants have considerably more negative attitudes towards Soviet past than the low class family ones. An experience of work in nomenklatura structures is also a strong differentiating factor. Those who have such an experience have less negative attitudes towards the Soviet system. Indoctrination and a professional experience largely define attitudes towards the former social system as well.

In general it is possible to argue that there is a shift in the respondents' answers to the negative attitudes towards Soviet past. In contrast to results of national mass surveys (see Gorshkov, *et al.*, 1998 and Levada, 1999a), the regional elite does not feel nostalgia for the pre-perestroika time. In our case there is a quite clear negation of the past.

Accepting the new regime?

Instrumental legitimacy is based on ideas about effectiveness of the country's political leadership, its ability to create conditions in which individuals and groups are able to satisfy their interests their needs. It is linked to the perception of the situation in the country and the responsibility of authorities for this situation.

Ninety-three per cent of the respondents are not satisfied with the present situation in Russia. However, the younger respondents are more optimistic. Among the youngest respondents the proportion of dissatisfied is twice less than among the older generation; and the proportion of fully satisfied among the youngest generation is six times more than among the oldest age group.

As one can see, the political leadership of the country deserves the highest credit first of all among young members of the regional elite though this credit is not very large.

Table 9.9 Satisfaction with the situation in the country and age, N = 159 (%)

Age group	Satisfied fully	Satisfied partly	Dissatisfied
23–40	19	46	35
41–55	4	62	35
56–68	3	27	71
Total	7	50	43

Differentiation of new institutions

Political institutions

We assumed that one key fundament of democratic institutions in post-Soviet Russia is the attitude towards the idea of checks and balances. The Soviet political system had two main principles: the leading role of the Communist Party and democratic centralism. In fact, a destruction of these principles provided the opportunity for a transition to a democratic system.

We asked the respondents about expediency for officers of executive bodies to be members of legislative bodies simultaneously. Less than one-third of the respondents think that this is expedient. It is interesting that our respondents who are members of legislative bodies agree with such a combination of duties, even to a lesser extent. Only 11 per cent have positive opinions about such a possibility.

Different sectors of our respondents have different attitudes to this problem. Politicians are the most democratic. Only 6 per cent of them answer this question positively. Seventeen per cent of the administrators think that such a combination is useful. The respondents who belong to the political elite are more tolerant of a situation when administrators are at the same time members of legislative bodies: 14 per cent of the politicians do not mind such a combination of duties for administrators. The same attitudes are held by 35 per cent of the administrators. Thus we have an evident asymmetry in the notions about a possibility to combine positions in the two branches of authority. At the same time, one can state that *most of the regional elite members view the idea of checks and balances as a positive value*.

The respondents' age also affects their attitudes to the above-mentioned idea. Youth is more rigorous towards this problem. Nevertheless there are some specific features in their attitudes. The younger people adopt a more negative position with respect to politicians: 71 per cent of the respondents from this cohort without any doubt reject the idea of the combination of the duties. Sixty per cent of the respondents from the elder group and 52 per cent from the middle cohort reject this idea.

Government and business

A separation of political and administrative activities from economic activity is another important aspect of a diversification of powers when nomenklatura-type power groups transform themselves in elite groups. The institutional design of the Soviet system required politicization of economics and 'economization' of politics, and the state used administrative measures in order to regulate these large areas of social life.

For the post-Soviet society, tasks of a social restructuring are largely similar to pre-capitalist societies: these are the necessity of 'destatization' and 'depoliticization' of social life and of the formation of a civil society. However, significant differences between the post-Soviet society and pre-capitalist societies also exist. Soviet socialist society was not a traditional one, but an industrial society. Interconnections among spheres of social life are a structural/functional characteristic of industrial societies. Consequently, demands for a diversification of social spheres and power structures coexist simultaneously with the necessity of their interconnections. These complexities of social tasks reflect activities and attitudes of the power elites at all levels of authorities.

One more circumstance exists. Privatization as one of cornerstones of Russian society's transformation cannot last without the decisive influence of the political and administrative spheres. On the one hand, a chosen strategy of the 'destatization' of properties creates a possibility for politicians and administrators to join an economic activity combining their administrative duties with work in commercial structures. This makes it possible to characterize Russian privatization as a nomenklatura privatization. On the other hand, the objective situation pushes the financial and business elite towards political activities. Members of the financial and business elite come to the political elite. 'Plutocratization' of the political elite occurs.

We tried to clarify attitudes of our regional elite towards the combination of power positions in the economic and political spheres. Using interconnected variables we constructed an index of 'plutocratism' that shows the respondents' orientations towards the combination of positions in legislative bodies and business. More than half of the respondents (55 per cent) do not have such an orientation. One-fifth of them showed a low inclination towards plutocratism. Fourteen per cent of the respondents showed a moderate orientation and 12 per cent a strong orientation towards plutocratism. So, most of the St Petersburg and Leningrad Oblast elite supports institutional pluralism of the political space.

As is well known, the privatization and development of legal private business in Russia started from Komsomol structures. Professional work in Komsomol organizations at the end of perestroika period required maximum utilization of political/administrative resources in order to create favourable conditions for new economic structures that were separating themselves from the state economy. The paradox in this case is that private enterpreneurship could not develop without protection of the executive power. This can explain why plutocratic attitudes of the former Komsomol workers are different from the others (Table 9.10).

The orientations towards separation of powers and among spheres of competence are linked to the new principle of institutional differentiation and dominate among members of regional elite. At the same time, one-third of the respondents supports 'monocratic' attitudes towards the public space. Modes of interaction between the political power and entrepreneurship, which formed in the early period of 'Komsomol' business, can become important for an evolution of economic relations if these tendencies turn the 'beaten tracks' of Russian market economy's development.

Conclusion

This study shows that there is no such thing as unity of regional elites as far as basic political values are concerned. There are differences pertaining to the development of economic institutions, the structuring of political power, the evaluation of the federal government's activities, and Russia's place in international affairs. With no value consensus, a consolidation of the regional elites has a rather poor basis. Regional elites are acting within the boundaries of possibilities. They have some limits and simultaneously create others. These limits exist at the level of habitualized and routine practice.

The forms that existed before the transformation period have a great impact at the country's development. Past legacies are connected with the specific attitudes and values shaped in the Soviet period, and are based on a corresponding sub-universe of meaning. One may state that a certain deficiency of legitimation of the federal authority exists. But, at the same time,

Table 9.10 Experience of professional work in Komsomol and orientations towards plutocracy (a combination of membership in legislative bodies and entrepreneurship), $N = 163$ (%)

An experience of professional work in Komsomol organisations	Orientations towards plutocracy			
	Orientations are absent	Low orientations	Moderate orientations	Strong orientations
Do not have such an experience	64	19	9	8
Have such an experience	46	16	22	16
Total	55	19	14	12

we may speak about significant legitimacy of basic democratic institutions. It means that there is important support of democratic reforms among regional elite.

The sphere and character of activity influence attitudes and value orientations. There are significant associations between support for private ownership, economic individualism, acceptance of new institutional order and respondents' membership of the elite sector. The political elite is less oriented towards a market economy than economic elites. At the same time politicians demonstrate more support for political democracy than administrators and economic leaders.

The factor of socialization plays an important role in determining value preferences. A preference for the new institutional order – with a market economy and democratic institutions – is manifest to a greater degree in the young representatives of the elite. Secondary socialization, proceeding from work in Soviet official structures (primarily as Communist party functionaries) shows itself in a greater bias toward the former system's values.

The future of Russia depends on the development of the elite's orientations. Disagreements among elite's factions make coordinated actions on stabilization of the political, economic and social situation more difficult. Besides, these disagreements reduce cooperation of different groups and do not help mutual confidence and social equilibrium. Deficiencies of legitimatization can intensify regionalization and reinforce a competition between the federal and regional elites, and among elites in different regions. When procedural legitimacy is weak, competitive relations among different factions of the elite can also impede formation of democratic institutions. Democratic values of the elite may counterbalance or at least soften the above-mentioned negative tendencies.

Appendix

Table 9.11 Elite of St Petersburg and Leningrad Oblast (positions in 1998)

Elite sectors	St Petersburg	Leningrad Oblast	Total
Political elite	88	59	147
	(11%)	(8%)	(19%)
Economic elite	315	104	419
	(40%)	(13%)	(54%)
Administrative elite	123	91	214
	(16%)	(12%)	(27%)
Total	526	254	780
	(67%)	(33%)	(100%)

Table 9.12 Composition of sample: age and elite sectors, $N = 159$ (%)

Age group	Elite sectors		
	Political elite	Administrative elite	Economic elite
23–40	8	25	67
41–55	16	31	53
56–68	38	23	39
Total	19	27	54

Notes

1 The research was funded by Fridrich Ebert Foundation.
2 Comparison with results of an all-Russian survey conducted at the same time demonstrate that 'ordinary people' more often identify Russia with Europe and less as 'the Eurasian country', then St Petersburg elite (Gorshkov *et al.*, 1998: 75–76).

References

Bahry, D. (1993) Society Transformed? Rethinking the Social Roots of Perestroika. *Slavic Review*, Vol. 52, No. 3, pp. 512–554.
Berger, P.L. and Luckmann, T. (1967) *The Social Construction of Reality: A Treatise in the Sociology of Knowledge*. Garden City, NY: Doubleday & Company, Inc.
Burmykina, O. and Nechaeva, N. (1998) *Sotsiokul'turnye aspekty adaptatsyi naseleniya k rynochnoy ekonomike*. St Petersburg: SPbF Instituta sotsiologii.
Burton, M. and Higley, J. (1987) Elite Settlements. *American Sociological Review*, Vol. 52, No. 3, pp. 295–307.
Burton, M., Gunther, R. and Higley, J. (1992) Introduction: Elite Transformations and Democratic regimes, in J. Higley and R. Gunther (eds) *Elites and Democratic Consolidation in Latin America and Southern Europe*. Cambridge: Cambridge University Press.
Calista, D.J. (1994) Policy Implementation, in S.S. Nagel (ed.) *Encyclopedia of Policy Studies*, second edition, revised and expanded. New York: Marcel Dekker, Inc.
Devlin, J. (1995) *The Rise of the Russian Democrats: The Causes and Consequences of the Élite Revolution*. Aldershot: Edward Elgar.
Field, G.L. and Higley, J. (1980) *Elitism*. London; Boston: Routledge and Kegan Paul.
Gaidar, Ye. (1995) *Gosudarstvo i evolyutsiya*. Moscow: Evrasiya.
Gerber, T.P. (2000) Market, State, or Don't Know? Education, Economic Ideology, and Voting in Contemporary Russia. *Social Forces*, Vol. 79, No. 2, pp. 477–521.
Golovachev, B.V. and Kosova, L.B. (1995) Tsennostnye orientatsii sovetskih i postsovetskih elit, in T. Zaslavskaya (Ed.) *Kuda idet Rossia? Al'ternativy obshchestvennogo razvitiya*. Moscow: Aspekt Press.
Gorshkov, M.K., Chepurenko, A.Yu. and Sheregi, F.E. (eds) (1998) *Osenniy krizis 1998 goda: rossiyskoye obshchestvo do i posle*. Moscow: ROSSPEN.
Hahn, J. (1993) Attitudes Toward Reform Among Provincial Russian Politicians. *Post-Soviet Affairs*, Vol. 9, No. 1, pp. 66–85.

Higley, J., Field, G.L. and Grøholt K. (1976) *Elite Structure and Ideology: A Theory with Applications to Norway.* Oslo: Universitetsforlaget; New York: Columbia University Press.
Inglehart, R. (1990) *Culture Shift in Advanced Industrial Society.* Princeton, NJ: Princeton University Press.
Kapustin, B.G. and Klyamkin, I.M. (1994) Liberal'nye tsennosti v soznanii rossiyan. *Polis*, No. 1, pp. 68–92.
Keller, S. (1968) *Beyond the Ruling Class: Strategic Elites in Modern Society.* New York: Random House.
Khakhulina, L. (2001) Dinamika otnoshenia k rynochnoy ekonomike (analiz molodezhnyh kogort nachala i kontsa 90-h godov). *Ekonomicheskiye i sotsial'nye peremeny: Monitoring obshchestvennogo mneniya*, No. 1, pp. 30–38.
Kryshtanovskaya, O. and White, S. (1996) From Soviet Nomenklatura to Russian Elite. *Europe-Asia Studies*, Vol. 48, No. 5, pp. 711–733.
Lane, D. (1996) The Transformation of Russia: The Role of the Political Elite. *Europe-Asia Studies*, Vol. 48, No. 4, pp. 535–549.
Levada, Yu. (1995) Tri pokoleniya perestroiki. *Ekonomicheskiye i sotsial'nye peremeny: Monitoring obshchestvennogo mneniya*, No. 3, pp. 7–10.
Levada, Yu. (1999a) 'Chelovek sovetskiy' desyat' let spustya: 1989–1999 (predvaritel'nye itogi sravnitel'nogo issledovaniya'. *Ekonomicheskiye i sotsial'nye peremeny: Monitoring obshchestvennogo mneniya*, No. 3, pp. 7–15.
Levada, Yu. (1999b) Piatiletniye gruppy – piatiletniye sdvigi (opyt retrospektivnogo longit'uda). *Ekonomicheskiye i sotsial'nye peremeny: Monitoring obshchestvennogo mneniya*, No. 2, pp. 19–24.
Maiminas, E. (1996) Rossiyskiy sotsial'no-ekonomicheskiy genotip. *Voprosy ekonomiki*, No. 9, pp. 131–141.
Mannheim, K. (1940) *Man and Society in an Age of Reconstruction: Studies in Modern Social Structure.* New York: Harcourt.
Matějů, P. (1997) Elite Research in the Czech Republic: A Report on Major Research Projects, in H. Best and U. Becker (eds) *Elites in Transition: Elite Research in Central and Eastern Europe.* Opladen: Leske und Budrich.
Meisel, J. (1962) *The Myth of the Ruling Class: Gaetano Mosca and the 'Elite'.* Ann Arbor: University of Michigan Press.
Miller, A.H., Hesli, V.L. and Reisinger, W.M. (1995) Comparing Citizen and Elite Belief Systems in Post-Soviet Russia and Ukraine. *Public Opinion Quarterly*, Vol. 59, No. 1, pp. 1–40.
Miller, A.H., Hesli, V.L. and Reisinger, W.M. (1997) Conceptions of Democracy Among Mass and Elite in Post-Soviet Societies. *British Journal of Political Science*, Vol. 27, Part 2, pp. 157–190.
Miller, A.H., Reisinger, W.M. and Hesli, V.L. (1998) Establishing Representation in Post-Soviet Societies: Change in Mass and Elite Attitudes Toward Democracy and the Market, 1992–1995. *Electoral Studies*, Vol. 17, No. 3, pp. 327–349.
Montero, J.R. and Morlino, L. (1996) Legitimacy and Democracy in Southern Europe, in *Reis. Revista Española de Investigaciones Sociológicas.* English edition. Madrid.
North, D.C. (1990) *Institutions, Institutional Change and Economic Performance.* New York: Cambridge University Press.
Pakulski, J. (1999) Elites, Ethnic Mobilizations and Democracy in Post-Communist Europe, E.S. Brezis and P. Temin (eds) *Elites, Minorities and Economic Growth.* Amsterdam: Elsevier Science BV.

Rukavishnikov, V., Halman, L. and Ester, P. (1998) *Politicheskie kultury i sotsialnye izmeneniya. Mezhdunarodnye sravneniya*. Moscow: Sovpadenie.

Safronov, V. (1996) Obshchesvennoye razvitie, politicheskaya kultura i demokratiya: sravnitel'nyi makroanaliz, in B.M. Firsov (ed.) *Kachestvo naseleniya Sankt-Peterburga II*. St Petersburg: SPbF Instituta sotsiologii.

Safronov, V., Burmykina, O., Kornienko, A. and Nechaeva, N. (1999) Rossiyskaya kul'tura i otnosheniye grazhdan k obshchestvennym preobrazovaniyam. *Zhurnal sotsiologii i sotsial'noy antropologii*, Vol. 2, No. 2, pp. 133–165.

Stein, A.J. (1998) The Consequences of the Nicaraguan Revolution for Political Tolerance: Explaining the Differences Among the Mass Public, Catholic Priests and Secular Elites. *Comparative Politics*, Vol. 30, No. 3, pp. 335–353.

Stouffer, S. (1992) *Communism, Conformity and Civil Liberties*. New Brunswick, NJ: Transaction.

Sullivan, J.L., Walsh, P., Shamir, M., Burnum, D.G. and Gibson, J.L. (1993) Why Politicians are More Tolerant: Selective Recruitment and Socialization Among Political Elites in Britain, Israel, New Zealand and the United States. *British Journal of Political Science*, Vol. 23, Part 1, pp. 51–76.

Toffler, A. (1981) *The Third Wave*. New York: Bantam Books.

Toneva, Z. (1997) Research on Economic and Political Elites in Bulgaria in the Period 1990–95, in H. Best and U. Becker (eds) *Elites in Transition: Elite Research in Central and Eastern Europe*. Oplanden: Leske und Budrich.

Veblen, T. (1984) *Teoriya prazdnogo klassa*. Moscow: Progress. Russian edition of Veblen, T. (1953) *The Theory of the Leisure Class: An Economic Study of Institutions*. New York: Mentor.

Wasilewski, J. (1997) Elite Research in Poland: 1989–1995, in H. Best and U. Becker (eds) *Elites in Transition: Elite Research in Central and Eastern Europe*. Oplanden: Leske und Budrich.

Wesolowski, W. (1992) The Role of Political Elites in Transition from Communism to Democracy: The Case of Poland. *Sisyphus*, Vol. 2, No. 8, pp. 77–100.

Whitefield, S. and Evans, G. (1994) *The Popular Bases of Anti-Reform Politics in Russia*. Paper presented at the Second Thematic Workshop funded by the ESRC 'The Political Process and its Emerging Discourse', 11–12 February, 1994.

10 Elite transformation and regime change
The case of Tomsk Oblast

Inessa Tarusina

Introduction

The crucial role of elites in the process of change towards more democratic rule is unequivocally assumed by most political scientists. This has certainly been the case for successful democratizations throughout the entire world. But what about Russia, where the 'transition to democracy' after ten years of post-Communist rule casts some serious doubts? Although the configuration of Russia's elites has been changed to a significant degree, the progress towards democracy is unclear. For the last few years, Freedom House has regularly considered Russia to be a partially free country. The question of my research is how these elite transformations have affected political development towards a more democratic rule in Russia.

One could assume that the dynamics of the composition of elites in Russia was decisive for the major dimensions of intra-elite relations, such as their integration and differentiation (see Higley *et al.*, in this volume). As cross-national studies show, the breakdown of ideologically unified elites leads to disunified elites who could turn into consensually unified elites through elite settlements, thus forming a basis for further democratic stability (Higley and Gunther, 1992; Higley and Burton, 1998). But this is a relatively rare outcome of elite transformation and its impact on change towards a more democratic rule. However, elites in transition could try to overcome conflicts through agreements, or 'pacts'. The outcome of these agreements for elites, as well as for regimes, might be different from case to case. In this chapter, I shall analyse the impact of elite 'pacts' on changes towards more democratic rule using a single case study of regional elites in Tomsk Oblast. Without comparative research, it is hard to say whether conflicts and agreements among Tomsk regional elites are typical or whether this is a unique case. But hopefully this analysis will also shed some light on the more general causes and consequences of intra-elite relations in Russia.

Elite transformations

The vast literature on post-Soviet Russian elites that has appeared throughout the last decade (for an overview, see Gel'man and Tarusina, in this volume) has presented different perspectives on elite transformations. As for stratification studies of elites as distinctive social groups in Russia, the two basic approaches are the concept of nomenklatura (Olga Kryshtanovskaya and Stephen White) and the 'generation change' (David Lane). These models pay more attention to the Russian post-Soviet elite genesis and dynamics.

Olga Kryshtanovskaya and Stephen White suggested that a part of the former Soviet nomenklatura in the late 1980s had converted its political power into economic capital in the wake of Gorbachev's perestroika, and then in the mid-1990s the nomenklatura converted this economic capital back into political power, thus returning to their position of domination (Kryshtanovskaya and White, 1996). This model corresponds to the model of political capitalism in Eastern Europe by Elemer Hankiss (Hankiss, 1990). The data on Russia's elites in 1993 clearly showed the huge domination of former nomenklatura members in Russia in comparison with Poland and Hungary. As for Russia's regional elites, according to Kryshtanovskaya, as many as 85 per cent in the mid-1990s had a nomenklatura background (Kryshtanovskaya, 1995). Using this approach, the explanation of the troubles of Russia's democratization could be easily linked to the restoration of an ideologically unified elite. If those 'bad guys' from the nomenklatura were to win over the 'good guys' without such a background, there would be a pending democratic transition in Russia.

However, the nomenklatura model has little explanatory power. First of all, this broad category included the former segments of elites and ruling groups at all levels, not only political leaders but also managers and high-level professionals. Thus, virtually all positions in post-Soviet Russia's elites were doomed to be occupied by former nomenklatura members, since Communist rule left no room for alternative pools of elite recruiting. Another weakness of this model is that the nomenklatura looks like a single group with common goals and values. But the in-depth studies of the late-Soviet and post-Soviet elite by David Lane and Cameron Ross (Lane, 1997; Lane and Ross, 1999) challenged this statement and demonstrated that Soviet elites under Gorbachev had a high degree of differentiation. Furthermore, this differentiation broadened and even advanced under Yeltsin. If this is the case, then the prevalence of former elite members in post-Soviet elites should not be considered as a clear sign of a return to an ideologically unified elite. Finally, the nomenklatura model failed to explain the regional diversity of elite changes (see McAuley, 1997). Although the nomenklatura members survived in the post-Soviet period across all of Russia, the political consequences of their survival and/or replacement differ widely.

Contrary to this approach, David Lane's model of elite transformation in Russia is based on the idea of a conflict of generations among Russia's elites. He suggested that the different attitudes of Gorbachev's elite cohort (more conservative) and Yeltsin's elite (more reform-oriented) were the major sources of elite differentiation and, simultaneously, of the lack of elite integration in Russia (Lane, 1997; Lane and Ross, 1999). This means that the conflict between elite generations was the crucial determinant of elite transformation in Russia. This model has been used by several scholars in studies of regional elites in Russia (see Magomedov, 2000; Hughes and John, in this volume). The premise of this model, however, has been based on data on attitudes rather than on analysis of the behaviour of the 'new' and 'old' elite cohorts. Thus, the question remains open: are the practices of 'new' elites really more democratically oriented than those of 'old' ones?

Other scholars have sought alternative explanations of elite transformations in Russia based on the analysis of patron/client relationships (Coullodon, 1998; Willerton, 1998; Afanas'ev, 2000). They focused attention on the decisive role of informal Mafia-like networks as a source for recruitment and the survival of Russia's national and regional elites in the post-Soviet period. Vladimir Gel'man and his co-authors proceeded on the assumption that the regional governance structure has a strong impact on regional elite transformation (Gel'man et al., 2000). As their comparative study shows, the diversity of regional elites depends heavily upon regional resource dynamics in the post-Soviet period as well as on the configuration of regional interest groups in the late-Soviet period. The applicability of all of the above models will be tested in my case study.

The dynamics of intra-elite relations

The problems of elite integration and differentiation and their changes in post-Soviet Russia have also been the focus of debate. Despite the different evaluations of late-Soviet elite features (see Higley et al., in this volume), it has obviously not transformed into a consensually unified elite through elite settlement in the manner of post-Communist democratization in Hungary and Poland (Higley and Pakulski, 1995; Higley and Burton, 1998). Similar conclusions were reached in analyses of regional elites (Melvin, 1998; Duka et al., 1999; Stykow, 1999; Gel'man et al., 2000). In fact, conciliatory elite agreements as outcomes of intra-elite conflicts were easily found, but their consequences were different from those elite settlements.

It is no wonder that elite 'pacts' were variously interpreted. While some scholars suggested that elite 'pacts' are necessary for democratization and political stability in Russia (Kliamkin and Shevtsova, 1999), the agreements among Russian elites were criticized as being a 'collusion' (Kholodkovskii, 1997) or a 'perverted pact' (Melville, 1999: 63). Moreover, the elitist concept of democratization through pacts was charged as being irrelevant for Russia (Elizarov, 1999). This view corresponds with those who declared that elite 'pacts' may lead not to democratic consolidation but to a hybrid type of non-democratic regime if these agreements are oriented toward the restriction of political competition and informal rules of the game (Knight, 1992; Case, 1996).

Even so, non-democratic consequences of elite pacts in Russia have not led towards political stability. This kind of consensus is very short-lived because it is oriented solely towards immediate conflict resolution (Elizarov, 1999: 76). Rather, this is a model of the survival of the fragmented elite groups (Coullodon, 1998) that did not form clearly defined competing political camps but traversed them. Under these circumstances, new intra-elite conflicts could arise repeatedly without the emergence of a stable regime, whether representative or not (see Higley *et al.*, in this volume).

Regime transitions: a regional perspective

As for Russian national politics, most scholars agree that the 'imposed' post-Soviet transition (see Gel'man, in this volume) and further political changes led to the emergence of the current 'semi-democratic' or 'hybrid' regime (Elizarov, 1999; Kliamkin and Shevtsova, 1999; Melville, 1999). Certainly, the new Russian national regime contributes to political developments across the regions. However, recent studies have demonstrated various patterns of regional political regimes (McAuley, 1997; Gel'man *et al.*, 2000; Magomedov, 2000).

The most popular explanation of these features of post-Soviet regional politics in Russia is based on an analysis of socio-economic backgrounds and/or economic reforms in particular regions (Stoner-Weiss, 1997; Afanas'ev, 1998). Although some scholars have examined the political/cultural factors of regional transition, they were restricted to aspects of electoral behaviour (see McFaul and Petrov, 1998). The conclusions about the role of these factors are controversial because causal links between regional social and economic development, economic reform policies, mass voting and democratization in Russia's regions are unclear. Although no commonly accepted indicators like Freedom House ratings of political rights have been established for Russia's regions as yet, and systematic comparative large-N studies of regional democratization are more or less speculative, evidence from small-N comparisons and case studies have not confirmed any of those assumptions.

Here, I will try to explain the causes and consequences of the development of regional political regimes that employ an elite perspective. The most obvious way is to analyse the changes in regional elites both in terms of their composition and their integration or differentiation on regional stages of regime transition. The role of intra-elite conflicts and 'pacts' as a model of their resolution in this regard deserves primary attention.

Elites and regime in Tomsk Oblast

I have chosen Tomsk Oblast as a principal case for the following reasons: (1) regional elite composition has changed substantially but not fully since the late-Soviet period, and differs from two extreme cases – for example, the fully fledged survival of the 'old' (Soviet) elite as in Tatarstan (Farukshin, 1999) and its total replacement as in St Petersburg (Duka *et al.*, 1999); (2) this region has been examined in a comparative research study by Mary McAuley as a case of a transition from a 'pluralist' to a 'consensual' politics model (McAuley, 1997: 156–220). Thus it might be suitable for testing the above models and assumptions.

During my research, I have collected and analysed more than twenty in-depth interviews with members of Tomsk regional elites and local experts, newspaper material and Internet sources, biographical and statistical information, data from regional political monitoring conducted by IGPI (the Moscow-based think-tank) in 1993–1999, and also official documents of regional authorities. The regional political and economic elites were defined using a combination of positional and reputational approaches (on the use of these methods, see Duka *et al.*, 1999). First, I formed a list of leading positions in Tomsk regional political and economic life, based on various reference sources. Then, I checked this list with regional experts, such as Tomsk political journalists, activists of political parties and social movements, officials from local and regional government, social scientists and electoral campaigners. These experts made their evaluations of the list and also made judgements about the degree of influence 'real' elite members had on the policy-making process in several areas. Major topics of interviews focused on elite changes and intra-elite relations in Tomsk Oblast in late-Soviet and post-Soviet periods, on formal and informal rules, norms and practices of regional elites, including conflicts, and the means of their resolution such as 'pacts' and agreements.

Background

Tomsk Oblast is located in the south-eastern part of Western Siberia. The basic natural resources of the region are oil and gas. The city of Tomsk was founded in 1604 and, from the beginning of the nineteenth century, it was the capital of the 'guberniya' (province), which included most of the territory of contemporary Western Siberia and the eastern part of Kazakhstan. From the end of the nineteenth century Tomsk was considered to be a cultural, economic and political centre of Siberia ('Siberian Athens'). Then, the construction of the Trans-Siberian railroad that bypassed Tomsk in the late nineteenth century seriously affected the role of Tomsk, which became a periphery of Siberia *vis-à-vis* the new Siberian capital of Novosibirsk. And in 1944 Tomsk even lost its status as the regional capital. In the course of the Second World War and its aftermath a new regional economy emerged due to the development of a military/industrial complex in the region. The new 'golden age' of Tomsk Oblast was from 1965 to 1983, when Yegor Ligachev served as a first secretary of the regional Communist Party committee (he was then a leader of the conservative wing of the national elite under Gorbachev). Institutions of higher education and high-tech industries developed in Tomsk Oblast at this time due solely to investments from the central authorities. The emergence of oil production in the northern part of the region was a new innovative step in regional economic development. Since the late-Soviet period, Tomsk Oblast's governance structure has typified an intermediate position between two major tendencies – 'localism' and 'departmentalism' (Rutland, 1993; Gel'man et al., 2000). On the one hand, this was possible because Tomsk was the location of many large federal industrial complexes which were governed from Moscow. On the other hand, agriculture as well as small- and medium-sized enterprises that oriented to the regional market were, and still are, important for this relatively remote area with its large territory.

The centralized government and Communist rule enabled the preservation of an ideological unity of regional elites. But its stability was undermined by the very fact that social and economic modernization does not correspond to the regional elite dynamics. First of all, elite mobility was very slow and moved only horizontally, from one niche to another, especially under Ligachev's eighteen-year-long rule. For example, Communist Party officials could be transferred to the regional administration and an enterprise director could occupy a position in the Communist Party committee etc. The regional elites were dominated by rural-born leaders and those associated with the historic sectors of the economy. Thus, major contemporary interest groups, such as city government managers, university rectors, directors of research and development institutions and directors of energy complex enterprises, were underrepresented in the regional elite, including the Communist Party committee. At the same time, previously established groups, such as agrarians and directors of military/industrial complex enterprises, still had power in the region. Finally, a split between the city of Tomsk and the rest of the region emerged after the Second World War. The city (where 67 per cent of the Oblast's population lived) developed faster than the rest of the territory, but was at the same time poorly reflected in regional elites. In fact, regional elite integration was preserved in the Soviet period, but its growing differentiation led to hidden tensions that turned into open conflicts during the late 1980s.

Actors and regional development

The regional elite changed radically in the time of perestroika. On the one hand, the liberalization initiated the ideological diversity of Russian elites (Lane, 1997; Coullodon, 1998; Elizarov, 1999). Following the lines of transitology, the major camps could be defined either as 'hard-liners' or 'soft-liners' (O'Donnell and Schmitter, 1986). Thus, the process of the disintegration of elites was launched at a regional level from Moscow. Simultaneously, the effect of decentralization under Gorbachev caused further regional elite differentiation. Some economic interest groups of the Tomsk regional elite began to seek their political autonomy outside of

Communist Party control. This primarily concerned the directors of building industry enterprises and the leaders of the emerging new economy (such as bankers etc.) who were mostly recruited from the former Komsomol nomenklatura. This process of differentiation and disintegration of regional elites partly overlapped and fuelled each other. This led to a polarization of regional elites within the framework of a one-dimensional ideological conflict among the regional elite that developed simultaneously. The 'hard-liners' belonged to the old interest groups like military/industrial energy complexes and agricultural groups. The 'soft-liners' were linked to the new interest groups and represented a younger generation of elites.

The influence of democratization and the impact of competitive elections on the national parliament in March 1989, and on the regional and local Soviets in March 1990, launched the open intra-elite conflict that tended to the emergence of the anti-Communist opposition and pressure for the exclusion of 'hard-liners' from the elite. The 'hard-liners' did not have any stable connections with the new interest groups and declined to make any compromise with their opponents. At the same time, the opposition became divided into 'radicals' and 'moderates' (McAuley, 1997: 168–171), although they remained a single camp vis-à-vis their common enemy. In 1990–1991, the regional elite in Tomsk, as well as in several other Russian regions (see McAuley, 1997; Stykow, 1999; Gel'man, et al., 2000), had divided into two rival camps.

However, this intra-elite conflict was resolved in 1991 due to the breakdown of Communist Party rule. 'Hard-liners' lost their power in Tomsk Oblast and were removed from leading positions. They were not excluded from the regional elite altogether and occupied several important posts in agriculture, the municipal services, universities and business. The leadership in the region was completely changed: the leader of the agrarians, Viktor Kress, was appointed as head of regional administration and leader of the opposition, and the radical 'democrat' Stepan Sulakshin took the position of presidential representative (McAuley, 1997: 172). But the disappearance of Communist rivals resulted in a lack of integration among their former opponents, since their unity had previously been based on negative consensus. It was not long before fragmentation of the regional elite became manifest.

In the wake of economic reforms beginning in early 1992, and especially during the period of privatization, the conflict of interest groups became more important for elite development. The inflow of resources from Moscow to the region was shrinking, especially when compared to that of the 'golden age' of Ligachev. In search of regional elite (re)integration, the new regionalist ideology (*oblastnichestvo*) became popular in Tomsk, as it did elsewhere throughout Siberia (Hughes, 1994: 1134). At the beginning of the 1990s, new regionalist factions were established in Tomsk regional and city legislatures. These developments partially resembled similar intellectual trends in Tomsk in the early twentieth century when regionalist ideology developed in the region which had previously lost its importance in Russia.

The dissolution of the Soviets in 1993 had limited public activity of political parties and movements. The 'new' politicians (regionalists and 'democrats') lost positions of power. Even though the 'democrat' Stepan Sulakshin was elected in 1993 and 1995 as a deputy of the State Duma, he became increasingly engaged in lobbying for the interests of military/industrial groups without any party label. Political parties, regardless of their colours, gradually lost their importance in regional politics in Tomsk Oblast, as elsewhere (see Golosov, in this volume). In the Tomsk Oblast Soviet of 1990–1993, more than 100 of 230 deputies belonged to political parties or factions (McAuley, 1997: 198–199). The party representation of 21 deputies in the new Oblast Duma, elected in 1994, declined to just 3 Communists and 4 agrarians. Then, one Oblast Duma deputy joined the Yabloko party. During the next regional legislative elections of 1997, only 3 party candidates of 42 deputies were elected to the regional parliament (Vybory, 1998; Golosov, 1999). No wonder the chairman of the Oblast Duma Boris Mal'tsev described the legislature as 'the structure above parties, where there is no room for political activity'. Thus, the 'newest' politicians – local or sectoral 'bosses' and managers or their nominees – replaced the 'new' party-oriented politicians. In other words, interest groups replaced political parties as channels of representation of the masses and as a tool of the integration of elites. Similar trends have been observed in the other regions of Siberia (Golosov, 1997; Hughes, 1997) and throughout all Russia (Vybory, 1998). This process was accompanied by the decline of parties and legislatures.

The Tomsk City Duma replaced the City Soviet which had been the centre of activity of the 'democrats' in the early 1990s. In 1996, the number of seats in the City Duma was reduced to eighteen, and its political significance was lost. No chair had been elected by the City Duma and its activities were run by the Mayor of Tomsk, Alexander Makarov, who was also the deputy of the regional Duma. One-quarter of City Duma deputies simultaneously served as regional or local executive branch officers which undermined democratic accountability. Although in 1996 representatives of three national parties were elected to the City Duma, most local political activists left politics for business as they understood that there was no longer any opportunity for party organizational development.

As to party representation within the executive branch, the only party that could exist in Tomsk was a so-called 'party of power', for example 'Our Home is Russia' in 1995–1998 or 'Unity' in 1999–2000. The very existence of these party organizations is mostly informal and based on the 'political machine' of electoral mobilization through the administrative apparatus (Brie, 1997). Any presence of other political parties and movements in the executive branch is excluded. As a result, 50 parties and 400 political movements nominally exist but have no influence on regional politics.

These declining trends could also be observed in the Oblast Duma. The share of district-level executive officials among its deputies is significant (28.6 per cent in 1994 and 14.2 per cent in 1997). According to experts, more than one-quarter of deputies act poorly as legislators and only voted following the commands of the regional administration. Despite the effects of some business leaders elected to the regional assembly in 1994 and 1997, the impact of the Oblast Duma (not to mention the City Duma) on the decision-making process is restricted. These restrictions are imposed by the formal institutional design and the subordinate role of the Oblast Duma in the policy-making process, including budgetary and fiscal regulations. The key policy decisions belong to regional government under the control of the governor and his administration. But informal practices of intra-elite relations make the policy-making process even less accountable.

Since 1988, the configuration of Tomsk Oblast political elites has changed significantly. First of all, the number of elite members increased for a short period during the early 1990s, and then decreased again. In 1988, 48 people were considered to comprise the regional political elite, but in 2000, they numbered only 29. None of the leaders of the institutions of science, culture and higher education were recognized as elite members in 2000 in comparison with 1988, when there was a clear, visible presence of this group (14.6 per cent of Tomsk Oblast political elite). The representation of officials of the regional administration among the elite has changed in the opposite direction, from 8.3 per cent in 1988 to 34.4 per cent in 2000. The only group which represented the elite even more strongly was the deputies of Tomsk Oblast Duma (41 per cent), but this is not evidence of Duma influence within the elite. On the contrary, the elite position is one of the most important factors of electoral success in regional legislative elections. The enterprise directors (both giant plants and small and medium business) comprise the third group, which also increased their proportion of the regional elite. Finally, the new group of the heads of the law-enforcement agencies – i.e. regional branches of the Ministry of Internal Affairs, Federal Security Service, prosecutors' office etc. – is a small but highly integrated segment of the regional elite, which is informally known as the 'club of generals'. Experts have suggested that this 'club' is one of most influential groups of the regional elite.

Thus, at the beginning of 1990s the recruitment pool of regional elites was enlarged, but will become increasingly smaller in the future. At the beginning of the 1990s, social interest groups, including leaders of school education and public health institutions as well as 'third sector' NGOs, were also visible in regional politics. Now they are out of the political game. As for other 'old' interest groups, the military/industrial enterprises lost their influence due to economic hardship in the region (as well as in Russia as a whole). After a serious accident in 1993 in one of the regional industrial giants, the Siberian Chemical Industry, the regional authorities decided to close some military/industrial enterprises in Tomsk Oblast. Neither did the agrarians have any positive political perspectives in the region. They had no political structure for lobbying their interests within the region and they had no money for sponsoring the election campaigns of their candidates.

All of these groups were replaced by new groups comprising representatives of the oil, gas and food industries. The building industry group led by the chairman of Tomsk Oblast Duma, Boris Mal'tsev, is still in power. The elite members, as well as some experts, suggested in their interviews that some criminal groups should also be involved in the elite recruitment process.

How does elite change in Tomsk Oblast fit into the framework of the above models of elite transformations? As for 'nomenklatura conversion', this has certainly not been the case in Tomsk Oblast, because the share of members of the nomenklatura in the regional elite fell between 1990 (91.7 per cent) and 2000 (24.1 per cent). This kind of gradual extinction of the nomenklatura could be explained by the mode of regime transition in Tomsk and economic changes. In 1991, the former elite members lost their political power and had no resources to convert them into economic power. In the course of economic reform, even those sectors which had been linked to the former elite (military/industry and agriculture), have lost economic influence, thus leaving no chance for the nomenklatura to return to power.

Regarding the elites' generation change, the evidence from Tomsk Oblast contrasts with the previous model. Although the average age of elite members was about 50.8 years in 1988 and 49.9 in 2000, the personal structure of the regional elite has changed following two new waves of recruitment. The first wave reflects the period 1990–1991 when new regional governing bodies were elected and non-elite members entered into regional politics. The second wave commenced in 1997–1998 when the composition of the Oblast Duma and administration was changed and the cohort of politicians and bureaucrats aged 50–60 was partially replaced by their younger members (the average age of the 'newest' elite is now 43 years). But the impact of these waves on regional elites was different. The first wave of generation changes led to an opening up of the regime, the development of political competitiveness, and the establishment of formal rules and norms of elite behaviour. The second wave led to regime closing, the limitation of political competitiveness, and the enforcement of informal rules and patterns of intra-elite relations.

In both cases of regional elite change, the conflict between generations of elites was obvious. But the consequences of these conflicts were different. In 1990–1991, the open clash between 'hard-liners' and 'soft-liners' (and then between 'old' and 'new' elites) was resolved as a zero-sum game. Since 1997–1998, the conflict between generations of elites has no longer been manifest, and, at least, has not been accompanied by open electoral competition. Rather, this is behind-the-door bargaining, which led to a step-by-step decline of the 'new' elites' influence in favour of the 'newest' members. For example, in 1999 two leading advisers to the governor who had held their positions since 1991–1992, were fired due to pressure from the 'newest' challengers.

Regarding patron/client relations within the regional elite, their role in Tomsk Oblast is undeniable, as elsewhere in Russia (Afanas'ev, 2000). But the very nature of clientelism in the region has two distinctive features. First of all, the patron/client ties and networks are not based on local or personal 'clan' politics (Willerton, 1998), but on sectional economic interest groups like the gas, building or food industries. The decline of the old interest groups (agrarians or military/industrial complex) and the rise of the new groups (oil and gas industry) determined the survival and/or breakdown of respective networks. The other point is that the leaders of major interest groups within the region (i.e. fuel and energy complex) are representatives of branches of nationwide companies. Thus, external actors have a decisive impact on Tomsk regional elites and on the decision-making process within the region.

Taking the decision-making perspective, I would say that the transformation of interest group politics within and outside the region is the major factor in the transformation of Tomsk Oblast political elites. Capital, generation, nomenklatura background, or any other social characteristic of the elite, are not resources of crucial importance for the survival of the regional elite. The only direct or indirect access to major economic resources – i.e. the circulation of oil, gas, or money – makes the political domination in Tomsk Oblast possible. This explanation of elite transformation is also plausible for an analysis of intra-elite relationships in this region.

Conflicts and agreements

In comparison with the elites of some other Russian regions (see McAuley, 1997; Stoner-Weiss, 1997; Magomedov, 2000; Gel'man *et al.*, 2000), Tomsk Oblast is one of the most 'quiet'. This observation is particularly so in connection with federal/regional relations, because Tomsk Oblast was one of the most loyal regions in its relationship to the Centre during the 1990s due to the high economic dependence of the region on the Centre. But the picture is somewhat different in connection with intra-elite relations within the region. Throughout the 1990s, regional elites oscillated between two types of strategies – compromise and force-oriented. In other words, cycles of intra-elite conflicts and agreements could be observed in Tomsk Oblast.

What kind of agreements among elites have been achieved in Tomsk Oblast? Were they were steps towards democratization or did they serve as 'cartels of incumbents against contenders, cartels that restrict political competition'? (Przeworski, 1991: 90). The answer to this question is closely related to the analysis of crises and conflicts among Tomsk Oblast elites. The major conflicts arose around two basic factors: (1) the distribution of political power between different branches and elite groups and (2) the distribution of control over property in existing or newly emerging sectors of regional economy, which appeared to be contradictory to each other. Political leaders, branches of federal, regional and local authorities, and interest groups were involved in these conflicts in different constellations. Most of these conflicts resulted in a compromise based either on preserving the status quo or on a negative consensus of incumbent elite groups versus outsiders or so-called 'rebels'. But these agreements were fragile and volatile, and new conflicts arose among fragmented regional elites soon after a compromise had been reached.

The foundations of elite agreements were established in October 1993 as a consequence of the national political crisis. After Boris Yeltsin's decree on the dissolution of the Supreme Soviet, some deputies of the Tomsk Oblast Soviet expressed their solidarity with the ousted national parliamentarians. These deputies, backed by 'regionalists' and some other parties and movements, applied to their constituencies for public support. The Oblast administration decided to show its loyalty to the President by the dissolution of the regional legislatures. But they needed public or legislature support for such a decision. This was the reason that the administration sought the consent of the regional deputies' majority. The chairman of the Oblast parliament was loyal to the regional administration. On meeting with the Oblast governor and with members of the 'club of generals' he promised to put to the vote the question of regional Duma self-dissolution and to organize a majority's approval. They were in agreement on the dissolution of the Oblast Soviet by the joint decision of its chairman and governor. The former deputies that were still loyal to the regional administration received informal support during the new legislative elections, thus securing the status quo. This informal intra-elite agreement launched the chain of subsequent events which was becoming routine practice in the Tomsk Oblast.

The natural conflict of interests of the executive and legislative branches makes these compromises very fragile under conditions of regional elite fragmentation. In 1997, on the eve of the new regional legislative elections, the new chairman of the Oblast Duma claimed more powers for the regional legislature in regional media. His claims were backed by the very fact that the major interest groups were represented in the Oblast Duma. If more powers could be granted to the Duma, its chairman would be in a strong position at the next gubernatorial election. But after the bargaining between himself and the incumbent governor, these conflicts were resolved. The chairman withdrew his claims, being supported by the governor during the elections and as chairman of the new convocation of the Oblast Duma. For his part, the chairman took control of the pro-governor legislative majority which excluded open inter-branch conflict in the region. Again, this agreement limited public contest in favour of the executive branch and strengthened the informal practices of elites.

Nevertheless, the new interest groups who entered the Oblast Duma required a new redistribution of power. In early 1999, some junior deputies and leaders of the food industry revitalized the idea of widening the powers of the regional legislature in terms of the policy-making process. Their claims in the regional media made this conflict more open. The new compromise was based on resource exchange. The formal powers of the Duma have been expanded. For example, a legislative commission on control over budget expenditures has been established. But informal control of the administration over the Duma was enforced and the governor's nominee (who had previously served as an executive official) was elected as First Vice-Chairman of the legislature in charge of the above commission. Thus, the status quo was re-established at the expense of contest and accountability. Soon after, the 'rebels' were punished and excluded from the new economic project. Although their idea to build a new alcohol production plant in the region was adopted and partially funded by administration, none of these Duma deputies or their supporters participated in this business.

It was no wonder that the conflicts emerged again on the eve of the gubernatorial elections in May 1999. The chairman of the Oblast Duma claimed possible nomination as a candidate for governorship. In response, the governor advanced the idea of early elections that could minimize the chances of his contenders. After a series of bargains with the chairman and vice-chairmen of Oblast Duma as well as with members of the 'club of generals', the election date was changed from 19 December to 19 September 1999. The loyal Duma voted for this proposal without any protest either from the parties or interest groups.

But the incumbent governor was not the only possible contender in the early elections. In June 1999, Tomsk Mayor Makarov declared his participation in the gubernatorial race. After this declaration, the governor met with the mayor and forced him to withdraw his candidacy in exchange for gubernatorial support of Makarov in the new mayoral elections. The agreement was reached: Makarov openly expressed his loyalty to Kress, while the governor's nominees were appointed to two senior positions in the Tomsk city administration in charge of Oblast–city relations. On the eve of the mayoral elections, Makarov called early elections in the same manner as Kress had done previously. The City Duma majority enthusiastically supported his idea of the incumbent mayor, but, following the protest of one Communist deputy of the City Duma, this decision was quashed by the court as being illegal. However, Makarov resigned from his post, thus making early elections inevitable anyway. Nevertheless, Makarov was unable to win in the first round of elections in which he received 34.9 per cent of votes against two major challengers with 21.8 per cent and 18.4 per cent respectively. He certainly needed guarantees of survival within the regional elite and sought the support of the electorate. The only political machine available was the 'party of power' (Brie, 1997) which was based on the regional administration. Following an effective campaign organized by the first deputy governor, Makarov won the second round with 54.3 per cent of the votes cast.

In addition to these problems, Sulakshin also proclaimed his participation in the gubernatorial elections. However, under threat of the publication of compromising material, he was forced to meet with his major rivals – Kress and Makarov – and then withdrew his candidacy. Both the governor and the mayor rewarded Sulakshin and expressed their open support to him at the 1999 State Duma elections, but the latter lost to 79-year-old Ligachev whose popularity in the region remains high.

However, the most powerful actors in regional politics were located outside of Tomsk Oblast – first and foremost, the national oil company YUKOS. The regionally based Eastern Oil Company (which included eight oil factories), the owner of major oil resources of the region, was acquired by YUKOS in 1997. In 1999, the regional authorities received credit for more than 1 billion roubles from YUKOS and the regional administration was forced to take up a new loan of 1,760 million roubles. This meant that the candidacy for the governorship was supposed to be coordinated with YUKOS authorities. At the same time, YUKOS was more interested in political stability in its subordinate region than in the escalation of new conflicts. This was the reason for the resolution of the new conflict about the gubernatorial elections. The head of Eastern Oil Company, Viktor Kalyuzhnyi, announced his own plans to compete in the gubernatorial elections. The threat of defeat for Kress was serious, and he applied to the head of YUKOS for political support. The assistance of YUKOS was principal: the electoral campaign of Kress was well paid by the new sponsor, while YUKOS bought major stakes of regional oil enterprises. It was not surprising that Kress had no visible contenders during the elections and easily won in the first round with 72.9 per cent of the votes. The head of Eastern Oil Company obtained a prominent post in Moscow, left Tomsk and relinquished his influence in the region.

Despite the powerful influence of YUKOS, this company has no monopoly on the natural resource-based economy of Tomsk Oblast. A new conflict in the region emerged in 1999–2000 concerning the control of the oil and gas industries. In 1995, the backbone of the regional economy – Oil-Chemical Industry of Tomsk – was split into several joint-stock companies, but was then bankrupted in 1997. The major part of its corporate stocks was transferred to the Ministry of Atomic Energy. Two years later Gazprom attempted to purchase these shares, but its interests were confronted by the holding Alliance-Group and YUKOS. As a result, various groups (and not one stakeholder) have the largest holdings of corporate stocks for the different parts of this industry. Looking for new resources, the regional administration of Tomsk Oblast launched a project on the development of the gas industry that could provide gas to sixteen regions in Siberia and the Far East. The interests of YUKOS here clashed with those of Gazprom whose interests were represented by its regional affiliated company, Eastgazprom. According to some estimates, the possible winner of this conflict would not only have supplied gas in the Tomsk region, but could also have won control over the prospective energy market for the whole of Siberia.

As may be seen, the balance of localism and departmentalism is still relevant for Tomsk regional politics. While the heads of the local administration and the Mayor of Tomsk have become more powerful, the oil and gas companies have also increased their influence. But the regional elite in the Soviet period was integrated owing to the dominance of the Communist Party. In contrast to this, the post-Soviet elite was fragmented into several groups and their agreements could not supply political stability. Therefore, after triumphant and actually non-competitive gubernatorial elections, Kress was once again faced with the regional elite differentiation and lack of integration. He had no resources with which he could impose control over regional politics and economies, and groups of the fragmented regional elite could not serve as his strategic allies.

In search of effective tools of elite integration, some of the 'newest' members of the Tomsk Oblast political elite attempted to return to the use of forceful strategies rather than compromise. But if the conflicts among the elites in the late 1980s and early 1990s had initially been developed in the field of mass politics, recent conflicts do not include electoral contest. Instead, some groups of the 'newest' elites proposed other means of conflict resolution, such as the use of informal influence within the decision-making process, including administrative pressure and (last but not least) threats of violence towards political outsiders, the media and the business community. The proponents of the strategy of force are an informal group of elites calling themselves 'the politicians of the new generation' (or 'new-type politicians') who tried to capture dominant positions among the regional elite. The leader of this group, Vladimir Zhidkikh, a former senior executive officer of Eastern Oil Company, was appointed in 1999 as a presidential representative in the region. He was then the major organizer of electoral campaigns for the incumbent governor and for President Putin. Kress was forced to reward Zhidkikh, and appointed him as First Vice-Governor. The influence of the 'new-type politicians' has been increased, and the regional administration has strengthened its position among the regional elite.

However, opportunities for the forced integration of the regional elite are quite limited due to the resource crisis and dependence of regional political actors upon external actors who also contend with each other (such as Gazprom and YUKOS, for example). Furthermore, the differentiation of elite groups in the region is based on their resource autonomy, which makes the domination of one single actor virtually impossible.

Conclusion: a political regime in flux

Ten years after the breakdown of Communist rule, the Tomsk regional elite is still fragmented, despite a number of attempts to achieve integration. The reinforcement of elite fragmentation in Tomsk Oblast had a decisive impact on the regional political regime. The generation change led first to the opening up of the political regime and then to its closing in, which meant the domination of informal rules in elite relations. According to the typology of elites and regimes by John Higley and his co-authors (see Higley *et al.*, in this volume), the political regime in Tomsk Oblast corresponded with an unstable representative type. But the representativeness here means only the inclusion of major elite groups into decision-making processes that were based on the non-democratic practices of representation.

In fact, regional elites operated not within the framework of formal institutions such as political parties or legislation, but within the informal practices of elite agreements. Although intra-elite bargains and compromise in Tomsk Oblast are similar to the model of elite settlement in certain points (Higley and Gunther, 1992; Higley and Burton, 1998), these led to an incidental consensus that does not transfer into a stable set of formal rules and norms. This is not to say that the formal institutions have had no impact in Tomsk Oblast. But most elite members and experts considered that the formal rules were a façade rather than real decision-making. They are purely instrumental and often change due to current affairs. For example, there are many situations where the regional government has made decisions about economic preferences of certain companies or regional legislation has been changed in favour of certain persons and/or groups.

The major features of the Tomsk regional political regime are the following: (1) the predominance of regional executive authorities over other branches and levels of governing bodies; (2) the informal contract about mutual loyalty between regional and federal elites as well as between some groups of regional elites; (3) the indirect control of regional administration over regional mass media; (4) the neutralization or suppression of real and potential opposition; (5) the patronage of regional executive authorities over the public sphere. The rules of the political game in Tomsk Oblast are oriented towards the restriction of political competition. The elite members are agreed that they have no interest in the loss of power. It is no wonder that, although elections remain virtually the only formal institution whose significance is indisputable, it is difficult to call them 'democratic'. For example, the governor insisted on amendments to regional legislation (and, then, to national legislation), allowing him to be elected for a third term of office. These amendments were passed to his satisfaction. There are no guarantees against the abolition or postponement of elections or for holding early elections, as occurred in the gubernatorial and mayoral elections of 1999–2000. Indeed, to ensure their own survival, the regional elites gave mutual assistance in this respect. In September 2000, the Oblast Duma prolonged its term of office until 2002 (instead of holding the elections scheduled for 2001). Simultaneously, the same decision was passed by the City Duma. One member of the elite explained these decisions to the general public as being due to the need for the continuity of power.

The other feature of elections in the region (especially gubernatorial and mayoral elections) is the use of 'administrative mobilization' based on the use of the political machine of state apparatus in the form of the 'party of power' (Brie, 1997). The effect of pressure by enterprise managers and local bosses on the voters was clear. In the interviews, some members of the regional elite described their method of preparing for the elections as so-called 'cleaning of the area' (*raschistka territorii*). It means bargaining with powerful contenders within the regional elite and applying pressure towards irreconcilable challengers and competitors outside of this.

The case of the gubernatorial elections of 1999 is a clear example of the use of such methods. Therefore, the function of elections in the Tomsk regional political regime is different from electoral democracies. They did not serve as a mechanism for ensuring a shift of power, but rather served as a mechanism of the legitimization of the status quo in the region, because the elite insured themselves against the threat of loss of power.

As stated above, the regime transformation in Tomsk does not correspond to the normative models of 'democracy'. This particular case study has not permitted an explanation of the similarities or differences between 'Western' and 'non-Western' democracies. In this sense, the cultural and historical preconditions of regional political development need special comparative investigation. Now it is only possible to say that, when comparing the Tomsk transition to some other regional case studies (see McAuley, 1997; Magomedov, 2000; Gel'man et al., 2000), I would consider Tomsk neither as a case of 'transition to democracy', nor as a case of 'breakdown of democracy'. The transformation of political regime in Tomsk is not yet complete. Despite the number of regional elections held, not only the configuration of the most powerful regional political actors, but also the rules of intra-elite relations are still unstable. Reducing the resources of the regional elites and the growth of the influence of external actors makes the regime instability even more visible. Under these conditions, informal agreements can only be temporary solutions for regional elites, while the lack of formal institutions cannot guarantee the fulfilment of the conditions of the agreements. This cycle of conflicts and agreements could be endless as long as the present regional elite survives.

Further possible changes in the Tomsk regional political regime depend upon new trends of elite transformation. In the long haul, these trends could include either the emergence of some large camps of elites (i.e. divided elites) which are able to achieve real elite settlement, or gradual step-by-step acceptance of formal rules and norms imposed by external actors. However, in the short term, this 'halfway house' (Case, 1996) state of the elite and intra-elite network transformation in Tomsk Oblast cannot be overcome easily.

Acknowledgement

The chapter is based on a project supported by the Research Support Scheme of the Open Society Support Foundation, grant N 1540/2000.

References

Afanas'ev, M. (1998) Ot vol'nykh ord do khanskoi stavki. *Pro et Contra*, Vol. 3, No. 3, pp. 5–20.

Afanas'ev, M. (2000) *Klientelizm i rossiiskaya gosudarstvennost'*, second edition. Moscow: Moskovskii Obshchestvennyi Nauchnyi Fond.

Brie, M. (1997) *The Political Regime in Moscow – Creation of New Urban Machine?* Berlin: WZB Working Paper No. P97–002.
Case, W. (1996) Can the 'Halfway House' Stand? Semidemocracy and Elite Theory in Three Southeast Asian Countries. *Comparative Politics*, Vol. 28, No. 4, pp. 437–464.
Coullodon, V. (1998) Elite Groups in Russia. *Demokratizatsiya*, Vol. 6, No. 3, pp. 535–549.
Duka, A., Bystrova, A., Daugavet, A., Gor'kovenko, V. and Kornienko, A. (1999) *Regional'nye elity Rossii: problemy, podkhody, gipotezy: programma issledovaniya*. St Petersburg: St Petersburg Branch of the Institute of Sociology RAS.
Elizarov, V. (1999) Elitistskaya teoriya demokratii i sovremennyi rossiskii politicheskii protsess. *Polis*, No. 1, pp. 72–78.
Farukshin, M. (1999) The Ruling Elite in Tatarstan: Contemporary Challenges and Problems of Adjustment, in V. Shlapentokh, C. Wanderpool and B. Doktorov (eds) *The New Elite in Post-Communist Eastern Europe*. College Station, TX: A&M University Press, pp. 223–240.
Gel'man, V., Ryzhenkov, S. and Brie, M. (eds) (2000) *Rossiya regionov. Transformatsiya polititsheskikh rezhimov*. Moscow: Ves' Mir.
Golosov, G.V. (1997) Russian Political Parties and the 'Bosses': Evidence from the 1994 Provincial Elections in Western Siberia. *Party Politics*, Vol. 3, No. 1, pp. 3–21.
Golosov, G.V. (1999) From Adygeya to Yaroslavl': Factors of Party Development in Russia's Regions. *Europe-Asia Studies*, Vol. 51, No. 8, pp. 1333–1365.
Hankiss, E. (1990) *East European Alternatives*. Oxford: Clarendon Press.
Hanley, E., Yershova, N. and Anderson, R. (1995) Russia – Old Wine in a New Bottle? *Theory and Society*, Vol. 24, No. 5, pp. 639–668.
Higley, J. and Burton, J. (1998) Elite Settlements and the Taming of Politics. *Government and Opposition*, Vol. 33, No. 1, pp. 98–115.
Higley, J. and Gunther, R. (eds) (1992) *Elites and Democratic Consolidation in Latin America and Southern Europe*. Cambridge: Cambridge University Press.
Higley, J. and Pakulski, J. (1995) Elite Transformation in Central and Eastern Europe. *Australian Journal of Political Science*, Vol. 30, No. 3, pp. 415–435.
Hughes, J. (1994) Regionalism in Russia: The Rise and Fall of Siberian Agreement. *Europe-Asia Studies*, Vol. 46, No. 7, pp. 1133–1161.
Hughes, J. (1997). Sub-National Elites and Post-Communist Transformation in Russia: A Reply to Kryshtanovskaya and White. *Europe-Asia Studies*, Vol. 49, No. 6, pp. 1017–1036.
Kholodkovskii, K. (1997) Konsolidatshiya elit: obstshestvennii pakt ili verchushetshnii sgovor?, in T. Zaslavskaya (ed.) *Kuda Idet Rossiya?* Moscow: Intertsenter, pp. 125–132.
Kliamkin, I. and Shevtsova, L. (1999). *This Omnipotent Impotent Government*. Moscow: Moscow Carnegie Center.
Knight, A. (1992) Mexico's Elite Settlement: Conjuncture and Consequences, in J. Higley and R. Gunther (eds) *Elites and Democratic Consolidation in Latin America and Southern Europe*. Cambridge: Cambridge University Press, pp. 113–145.
Kryshtanovskaya, O. (1995) Transformatsiya staroi nomenklatury v novuyu rossiiskuyu elitu. *Obshchestvennye Nauki i Sovremennost'*, No. 1, pp. 51–65.
Kryshtanovskaya, O. and White, S. (1996) From Soviet Nomenklatura to Russian Elite. *Europe-Asia Studies*, Vol. 48, No. 5, pp. 711–733.

Lane, D. (1997) Transition Under Eltsin: The Nomenklatura and Political Elite Circulation. *Political Studies*, Vol. 45, No. 5, pp. 855–874.
Lane, D. and Ross, C. (1999) *The Transition from Communism to Capitalism: Ruling Elites from Gorbachev to Yeltsin*. London: Macmillan.
Magomedov, A. (2000) *Misteriya regionalizma*. Moscow: Moskovskii Obshchestvennyi Nauchnyi Fond.
McAuley, M. (1997) *Russia's Politics of Uncertainty*. Cambridge: Cambridge University Press.
McFaul, M. and Petrov, N. (eds) (1998) *Politicheskii Al'manakh Rossii*. Moscow: Moscow Carnegie Center.
Melville, A. (1999) *Demokraticheskie tranzity. Teoretiko-metodologicheskie i prikladnye aspekty*. Moscow: Moskovskii Obshchestvennyi Nauchnyi Fond.
Melvin, N. (1998) The Consolidation of a New Regional Elite. The Case of Omsk (1987–1995). *Europe-Asia Studies*, Vol. 50, No. 4, pp. 619–650.
O'Donnell, G. and Schmitter, P. (1986) *Transitions from Authoritarian Rule. Tentative Conclusions about Uncertain Democracies*. Baltimore and London: Johns Hopkins University Press.
Przeworski, A. (1991) *Democracy and the Market. Political and Economic Reforms in Eastern Europe and Latin America*. Cambridge: Cambridge University Press.
Rutland, P. (1993) *The Politics of Economic Stagnation*. Cambridge: Cambridge University Press.
Stoner-Weiss, K. (1997) *Local Heroes. The Political Economy of Russian Regional Governance*. Princeton: Princeton University Press.
Stykow, P. (1999) Elite Transformation in the Saratov Region, in V. Shlapentokh, C. Wanderpool and B. Doktorov (eds), *The New Elite in Post-Communist Eastern Europe*. College Station, TX: A&M University Press, pp. 201–222.
Vybory (1998) *Vybory v zakonodatel'nye (predstavitel'nye) organy gosudarstvennoi vlasti sub"ektov Rossiiskoi Federatsii, 1995–1997*. Moscow: Ves' Mir.
Wasilewski, J. (1998) Hungary, Poland and Russia: The Fate of Nomenklatura Elites, in M. Dogan and J. Higley (eds) *Elites, Crises and Origins of Regimes*. Lanham, MD: Rowman and Littlefield, pp. 147–167.
Willerton, J. (1998) Post-Soviet Clientelist Norms at the Russian Federal Level, in G. Gill (ed.) *Elites and Leadership in Russian Politics*. London: Macmillan, pp. 52–80.

11 Studies of political elites in Russia

An overview

Vladimir Gel'man and Inessa Tarusina[1]

Introduction

Until the late 1980s, the field of elite research – both theoretical and empirical – was still a kind of taboo in Russian social sciences. Although the field itself was recognized among scholars, and, for example, C. Wright Mills' classical *The Power Elite* (1956) was published in Russian as early as 1959, the use of elite theories was limited to the so-called 'critique of non-Marxist concepts' (see Ashin, 1985; Burlatskii and Galkin, 1985). Recently, the situation has looked completely different. Since 1989, when a section on elite research was established at the Institute of Sociology of Russian Academy of Sciences (Steiner, 1997: 118), studies in this field have been rapidly expanded and quickly institutionalized. 'Elite' became a key word in political science and sociological discourse. Dozens of books and hundreds of articles on elites have appeared (for a bibliography, see Kukolev and Stykow, 1996: 109–113, 1998: 132–137; Steiner, 1997: 125–132; Duka, 2001). Dissertations on elites have been written, conferences on elites have been held, lecture courses on elites have been taught and even the first Russian textbook on 'elitology' has been published (see Ponedelkov and Starostin, 1998).

So, from a quantitative point of view, elite research as a new subdiscipline became a distinct area of Russian social science studies – relatively more developed, than, for example, comparative politics or political theory. But what about the qualitative assessment of this growth? Did the new theoretical frameworks provide new methodologies to be applied? Did the new findings stimulate a research agenda relevant to contemporary international standards? This chapter is focused on these issues through an analysis of current trends in elite research in Russia. It is primarily concerned with the studies of political and, partially, economic elites – and not with cultural or academic elites, even though some scholarly works have appeared on those topics. We shall start by discussing the emergence of elite studies in Russia and their features, and then turn to two different dimensions of research – stratification and transition studies. Finally, we shall discuss some achievements and shortcomings of Russia's elite research as well as present an agenda for future research.

Developing research: scholars, institutions and works

The early 1990s was a period of a major turn on the part of Russian scholars toward research on elites as well as different aspects of elite influence on political, economic and social developments in Russia (see Steiner, 1997). The reasons for such a turn combine some academic and non-academic developments. First and foremost, elites became a major actor in the process of transition in Russia, especially after the decline of the wave of social movement mobilization in 1988–1991. Thus, Russian social scientists began to focus their attention on the elite, rather than the mass level of politics (Gel'man, 1997: 70). Meanwhile, changes in academic infrastructure – that is, the lack of state funding for social research as well as the emergence of opportunities for collaboration between Russian scholars and Western foundations and researchers – increased the value of elite research on the academic market. The demand for data and analysis on elites (such as directories, reference volumes, databases etc.) also expanded. At the same time, the Russian academic community was, and still is, highly influenced by overpoliticization, and, then, overcommercialization. A large number of scholars served as political observers, advisers, political campaigners, and so on. Their writings often expressed either political preferences or self-reflections. Finally, as one Russian sociologist noted, 'elite research is the best way to become a member of the elite' (as quoted in Gel'man, 1996: 19).

The infrastructure of elite research in Russia reflects the complexity of social science developments in general. Research teams and individual scholars vary greatly in their background and institutional affiliation. They can be classified in the following way: (1) standing groups and regular members of institutions of the Russian Academy of Sciences (RAS) and universities; (2) project teams, carrying out their research within institutions or groups of scholars from different institutions; and (3) non-academic groups and individuals from think-tanks, the media and government working in this field. Although special divisions of elite research within the RAS system are limited to the section of elite research in the Institute of Sociology (led by Olga Kryshtanovskaya) and the group of political sociologists at the St Petersburg branch of the same institute (led by Alexandr Duka), individual or group projects dealing with elites have been established at the Institute of Employment Affairs, the Institute of World Economy and International Relations, the Institute of Scientific Information in Social Sciences, the Institute of Ethnology and Anthropology, the Institute of International Economic and Political Studies and some other RAS Moscow-based institutions. For universities, research was not the primary focus in the Soviet period as they specialized mainly in teaching. However, individual research projects have been launched elsewhere across Russia's provincial universities, even though most of them were limited to their 'own' regions. Scholars from the Russian Academy of Civil Service and its provincial branches have also produced some work on elites.

Special project teams that include scholars from different institutions (or from the same institution) are a relatively new phenomenon in the Russian social sciences, related to major changes in the system of funding social science research. First of all, the participation of Russian scholars in some comparative cross-national research teams sometimes requires attracting scholars with different specializations. This was the case with the elite research in Poland, Hungary and Russia conducted by Ivan Szelenyi.[2] The Russian project team was organized by VTSIOM (the most renowned Russian center for public opinion research), which carried out a large-scale elites survey as well as an in-depth analysis (Ershova, 1994; Golovachev *et al.*, 1995–1996). Some groups were organized around Russian-funded projects, such as the project based on elite interviews conducted in 1992–1993 by a group of scholars from the Institute of Employment Affairs and the Institute of Sociology RAS (Mikul'skii *et al.*, 1995). However, the lack of regular funding as well as other organizational problems made such teams quite fragile: according to our information, none of them survived as a group after the completion of those projects.

Finally, the non-academic groups and individuals in the field vary widely with respect to their tasks and organizational forms. Some of them are well known, such as 'Panorama,' a Moscow-based think-tank that collects very detailed data, including biographies of national and regional elites in Russia. While Panorama products are mainly commercial, an alternative is represented by the 'Vox Populi' expert surveys, which are public-oriented. Starting in early 1993, this group, led by the well-known Russian sociologist Boris Grushin, has provided monthly surveys of about 50 Moscow-based political scientists, journalists and other experts, as well as analysis of the degree of influence of politicians and other prominent figures on current Russian political issues. The results of such surveys have been published monthly in *Nezavisimaya gazeta* and serve as an interesting source for analysis (see Lysenko, 1994; Rivera, 1995). In 1999, however, this group split and some of its former members launched a new project with the same method of polling of regional (rather than Moscow-based) experts, which was published in *Literaturnaya gazeta*.

The number of conferences and seminars, either on Russian politics in general or specifically devoted to elite research, has increased dramatically in the past several years. The major cycle of conferences and seminars on post-Communist political elites, focused on Russia but with some reference to other CIS countries, was launched in 1996 by the Moscow Public Science Foundation with the support of the Friedrich-Ebert-Stiftung. Five meetings were organized with the participation of scholars from different regions of Russia and CIS countries as well as some Western specialists (Na Putyakh, 1997; Mel'ville, 1999b). Some local conferences on elites have been organized across Russia as well (Kugel', 1998). Major Russian journals in political science (such as *Polis, Vlast', Pro et Contra*), sociology (*Sotsiologicheskie Issledovaniya, Sotsiologicheskii Zhurnal*) as well as interdisciplinary journals (*Obshchestvennye Nauki i Sovremennost'*, *Mirovaya Ekonomika i Mezhdunarodnye Otnosheniya, Mir Rossii*) frequently publish both articles of Russian authors on elite research and some translations of modern Western authors, such as Dogan, Higley, Sartori and Lane, and even classical works by Mosca. However, while well-known writers on Communist elites have been widely published in Russia (Voslenskii, 1991; Djilas, 1992), recent Western elite research is still not well known among Russian scholars since most of them either have no access to English-language literature (especially in Russia's provinces) or do not know English well enough to read it. Although the most widely used Russian textbook on social stratification includes a special chapter on elite research (Radaev and Shkaratan, 1995: Chapter 7) that briefly summarizes contributions by Pareto, Mosca, Michels, Laswell, Mills, as well as Djilas and Voslenskii on Communist elites, it ends by discussing theoretical developments in the field in the 1950s–1960s, American elitist/pluralist discussions on community power like Hunter vs Dahl and others. (For an overview of those American debates in Russian, see also Tarusina, 1997.)

Themes and perspectives

The thematic diversity of elite research depends on both academic and non-academic factors. The latter, including a shortage of funding, priorities of sponsoring bodies (such as the Soros Foundation or the Russian Science Foundation for Humanities), opportunities for career promotion, poor information on theoretical and methodological achievements in the field and the lack of literature, have played a crucial role in recent developments in research. For a very rough classification, we shall use in our analysis three thematic categories: (1) historical elite research; (2) research on national elites; (3) regional elite research. These three directions poorly overlap with each other due to the different backgrounds of the specialists in the respective fields. The first one is still a primary area of interest to historians; the research on national elites is mainly conducted by sociologists; and finally, regional elite research usually attracts a limited number of Moscow-based specialists (mainly in geography) as well as scholars who live outside of Moscow in their 'own' regions (Gel'man and Ryzhenkov, 1998). Each group of scholars uses its own concepts and methods and rarely borrows or exchanges ideas either between or within such 'camps.' No wonder that in the short run these three sources of elite research have not become converted (at least yet) into three component parts of a common area and instead resemble what Lenin called in his article 'Three sources and three contentious parts of Marxism.' It is hard to say as yet whether this phenomenon is a consequence of the infancy of the field or whether it will be a long-term feature of Russia's political science in general, or whether it is simply waiting for its own Marx as a discipline integrator.

Historical elite research has focused mainly on interpreting the experiences of Soviet ruling elites in terms of patterns of authority and social mobility. Historians have analyzed details of the background of the Soviet nomenklatura (Gimpel'son, 1998) as well as the circumstances of its emergence and development (Korzhikhina and Figatner, 1993; Korzhikhina, 1995). Other historical research has concentrated on the dynamics of the composition of ruling groups in Soviet society in the late 1930s (Bonyushkina, 1995) as well as in the period 1960s–1980s (Mokhov, 1998, 1999). Although these studies contain many interesting quantitative and, sometimes, qualitative data, these authors pay less attention to causal sociopolitical explanations of the rise of the Soviet elite and to the prerequisites for its continuity and/or change in the post-Soviet period, save for some common sense notes. Historical elite researchers usually base their studies on documentary analysis and archival materials, but some works on the late-Soviet period have utilized oral history, such as the study of former district Communist Party leaders in Moscow based on in-depth interviews conducted by Koval' (1995).

While data-based historical research tends to be too descriptive, some macro-historical speculations on the role of elites in the history of Russian society have appeared as well. First and foremost, they are rethinking the Soviet experience using different interpretations. Dmitrii Badovskii analyzes the division of late-Soviet elites into 'political' (that is, Communist Party apparatus) and 'administrative' (that is, state bureaucracy and top managers) categories and traces the sources of differentiation that undermined Soviet elite unity and forced the Communist leaders to maintain a balance of interests among the competing ruling subgroups (Badovskii, 1994).[3] These complicated intra-elite relationships, according to Badovskii, played a significant role in post-Soviet elite transformation in terms of the emergence of intra-elite conflicts during the perestroika period as well as the survival of informal intra-elite networks and elite/mass connections. These interpretations come close to some other scholarly observations as well (for example, Shkaratan and Figatner, 1992).

Some scholarly attempts to trace patterns of elite development throughout pre-Soviet history deserve attention as well. The work of Oxana Gaman is typical in this respect (Gaman, 1998). She defines the main peculiarity of elites throughout Russia's history as their close relation to the state and sees it as a kind of vocation (in the Weberian sense) rather than simply as service, whether civil or military. This emphasis on state orientation is connected with her general framework of the 'mobilization' model of Russian development and seems to be an attempt to explain the continuity of elites and their inheritance of traditions of autocracy, etatism and collectivism. Gaman, however, does not draw a line between the elite as a social group and people who perform governmental functions (for a similar view, see also Kalugin, 1998). Mikhail Afanas'ev (2000) has provided an alternative historical explanation of the non-democratic character of Russia's elite in an interpretative study of Russian clientelism. The author has not only applied such an analytical concept to the Russian history of elite/mass relations, but has also developed his view on the role of patron/client relations in the Soviet period as a mechanism of adaptation of social groups to the late-Soviet political and economic system. According to Afanas'ev, both local communities and large enterprises functionally provided the ground for local-based or sectoral-based mass clienteles, thus developing the 'hidden' background for the emergence of the future post-Soviet elite. This form of 'nomenklatura quasi-corporatism' still survives even in the post-Soviet period as the only model of the political structuring of society based on vertical elite/mass linkages and networks. This concept, widely accepted by most Russian scholars, is a rare example of a successful interdisciplinary integrative approach to the interpretation of the role of elites in modern Russian history.

Research on national elites in Russia (and, probably, the general field of elite research in transitional societies) includes two different, although overlapping, dimensions. The first one might be called *stratification studies*, which focuses on the analysis of elites *per se* as a distinct social group (or strata) in terms of their characteristic features, such as composition, mobility (background, recruitment and career), relations with other social groups as well as values and attitudes. In other words, the different sociological theories and methods were applied here to provide answers to the complicated classical questions: 'Who governs?' and 'Who gets what, when, how?' The second dimension of elite research concerns the impact of elites on political regime in terms of transition from Communist rule. Thus, we might consider this dimension of research transition studies, which links continuity and change regarding elites to diverse prospects of democratization or other outcomes of post-Communist political transformation. Despite the fact that both of these dimensions of elite research are closely linked, they are based on different theoretical assumptions and methodological approaches. These deserve special attention.

The largest research projects on national elites have been undertaken in 1993–1994 by two groups of scholars. The first one, conducted by VTSIOM (as a part of the above-mentioned comparative research), is still the only Russia-wide quantitative study of the elite. This study is based on formalized face-to-face interviews with members of economic, administrative, political, media and intellectual elites in nineteen regions of Russia ($N = 1,812$). The sample was equally divided between the 'old' elite (that is, those who occupied elite positions in 1988) and the 'new' elite (those who occupied elite positions in 1993). The study focused mainly on elite background and patterns of mobility in the late-Soviet and post-Soviet periods as well as on the economic status and professional activities of elite group members (for results of the study, see Ershova, 1994; Golovachev *et al.*, 1995/1996; Golovachev and Kosova, 1995, 1996). The second one, conducted by the group led by Konstantin Mikul'skii, employed a qualitative approach. This study was based on 67 semi-formalized in-depth interviews with representatives of political, administrative, economic, intellectual, media and local elites, mainly Moscow-based (Mikul'skii *et al.*, 1995). The interviewed elite group members expressed their views on social, economic and political developments in post-Communist Russia, as well as on its prospects. Although this study makes available a considerable amount of evidence about the attitudes of elite group members, it is still deficient in terms of interpretative conclusions.

Some other empirical studies focus on distinct elite groups, for example conducting surveys of members of parliament – both upper (Diskin, 1995) and lower (Makarenko, 1996) chambers. Due to the weak influence of the military in domestic Russian politics (as well as the poor access of scholars to the field of military elite research), the classical Mills' triangle 'politics–business–military' does not seem to work in Russia's elite research, while research on the relationship between political and business elites has become much more popular in the post-Soviet period (Zudin, 1996; Mel'ville, 1999b; Peregudov *et al.*, 1999). However, there are only a few empirically oriented studies of the role of elite groups and sub-elites in the decision-making process, including institution-building or foreign policy-making. Finally, research on the political culture of elites is still neglected, although some elite attitudes toward current issues have been analyzed (Golovachev and Kosova, 1995).

Regional elite has become a rapidly expanding area of research since 1994, following the process of regionalization of Russia. For scholars located outside Moscow (even in St Petersburg), research in their localities became the only way for them to remain within the academic world. Thus, local research on local elites could be seen as a sort of 'political science for poor people.' Case studies seems to be the only methodological tool for such regional elite research utilized by local (for example, Tarasov, 1993; Okhotskii and Ponedelkov, 1994; Duka, 1995; Mel'ville, 1999b) as well as by some Moscow-based scholars (Shubkin, 1995; Kalugin, 1998). Sometimes, the works of local scholars simply repeated the similar findings of Moscow-based colleagues or represented purely descriptive studies, or even demonstrated collections of nonsensical statements. However, some local scholars have provided interesting observations and conclusions on local elites. For example, Rushan Gallyamov from the Republic of Bashkortostan in his longitudinal reputational analysis found two major trends in regional elite developments, 'etatization' and 'ethnocratization' (that is, the growth in the shares of state officials from the 'titular' ethnic group, the Bashkirs) (Gallyamov, 1998). However, despite the fact that the observations of Midkhat Farukshin from the neighboring Republic of Tatarstan are close to those of Gallyamov (Farukshin, 1994), no comparative study of the elites of these two republics has appeared as yet.

The lack of funds is not the only cause of the absence of comparative cross-regional elite research in Russia. The other problem is that maintaining research networks between local scholars requires coherent theoretical and methodological approaches as well as the development of a common academic language and research standards among scholars with very different backgrounds and orientations. But those rare attempts that have been made to provide comparative cross-regional analysis are interesting. Arbakhan Magomedov from Ul'yanovsk conducted a book-length study of political styles and the regionalist claims of local elites from four regions (Magomedov, 2000). He conducted almost 150 in-depth interviews of local political and administrative leaders in these regions using the methodological schemes of Robert Putnam (Putnam, 1973, 1976). His interpretation undermines public stereotypes about 'reform-minded' elites in some regions and 'conservative-oriented' elites in others. However, Magomedov's conclusions and the implications of his work are limited to the statement that the elites of ethnically-based republics have elaborated their regionalist claims (what he calls the 'ideology of regionalism') in much greater detail than have elites in non-ethnically based regions. Indeed, no causal explanation for these findings is elaborated.

Nataliya Lapina, in her comparative case study of relations between regional political and economic elites (based on in-depth interviews in four regions as well as secondary analysis in some others), has developed a typology of modes of business/politics interactions, including the categories 'patronage,' 'partnership,' 'privatization of power' and 'war of all against all' (Peregudov et al., 1999: 195–210), which is close to conclusions derived from other research (see Gel'man et al., 2000). Although some methodological questions, such as the general 'small N' problem, arise from case-oriented comparisons, the use of qualitative data mainly derived from the positional (institutional) analysis of regional elites in cross-regional research still provides for poor explanations (for some data and analysis, see McFaul and Petrov, 1998). But generally speaking, speculative/descriptive works are still more typical in this research area, although conceptual stretching weakens them (Badovskii and Shutov, 1995; Lapina, 1997; Mel'ville, 1999b).

Theory and methodology

With regard to theoretical issues of elite research in Russia, we should stress that they are similar to those of the general (mainly classical) social sciences literature and employ a wide range of models and empirical techniques. The functional approach to the definition of elites overwhelmingly dominates Russian scholarship. Some scholars either borrow definitions like 'power elite' by Mills (Ershova, 1994) and decision-making criteria by Higley (Diskin, 1995; Duka et al., 2001) or use their own terminology close to these (for example, Radaev and Shkaratan, 1995: 298; Mikul'skii,

1995: 10). Yurii Levada seems to be the only exception as a proponent of the 'meritocratic' approach (Levada, 2000: 204–215, 269–287). According to Levada, social groups that claim to be 'elite' in contemporary Russia in fact only represent themselves *vis-à-vis* the mass public. He has drawn a distinction between the 'public elite' (which demonstrates its desire to be like the 'real' elite) and the 'social elite' (which may provide new practices, patterns of attitudes and behavior). In this sense, Levada focuses his analysis on professional elites such as top managers, high-level professionals, experts and others. The typology of elites is also mainly based on functional divisions such as ideological, administrative, military, economic and political elites and/or elites vs counter-elites as well as national vs local elites (Mikul'skii *et al.*, 1995; Kryshtanovskaya, 1995a). As for stratification terms, scholars use different definitions of elites as 'stratas' (Mikul'skii *et al.*, 1995) or a 'ruling class' (Radaev and Shkaratan, 1995; Ryvkina, 1995). With regard to elite identification, most scholars widely accept the positional (or institutional) approach as the only reliable one for analysis in the transition period (for arguments, see Duka *et al.*, 2001), although the reputational approach was used in studies like Vox Populi's and some others. Finally, theoretical models of elite transformation – such as the classic 'lions vs foxes' (Pareto) or modern 'elite settlements' (Higley *et al.*, in this volume) are also applied to scholarly works on Russia's elites (see below).

Methodological issues of elite research are typical for post-Soviet political studies. First and foremost, the lion's share of published articles and, sometimes, books, still tends to be speculative and heavily dependent on the political or commercial interests of authors and publishers, while scholars here do not draw a clear line between their academic and non-academic activities. Second, the trend towards the dominance of qualitative, rather than quantitative, methodology tends to be characteristic of Russia's social sciences, reinforced by the lack of resources for large-scale projects and the decline in the activities of RAS institutions. Thus, most elite studies fit into this category. Scholars apply in their research respected methods of data collection: the analysis of documents, such as biographies of elite members (Kryshtanovskaya, 1995a; Kukolev, 1997), or in-depth semi-formalized interviews (Duka, 1995; Mikul'skii *et al.*, 1995). However, this tendency poses new problems of research design, case selection, data reliability and interpretation and comparability (King *et al.*, 1994), which are less reflected as yet within Russia's academic community. Third, the poor co-ordination of academic activities (both within the country as well as with foreign institutions) has resulted in the absence or commercialization of data archives, and this makes some data unavailable for scholars. Due to these problems, the academic value of empirical studies can be questioned. Finally, the lack of comparative studies of elites hinders further development of a research agenda.

Who governs? Continuity and change among Russian elites

The analysis of the circulation and reproduction of elites in a period of radical political change has become a natural priority area for contemporary Russian scholars. No wonder that these studies are highly influenced by current political developments and mainly by the dissatisfaction of most Russian scholars with the emerging post-Communist political regime (for example, Ol'shanskii, 1994; Ryvkina, 1995). One of the explanations of the unsuccessful democratization process was explicitly connected to the high level of reproduction of Soviet elites (or nomenklatura) in the post-Soviet period. The low elite circulation in the mid-1990s in comparison with the late 1980s was a common finding of various studies: various estimates of the degree of continuity in the late-Soviet elite differs from one-half to two-thirds in the business elite to 80–85 percent in local political and administrative élites (Ershova, 1994; Kryshtanovskaya, 1995a; Golovachev et al., 1995/1996). In the search for explanations for this U-turn in elite reproduction, Vadim Radaev has employed the concept of 'revolutionary breakthrough' and its aftermath (Radaev, 1994, 1997). He applies the classical Pareto dichotomy of lions vs foxes to the analysis of two stages of elite transformation: the first stage as a unilateral rise of newcomer office-seekers with different background and the second stage as a partial return of compromise-oriented former elite members with their professional skills, useful for routine duties in a post-revolutionary period. This view, however, has not become part of the mainstream of Russian elite research.

Alternatively, VTSIOM scholars who have been involved in cross-national elite research have regarded this phenomenon of 'political capitalism' as a common feature of post-Communist societies (Hankiss, 1990). At the same time, Olga Kryshtanovskaya independently postulated her model of the domination of the nomenklatura due to the double conversion of their previously privileged political status into privileged economic positions during the perestroika period, and, then, back to political power in post-Soviet period (Kryshtanovskaya, 1995a, 1995b; Kukolev, 1997). The 'nomenklatura conversion' approach has not only become accepted by most Russian scholars, but has also gained public support among liberal-oriented politicians, journalists and writers. Since Yurii Burtin and Grigorii Vodolazov have described Russian political and economic order as 'nomenklatura democracy' and 'nomenklatura capitalism,' respectively (Burtin and Vodolazov, 1994), the heritage of nomenklatura has been discussed in various contexts. Some authors have even describe the post-Soviet Russian elite as an entirely 'post-nomenklatura conglomerate' (Cheshkov, 1995; Afanas'ev, 2000). Kryshtanovskaya and her collaborators present evidence of the origins of the new Russian business class from the Communist Party and its satellites (Kryshtanovskaya, 1995a, 1995b; Kukolev, 1995), although some other studies do not confirm this conclusion (Bunin, 1994; Radaev, 1998). The close informal networks of the

Communist nomenklatura make the transformation of the Soviet elite into a post-Soviet oligarchy easier, based on the merger of political and business groups (Kryshtanovskaya, 1996), although no domination by a single elite financial/political group has been observed. Kryshtanovskaya and other scholars have recognized the merger of the former nomenklatura with some groups of organized crime as another major source for the formation of Russia's oligarchy (Kryshtanovskaya, 1995c, 1995d).

Although Russian scholars commonly accept the notion of the reproduction and high continuity of Russia's elites, the 'nomenklatura conversion' approach suffers from oversimplification and poor explanatory power. Yes, this model could show, *what* has happened to the Russian elite (and, to some extent, *how* it happened), but fails to explain *why* these changes occurred, what we might learn from them and what kind of future developments we might expect. Some other features of the 'nomenklatura conversion' model have been attacked as well. Iosif Diskin notes that the very thesis of 'conversion' is incorrect itself due to open political contestation and the need to acquire legitimacy by electoral means in the post-Communist period. According to Diskin, former elite members, if they get electoral support in a competitive environment, cannot be considered nomenklatura at all (Diskin, 1995). Another weak point of 'nomenklatura conversion' is that it fails to explain the sources of intra-elite conflicts in the post-Soviet period.

Instead, other views on elite transformation in the late-Soviet and post-Soviet period focus attention on the causes of patterns of intra-elite conflicts. They have been classified (Kukolev and Stykow, 1998: 118–121) as follows: (1) intergenerational conflict; (2) the 'rebellion' of radicals within the elite; (3) elite vs counter-elite conflict; (4) the 'rebellion' of managerial vs ideological elite. The first one started from the process of decay of the late-Soviet elite and the need for younger representatives of the subelite groups to gain access to power. Two shifts of powerful groups (under Gorbachev and early Yeltsin) provided a clash between these elite generations (Shkaratan and Figatner, 1992; Ol'shanskii, 1994). Meanwhile, other authors find other cleavage lines among elites more important: these lines involve ideological divisions, such as radical liberals vs gradual reformers (Diskin, 1995), or conflict between technocrats (economic managers and the government bureaucracy) and ideologically oriented politicians (Badovskii, 1994) or even between 'official' and 'unofficial' (like the shadow economy) segments of elites (see Zabelin, 1994). These discussions are still present on the research agenda, though.

Towards democracy? Political elites and Russia's transition

The distinction between the two theoretical approaches to the study of regime transition – the 'structural' (system-based) and 'procedural' (actor-based, or 'genetic') – is commonly accepted among Russian scholars

(Mel'ville, 1999a). The latter perspective poses new questions on the impact of political elites. Although the crucial role of political elites in the process of regime transition, recognized by most Western scholars of 'transitology' (Rustow, 1970; O'Donnell and Schmitter, 1986; Przeworski, 1991; Higley and Gunther, 1992), has attracted the attention of Russian researchers, the gist of these discussions is distinct from the focus of debates on the consolidation of new democracies in Latin America and Southern Europe as well as in Eastern Europe. While 'transitology' was based on the teleological scheme holding democratization to be the universal and inevitable goal of political development, Russia's experience with regime transition has cast some doubt on this. Indeed, some Russian scholars have evaluated Russia's post-Communist regime as a 'semi-democracy' (Gordon, 1995), a 'hybrid' (Shevtsova, 1999), or have applied various models such as O'Donnell's (1994) 'delegative democracy' (Gel'man, 1996; Tsygankov, 1997) or even 'competitive oligarchy' (Elizarov, 1999; Mel'ville, 1999a). Thus, such different conceptualizations of regime transition require relevant explanations from the perspective of elite research.

Regarding transitological analysis, Russian scholars focus attention on distinct features of Russia's model of the breakdown of Communist rule as well as on the installation of the post-Communist regime. First of all, Russia has not experienced any kind of pacts (or other forms of bargaining) between segments of the ruling elite of the previous regime and the opposition (or counter-elites) as happened in Hungary and, to some extent, in Poland. Indeed, using the typology of models of transition provided by Karl and Schmitter (Karl and Schmitter, 1991: 275), Russia's transition from Communist rule is considered an 'imposition' (Elizarov, 1999; Gel'man *et al.*, 2000), while the whole period of the demise of Communist rule under Gorbachev fits into this transitological scheme as a case of the failure of Gorbachev's attempts at liberalization without democratization – that is, of maintaining a balance between Communist 'hard-liners' and the democratic opposition (Gordon, 1995; Mel'ville, 1999a; Sogrin, 2001). The impact of 'imposition' on Russia's transition has been evaluated as negative, reflecting the non-democratic behavior of 'winners' in such a zero-sum conflict, including the rejection of the idea of holding new elections in 1991 for securing their powerful positions, large-scale clientelism and corruption, the dominance of informal patterns in the decision-making process, and others (Mel'ville, 1999a; Shevtsova, 1999; Gel'man *et al.*, 2000).

Second, the impact of intra-elite bargains and agreements in Russia after the breakdown of the Communist regime is not always evaluated as the establishing of 'democracy by undemocratic means' (O'Donnell and Schmitter, 1986: 38). While some authors explicitly considered the applicability of the model of 'elite settlement' (Higley and Gunther, 1992) and discuss possible gains from such a scenario (Diskin, 1995), some opponents either express their doubts regarding the effectiveness of pacts in Russia (Vozmozhen, 1996) or even criticize this as an approach to the study of

Russian politics (Kholodkovskii, 1997; Elizarov, 1999). As the co-author of this chapter has noted, the principal distinction lies between 'pacts' as a model of the breakdown of authoritarian rule (nearly the classic O'Donnell–Schmitter's scheme) and 'pacts' that occurred after the breakdown of authoritarian rule. While the former serve as a decisive step towards the installation of political competitiveness within the framework of formal institutions, the latter serve instead as a step towards the sharing of power between actors, the limitation (or even elimination) of competitiveness, the exclusion of political outsiders, and is mainly based on informal, rather than formal, institutions. Thus, these kinds of 'pacts' undermine rather than strengthen the transition to democracy (Gel'man *et al*., 2000).

Although there are no empirical studies of Russia's national elite that could confirm or reject such an assumption, some evidence from subnational elite research might be a point of departure for future research in this area. On the one hand, Alexandr Duka from the St Petersburg branch of the Institute of Sociology of RAS bases his research of local elites in St Petersburg on the use of Higley's model of transition from an ideologically unified elite to a consensually unified elite through the stage of disunified elite (see Duka, 1995; Duka *et al*., 2001). However, his empirical analysis has clearly shown that even if intra-elite consensus has been achieved, it has not led to local democratization, at least in the short-term perspective. On the other hand, one co-author of this chapter provides an alternative framework, influenced by the ideas of Case (Case, 1996) that elite consensus might be accompanied by non-democratic features (what he calls a 'semi-democracy'). The comparative study of political development in six regions shows that the pursuit of a strategy of pacts between key regional elite actors limits the frame of opportunities for political competition, pending the development of formal institutions (such as elections, local government, legislature, political parties) in a favor of informal practices of decision-making and in general, the emergence of arbitrary rule (Gel'man *et al*., 2000).

At the same time, the role of intra-elite conflicts in the transition process in Russia has been reconsidered as well. In the early and mid-1990s the view that those conflicts were an obstacle to the consolidation of democracy in Russia were more or less commonly accepted (see Myasnikov, 1993; Ol'shanskii, 1994; Diskin, 1995), while the idea of 'pacts' between old and new elites has flourished (Fadin *et al*., 1991; Vozmozhen, 1996). However, since the democratic virtues of the post-Communist elite 'consolidation' in Russia have become unclear, an alternative view of the positive role of intra-elite conflict in transition has been provided. As studies of the development of political parties in Russia's regions have shown, intra-elite conflict was a crucial political factor in the party performance in Russia's regions (Gel'man and Golosov, 1998; Golosov, 1999). From a broader theoretical perspective, these debates reflect two different macro-theoretical approaches to social and political developments, either from various forms of integration (Parsons) or from conflict (Darendorf, Coser) as the source of the development of society.

As we mention above, the lack of comparative studies (cross-national as well as cross-regional and multi-level comparisons) leaves these research questions open. But despite the fact that the implications of those regional case studies are hard to apply to other regions as well as to the level of national elites, they might be useful for the agenda of future research.

Conclusion: state of the art and research prospects

The first stage of the post-Communist development of elite studies in Russia as a new research subdiscipline is close to completion. The field has become institutionalized in terms of organizational matters as well as substantive issues. Using Thomas Kuhn's view on the sociology of science, we might mention that an academic community of elite researchers in Russia has emerged, and the pre-paradigm phase of its existence has been exhausted. Although conceptual frameworks that have been elaborated during the past several years by some Russian scholars can hardly be considered fully fledged paradigms, they are being utilized as convenient among most specialists across Russia. Despite the fact that such a community remains somewhat isolated from the mainstream of contemporary political science and is faced with the lack of common academic standards as well as other academic and non-academic problems, it is seen as the real state of the art in Russia's social sciences.

As to the substantive achievements of elite research in Russia, we should highlight the following:

- a wide array of empirical studies has been conducted on national and local elites; among them, two major research projects on elites that represent quantitative and qualitative research design (VTSIOM's part of the comparative study headed by Szelenyi and the study provided by Mikul'skii *et al.*, respectively);
- the appearance of original interpretative frameworks for understanding Russia's elite in historical perspective;
- the concept of 'political capitalism' or 'nomenklatura conversion' has become accepted by Russian scholars and the general public;
- modern Western theoretical and methodological approaches have been applied by advanced scholars for empirical research and theoretical considerations;
- some theoretical problems regarding the role of intra-elite relationships as well as elite/mass linkage in the post-Communist environment have been discussed.

Nevertheless, the future of elite research in Russia is faced with short-term and long-term problems. While some of these problems arise from the general organizational and substantive issues involved in the development of the social sciences in Russia, distinct problems with elite research include:

- the lack of value-free research frameworks;
- the lack of well-developed concepts of transformation of elites as well as of elites in transition;
- the lack of reliable data accompanied by the problem of their validity;
- the lack of comparative cross-national and cross-regional research.

It is unclear now whether these flaws will be overcome as a kind of 'growing pain,' and if they are, how long this will take remains to be seen. This task might be solved only with the collective efforts of the Russian and international academic communities, and the solution depends on the general success or failure of Russian social science's international integration.

Notes

1 The early version of the chapter appeared as a journal article in *Communist and Post-Communist Studies* (2000) Vol. 33, No. 3.
2 See *Theory and Society* (1995) Vol. 24, No. 5 (special issue).
3 As one can see, these arguments closely resemble the works of Western revisionist scholars on Soviet elites and interest groups.

References

Afanas'ev, M. (2000) *Klientelizm i rossiiskaya gosudarstvennost'*, second edition. Moscow: Moscow Public Science Foundation.
Ashin, G. (1985) *Sovremennaya teoriya elity*. Moscow Mezhdunarodnye Otnosheniya.
Badovskii, D. (1994) Transformatsiya politicheskoi elity Rossii: ot 'organizatsii professional'nykh revolutsionerov' – k 'partii vlasti'. *Polis*, No. 6, pp. 42–58.
Badovskii, D. and Shutov, A. (1995) Regional'nye elity v postsovetskoi Rossii: osobennosti politicheskogo uchastiya. *Kentavr*, No. 6, pp. 3–23.
Bonyushkina, L. (1995) Opyt izucheniya stanovleniya professional'noi sovetskoi elity: Sovnarkom 1937–1941 gg. *Mir Rossii*, Vol. 4, No. 3/4, pp. 108–130.
Bunin, I. (1994) *Biznesmeny Rossii: 40 istorii uspekha*. Moscow: Oko.
Burlatskii, F. and Galkin, A. (1985) Pravyashchaya elita, in F. Burlatskii and A. Galkin (eds) *Sovremmennyi Leviafan. Ocherki politicheskoi sotsiologii kapitalizma*. Moscow: Mysl', pp. 124–159.
Burtin, Y. and Vodolazov, G. (1994) V Rossii postroena nomenklaturnaya demokratiya. *Izvestiya*, 1 June.
Case, W. (1996) Can the 'Halfway House' Stand? Semi-Democracy and Elite Theory in Three Southeast Asian Countries. *Comparative Politics*, Vol. 28, No. 4, pp. 437–464.
Cheshkov, M. (1995) 'Vechno zhivaya' nomenklatura? *Mirovaya Ekonomika i Mezdunarodnye Otnosheniya*, No. 6, pp. 32–43.
Diskin, I. (1995) *Rossiya: transformatsiya i elity*. Moscow: Eltra.

Djilas, M. (1992) *Litso totalitarizma*. Moscow: Novosti.
Duka, A. (1995) Transformatiya mestnykh elit: institutsionalizatsiya obshchestvennykh dvizhenii: ot protesta k uchastiyu. *Mir Rossii*, Vol. 4, No. 2, pp. 106–117.
Duka, A. (ed.) (2001) *Vlastnye elity i nomenklatura: annotirovannaya bibliografiya rossiiskikh izdanii 1991–2000*. St Petersburg: M. Kovalevskii Sociological Society.
Duka, A., Achkasova, V., Bystrova, A., Daugavet, A. and Kornienko, A. (2001) *Regional'nye elity Severo-Zapada Rossii*. St Petersburg: Aleteia.
Elizarov, V. (1999) Elitistskaya teoriya demokratii i sovremennyi rossiiskii politicheskii protsess. *Polis*, No. 1, pp. 72–78.
Ershova, N. (1994) Transformatsiya pravyashchei elity v usloviyakh sotsial'nogo pereloma, in T. Zaslavskaya and L. Arutyunyan (eds) *Kuda idet Rossiya? Al'ternativy obshchestvennogo razvitiya*. Moscow: Interpraks, pp. 151–155.
Fadin, A., Bunin, I., Markov, S. and Salmin, A. (1991) Kto pravil i kto budet pravit' v SSSR. Bor'ba elit v perehodnom obshchestve: nomenklatura i demokratiya. *Vek XX i mir*, No. 5, pp. 30–37.
Farukshin, M. (1994) Politicheskaya elita v Tatarstane: vyzov vremeni i trudnosti adaptatsii. *Polis*, No. 6, pp. 67–79.
Gallyamov, R. (1998) Politicheski elity rossiiskikh respublik: osobennosti transformatsii v perekhodnyi period. *Polis*, No. 2, pp. 108–115.
Gaman, O. (1998) *Politicheskie elity Rossii. Vekhi istoricheskoi evolyutsii*. Moscow: Intellekt.
Gel'man, V. (1996) Regional'nye rezhimy: zavershenie transformatsii? *Svobodnaya Mysl'*, No. 9, pp. 13–22.
Gel'man, V. (1997) 'Transition' po-russki: kontseptsii perekhodnogo perioda i politicheskaya transformatsiya v Rossii. *Obshchestvennye Nauki i Sovremennost'*, No. 4, pp. 64–81.
Gel'man, V. and Golosov, G. (1998) Politicheskie partii v Sverdlovskoi oblasti: regional'nye praktiki v sravnitel'noi perspektive. *Mirovaya Ekonomika i Mezhdunarodnye Otnosheniya*, No. 5, pp. 133–144.
Gel'man, V. and Ryzhenkov, S. (1998) Politicheskaya regionalistka Rossii: ot obshchestvennogo interesa – k nauchnoi discipline?, in I. Oswald, R. Possekel, P. Stykow and J. Wiegohs (eds) *Sotsial'nye issledovaniya v Rossii: Germano-Rossiiskii monitoring*. Moscow: Polis, pp. 138–186.
Gel'man, V., Ryzhenkov, S. and Brie, M. (2000) *Rossiya regionov: transformatsiya politicheskikh rezhimov*. Moscow: Ves' Mir.
Gimpel'son, E. (1998) *Sovetskie upravlentsy 1917–1920 gg*. Moscow: Institute of Russian History RAS.
Golosov, G. (1999) From Adygeya to Yaroslavl': Factors of Party Development in Russia's Regions. *Europe-Asia Studies*, Vol. 51, No. 8, pp. 1333–1365.
Golovachev, B. and Kosova, L. (1995) Tsennostnye orientatsii sovetsikh i postovetskhikh elit, in T. Zaslavskaya (ed.) *Kuda idet Rossiya? Al'ternativy obshchestvennogo razvitiya*, Vol. II. Moscow: Aspekt-Press, pp. 183–187.
Golovachev, B. and Kosova, L. (1996) Vysokostatusnye gruppy: shtrikhi k sotsial'nomu portretu. *Sotsiologicheskie Issledovaniya*, No. 1, pp. 45–51.
Golovachev, B., Kosova, L. and Khakhulina, L. (1995/1996) Formirovanie pravyashchei elity v Rossii. *Ekonomicheskie i Sotsial'nye Peremeny: Monitoring Obshchestvennogo Mneniya*, No. 6, pp. 18–24/No. 1, pp. 32–38.
Gordon, L. (1995) *Oblast' vozmozhnogo*. Moscow: Institute of World Economy and International Relations RAS.

Hankiss, E. (1990) *East European Alternatives*. Oxford: Clarendon Press.
Higley, J. and Gunther, R. (1992) *Elites and Democratic Consolidation in Latin America and Southern Europe*. Cambridge, UK: Cambridge University Press.
Kalugin, O. (1998) Mekhanizmy elitoobrazovaniya v regione. *Polis*, No. 4, pp. 145–151.
Karl, T. and Schmitter, P. (1991) Models of Transition in Latin America, Southern and Eastern Europe. *International Social Science Journal*, Vol. 43, No. 128, pp. 269–284.
Kholodkovskii, K. (1997) Konsolidatsiya elit: obshchestvennyi pakt ili verkhushchnyi sgovor?, in T. Zaslavskya (ed.) *Kuda idet Rossiya? Obshchee i osobennoe v sovremennom razvitii*. Moscow: Moscow School of Social and Economic Sciences, pp. 125–132.
King, G., Keohane, R. and Verba, S. (1994) *Designing Social Inquiry. Scientific Interference in Qualitative Research*. Princeton, NJ: Princeton University Press.
Korzhikhina, T. (1995) *Sovetskoe gosudarstvo i ego uchrezhdeniya*. Moscow: Russian State University for Humanities.
Korzhikhina, T. and Figatner, Y. (1993) Sovetskaya nomenklatura: stanovlenie, mekhanizmy deistviya. *Voprosy Istorii*, No. 7, pp. 25–38.
Koval', T. (1995) Kto vy teper', poslednie pervye – pervye ili poslednie? *Mir Rossii*, Vol. 4, No. 3–4, pp. 56–107.
Kryshtanovskaya, O. (1995a) Transformatsiya staroi nomenklatury v novuyu rossiiskuyu elitu. *Obshchestvennye Nauki i Sovremennost'*, No. 1, pp. 51–65.
Kryshtanovskaya, O. (1995b) Kto nami pravit? *Otrkytaya Politika*, No. 1, pp. 13–19.
Kryshtanovskaya, O. (1995c) Nelegal'nye struktury v Rossii. *Sotsiologicheskie Issledovaniya*, No. 8, pp. 94–106.
Kryshtanovskaya, O. (1995d) Mafioznyi peizazh Rossii: vzglyad sotsiologa. *Izvestiya*, 21 September.
Kryshtanovskaya, O. (1996) Finansovaya oligarkhiya v Rossii. *Izvestiya*, 10 January.
Kugel, S. (ed.) (1998) *Sotsial'nye i politicheskie orientatsii Sankt-Peterburgskoi elity*. St Petersburg: St Petersburg University of Economics and Finance.
Kukolev, I. (1995) Formirovanie rossiiskoi biznes-elity. *Sotsiologicheskii Zhurnal*, No. 3, pp. 159–169.
Kukolev, I. (1997) Transformatsiya politicheskikh elit v Rossii. *Obshchestvennye Nauki i Sovremennost'*, No. 4, pp. 82–91.
Kukolev, I. and Stykow, P. (1996) Elitenforschung (1991–1996), in I. Oswald, R. Possekel, P. Stykow and J. Wiegohs (eds) *Sozialwissenschaft in Russland, Bd.1*. Berlin: Berliner Debatte Wissenschaftverlag, pp. 83–113.
Kukolev, I. and Stykow, P. (1998) Stanovlenie elitovedeniya, in I. Oswald, R. Possekel, P. Stykow and J. Wiegohs (eds) *Sotsial'nye issledovaniya v Rossii. Germano-Rossiiskii monitoring*. Moscow: Polis, pp. 107–137.
Lapina, N. (1997) *Regional'nye elity Rossii*. Moscow: Institute of Scientific Information in Social Sciences RAS.
Levada, Y. (2000) *Ot mnenii k ponimaniyu: sotsiologicheskie ocherki 1993–2000*. Moscow: Moscow School of Political Studies.
Lysenko, V. (1994) Parlamentarizm i formirovanie politicheskogo establishmenta v Rossii. *Polis*, No. 6, pp. 134–141.
Magomedov, A. (2000) *Misteriya regionalizma*. Moscow: Moscow Public Science Foundation.
Makarenko, B. (1996) Gosudarstvennaya Duma: pervaya godovshchina. *Vlast'*, No. 12, pp. 6–11.

McFaul, M. and Petrov, N. (1998) *Politicheskii al'manakh Rossii*, 2 vols. Moscow: Moscow Carnegie Centre.
Mel'ville, A. (1999a) *Demokraticheskie tranzity: teoretiko-metodologicheskie i prikladnye aspekty*. Moscow: Moscow Public Science Foundation.
Mel'ville, A. (ed.) (1999b) *Transformatsiya rossiiskih regional'nykh elit v spavnitel' noi perspektive*. Moscow: Moscow Public Science Foundation.
Mikul'skii, K., Babaeva, L., Tarshis, E., Reznichenko, L., Chirikova, A. and Lapina, G. (eds) (1995) *Elita Rossii o nastoyashchem i budushchem strany*. Moscow: Vekhi.
Mills, C.W. (1956) *The Power Elite*. New York: Oxford University Press.
Mokhov, V. (1998) *Evolutsiya regiona'noi politicheskoi elity Rossii: 1950–1990 gg.* Perm: Perm State Technical University.
Mokhov, V. (1999) Stratifikatsiya sovetskoi regional'noi politicheskoi elity 1960–1990 gg., in M. Afanas'ev (ed.) *Vlast' i obshchestvo v postsovetskoi Rossii: novye praktiki i instituty*. Moscow: Moscow Public Science Foundation, pp. 14–38.
Myasnikov, O. (1993) Smena pravyashchikh elit: 'koonsolidatsiya' ili vechnaya shvatka? *Polis*, No. 1, pp. 52–60.
Na Putyakh (1997) *Na putyakh politicheskoi transformatsii: politicheskie partii i politicheskie elity perekhodogo perioda*, 2 vols. Moscow: Moscow Public Science Foundation.
O'Donnell, G. (1994). Delegative Democracy. *Journal of Democracy*, Vol. 5, No. 1, pp. 55–69.
O'Donnell, G. and Schmitter, P. (1986) *Transitions from Authoritarian Rule: Tentative Conclusions about Uncertain Democracies*. Baltimore and London: Johns Hopkins University Press.
Okhotskii, E. and Ponedelkov, A. (1994) Politicheskaya elita Rstova: krupnyi plan. *Vlast'*, No. 10. pp. 37–46.
Ol'shanskii, D. (1994) Vzbesibshayasya elita. *Vlast'*, No. 6, pp. 23–34.
Peregudov, S., Lapina, N. and Semenenko, I. (1999) *Gruppy interesov i rossiiskoe gosudarstvo*. Moscow: Editorial URSS.
Ponedelkov, A. and Starostin, A. (1998) *Vvedenie v politicheskuyu elitologiyu*. Rostov-na-Donu: North Caucasus Academy of Civil Service.
Przeworski, A. (1991) *Democracy and the Market. Political and Economic Reforms in Eastern Europe and Latin America*. Cambridge, UK: Cambridge University Press.
Putnam, R. (1973) *Beliefs of Politicians. Ideology, Conflict and Democracy in Britain and Italy*. New Haven and London: Yale University Press.
Putnam, R. (1976) *The Comparative Study of Political Elites*. Englewood Cliffs, NJ: Prentice-Hall.
Radaev, V. (1994) Revolutsiya raznochintsev, in T. Zaslavskaya and L. Arutyunyan (eds) *Kuda Idet Rossiya? Al'ternativy obshchestvennogo razvitiya*. Moscow: Interpraks, pp. 136–140.
Radaev, V. (1997) Transformatsiya elit i stanovlenie natsional'noi elity v Rossii, in *Rol' gosudatstva v razvitii obshchestva: Rossiya i mirovoi opyt*. Moscow: Russian Independent Institute of Social and National Problems, pp. 207–216.
Radaev, V. (1998) *Formirovanie novykh rossiiskikh rynkov*. Moscow: Center of Political Technologies.
Radaev, V. and Shkaratan, O. (1995) *Sotsialnaya stratifikatsiya*. Moscow: Nauka.

Rivera, S. (1995) Tendentsii formirovaniya sostava postkommunisticheskoi elity Rossii: reputatsionnyi analiz. *Polis*, No. 6, pp. 61–66.

Rustow, D. (1970) Transition to Democracy: Toward a Dynamic Model. *Comparative Politics*, Vol. 2, No. 3, pp. 337–363.

Ryvkina, R. (1995) Vliyanie novoi pravyashhei elity na khod i rezul'taty ekonomicheskikh reform. *Sotsiologicheskie Issledovaniya*, No. 11, pp. 35–43.

Shevtsova, L. (1999) *Yeltsin's Russia: Myths and Realities*. Washington, DC: Carnegie Endowment for International Peace.

Shkaratan, O. and Figatner, Y. (1992) Starye i novye khozyaeva Rossii. *Mir Rossii*, Vol. 1, No. 1, pp. 67–90.

Shubkin, V. (1995) Vlastvuyushchie elity Sibiri (na primere Altaiskogo kraya). *Sotsiologicheskii Zhurnal*, No. 1, pp. 147–155.

Sogrin V. (2001) *Politicheskaya istoriya sovremennoi Rossii 1985–2001. Ot Gorbacheva do Putina*. Moscow: Ves' Mir.

Steiner, H. (1997) Elite Research in Russia. Characteristics of Russian Elite Research, in H. Best and U. Becker (eds) *Elites in Transition: Elite Research in Central and Eastern Europe*. Opladen: Leske+Budrich, pp. 107–132.

Tarasov, Y. (1993) Pravyashchaya elita Yakutii: shtrikhi k portretu. *Polis*, No. 2, pp. 171–173.

Tarusina, I. (1997) Elitisty i plualisty v sovremennoi politicheskoi teorii. *Polis*, No. 4, pp. 148–153.

Tsygankov A. (1997) Mezhdu liberal'noi demokratiei i spolzaniem v avtoritarizm: predvaritel'nye itogi politicheskogo razvitiya Rossii (1991–1996). *Sotsial'no-politicheskii zhurnal*, No. 1, pp. 15–37.

Voslenskii, M. (1991) *Nomenklatura: gospodstvuyushchii klass Sovetskogo Soyuza*. Moscow: Sovetskaya Rossiya.

Vozmozhen (1996) Vozhmozhen li pakt obshchestvenno-politicheskikh sil Rossii? (Kruglyi stol). *Polis*, No. 5, pp. 96–106.

Zabelin, A. (1994) Nastuplenie Provintsii. *Vlast'*, No. 3, pp. 40–47.

Zudin, A. (1996) Rossiya: Biznes i Politika. *Mirovaya Ekonomika i Mezhdunarodnye Otnosheniya*, Nos 3–5.

Index

Note: *italicised* page numbers indicate tables

administrative elites 130, 133, 137, 150, 152, 155, 164
Adygeya 110
Afanas'ev, Mikhail 191–2
Aganbegyan, Abel 134
Agrarian Party of Russia (APR) 112, 113, 119, 174
Akademgorodok 134, 142–3
All-Russian Center for Public Opinion Studies 159; see also VTSIOM
All Russia Party (*Vsya Rossiya*) 26, 75, 76, 85
Almond, Gabriel 62
Al Qaeda attacks (9/11) 27
apparatchiki 140, 142, 145
armed forces 25, 45, 55, 56, 57; see also military
authoritarianism 5, 6, 93, 128, 199; and economic growth 65–6; and elites 30, 47, 57, 62, 68; and Gorbachev 18; and Putin era 47, 51, 105, 106; regimes 65–6; regional 84, 90n, 115; and Yeltsin era 23

Badovskii, Dmitrii 191
Baltic States 68
Barry, Brian 54
Barylski, Robert V. 18, 19, 24
Bashkortostan Republic 101, 102, 193
Bednyakov, Dmitrii 34, 36, 37
Belarus 20, 128
Berezovsky, Boris 22, 24
Brezhnev, Leonid 17, 18
Bulgaria 128, 149
Bunce, Valerie 17–18

bureaucrats/bureaucracy 56–7, 59, 63, 64, 88, 157, 177; political 133, 137–8; procedures 83, 85
Burton, Michael 53, 127, 131

capitalism 4, 6; Eastern European 169; and elites 125, 155–8; political 196, 200; and Putin era 67–8, 103; and Yeltsin era 57, 67
'cartel of anxiety' 32, 42, 43
case studies 193; Novosibirsk 133–7; St Petersburg 152–65; Tomsk Oblast 171–84
Case, William 31, 199
Central Bank 12
Central Electoral Commission 110
central government 58–60, 77, 95–7; cabinet 56, 58–9; legitimacy crisis 61–2; and power-sharing 99–100; regional relations 101–3
Chechnya/Chechens 110; terrorist attacks 43; war (1994–1996) 42, 43–4, 57, 76, 95
Chernomyrdin government 22, 23
Chernomyrdin, Victor 151
Chubias, Anatoly 23
Church (Orthodox) 12, 55, 56, 57, 59, 126
civil servants 56, 59, 61
clientelism 6, 38, 82–6, 84, 88, 170, 177–8; research on 192
coalitions and alliances 40–4, 126, 127, 128, 183–4
Communism 3, 4; collapse of 51, 124–5, 127, 129; legacy 124
Communist Party 16, 19, 41, 113, 119; banning 33; elites 33; and recentralization 99, 106

Communist Party of Russian Federation *see* CPRF; KPRF
confidence, elite 56, 59
Congress of People's Deputies 78
Constitutional Court 80, 102
corruption 16, 19, 34, 95; political 23, 198
CPRF (Communist Party of Russian Federation) 20, 22, 26, *see also* KPRF
CPSU (Communist Party of the Soviet Union) 15, 124–5; Central Committee membership 19–20; disintegration 132; elites 16–20, 130, 131; Party Congresses 19, 20
Czechoslovakia 21, 128, 149

Dahl, Robert 37, 132
decentralization 2, 7, 83; and democracy 106; and federalism 92, 94, 97–8, 100–1, 106; of legislative process 79; and taxation 103–5
decision-making 5, 34, 38; and elites 13, 37, 125, 126, 134, 193, 194, 198, 199; and institutions 52; and networks 12, 137; political 12, 63; regional 97, 152, 178, 182–3; under Soviets 4, 16
democracy: definition/theory of 4–5, 65, 92, 128–9; development 51–2, 53, 129; and inter-elite trust 58–68; legitimacy 53, 54, 55, 61, 164; and pluralism 66, 67–8; and political culture 1–2, 53–5, 62, 109; and regime change 168–70; semi-democracy 31, 198, 199; stabilization of 51, 65, 131, 151, 164, 168; Western 126, 133, 184, 190
Democratic Reform group 33
democratization: consolidation 127, 128, 129; and de-/recentralization 2, 6, 7, 71, 77, 81, 106–7; and elite consensus 48, 127; and elite settlements 25, 33–40; elitist concept of 29–30; and governors 72; and old/new elites issue 5–6, 130–1, 132, 137–41, 192; path dependency 124; and political elites 1–2, 197–200; research prospects 200–1; *see also* transition(s)
'Dictatorship of Law' 47, 77, 80
differentiation (elites): and conflict 11–12; and integration 12–16, 25–6, 58–62, 125–6; regional 170–1, 173–4, 177, 182–4
Diskin, Iosif 197
Duchacek, Ivo 80
Duka, Alexandr 199

Easter, Gerald 16–18
Eastern Europe 1, 4, 125, 128, 169, 198
Eastern Oil Company 181, 182
Easton, David 53
economic issues 131, 148; crisis (1998–1999) 23, 24, 25, 39, 42, 67, 74, 95; deregulation/decentralization 2; elites 8, 130, 138, 142–3, 144, 145, 153, 159, 172, 187, 194; growth 65–6, 154–8; reforms 45, 51, 67, 68, 95, 100, 148, 157, 171, 174, 177; and regional elites 149, 154–8, 163–5, *see also* market economy
education: and democratic values 148; and elites 63, 136, 137, 139, 140, 148; institutions 52, 53, 55, 143, 172, 176; regulation 102; system 56, 57
elections 4–5, 25, 26, 42, 110; electoral cycles 110–12, 116–17, 120; gubernatorial 74, 84–5, 88, 180–1, 182, 183–4; legislative 113–14, 121; mayoral 180, 183–4; and party development 113–19; presidential 23–4, 25, 42–3, 44, 85; and proportional representation 116, 117, 121–2; regional 35–7, 39, 40, 109, 180–1, 183–4; State Duma 23, 26, 35, 41, 44, 46, 76, 110, 119, 121; under Yeltsin 73
elite research 187–201; conferences and seminars 189–90; development 188–90; methodology 194–5; political studies 187, 192, 196, 197–200; stratification studies 187, 192; studies/surveys 48–9, 52–3, 127–9, 188–95; themes and perspectives 190–4; transition studies 187, 192, 197–200; typology/theory 1, 2–3, 30–2, 182, 195
elites 2–3, 58, 93, 125–7, 129; alliances and coalitions 126, 127, 128, 183–4; cleavages/fragmentation 13, 14–15, 19–24, 30, 37–40, 61, 62, 93, 131, 182; and Communist legacy 124; consensus 11, 13, 14, 15, 29–33, 44–7, 48–9, 130, 183; continuity and change 196–7; and decision-making 13, 37, 125, 126, 134; definition and nature 2, 3–4, 126, 134; and East/West identity 149, 153–4; generation attitudes/effects 151, 159–61, 165; ideocratic 13, 14–15, 16–20; integration and differentiation 12–16, 25–6, 58–62, 125–6, 170; legitimacy 44, 51; networks 12, 17–18, 21–2, 134, 141, 196–7; old/new cleavage 5–6, 130–1, 132, 137–41, 192,

197; pacts/settlements 11, 30–2, 37, 47–8, 129, 168, 170–1, 198–9; and pluralism 2–3, 13, 126; and regime transformation/development 20, 24–7, 48, 127–30, 151, 154–8, 168–70, 197; trust/distrust among 62–4; typology 12–16, 30–2, 195; unified 30, 53, 58, 144; Western 126, 133, *see also* national elite; political elites; regional elites; *see also under* economic issues; local issues
ethnic republics/minority groups 53, 83, 94; and special agreements 102–3

Farukshin, Midkhat 193
Fatherland Party (*Otechestvo*) 26, 75, 76, 85, 112, 115, 119
federalism 92, 94–5, 97; and authoritarianism 106; bargained 92, 93, 95, 105, 107
federal laws 26, 80, 87; and central/regional relations 99, 101, 102; as regulating mechanism 102, 106; and special agreements 102–3, *102*
Federation Council 46; confidence in 56, 58, 59–60, 61–4, 95, 96–7; and Putin reforms 76–7, 86, 106; and regional government 74, 86–7, 106; and special agreements 103
Filatov, Sergei 80–1
For Socio-Economic Progress and Civil Accord Movement 115–16
fragmented elite(s) 13, 61, 62, 93, 131; and unstable representative regime 14–15, 20–4
Freedom House 29, 168, 171

Gabriel, Oscar 53
Gallyamov, Rushan 193
Gaman, Oxana 191
GAZ, privatization issue 36
Gazprom 46, 181, 182
Gel'man, Vladimir 21, 170
Gill, Graeme 21–2
Goodman, Leo 137
Gorbachev era 3, 130, 169, 198
Gorbachev, Mikhail 18, 19, 20, 43
government: and business 162–3; central/regional relations 101–3; de-/recentralization 2, 6, 7, 71, 77, 81, 99–100; federal 46, 98–9; institutions 55–7, 58, 60; local 56, 83, 106–7; ministries 103; power-sharing 98–101; Russian Constitution (1993) 3, 40, 68, 79, 92, 93; special agreements 101–2, *see also* central government; regional government; State Dumas
governors 71–2; appointed versus elected 72–5, 82; and democratization 72; evolution of institution 72–3, 81–2; fall of 75–7, 86–8; and federal influence/powers 74, 75–7, 80–1, 87; legitimacy 74, 75; and patron/client relationships 82–6; and proportional representation 117; and Putin era 76–7, 82, 85–6; and regional powers 87–8; roles of 77–82, 88; and Yeltsin era 71–6, 78–9, 81, 83, 84–5
Grabher, Gernot 64
Great Purges (1936–1938) 17
Grushin, Boris 189
Gusinsky, Vladimir 24

Hare quota 117, 122
health issues 102
Higley, John 53, 58, 62, 127, 128, 131, 182, 194
Hungary 21, 128, 170
Huntington, Samuel 65

Inglehart, Ronald 65
Institute of Sociology of Russian Academy of Sciences 187
institutional design 77–82, 110, 141; and elite groups 150; and political party development 114, 120
institutions 53–4, 58, 67, 101, 161; confidence in 55–7, *59*; and decision-making 52; differentiation of 55–7, 161–3; and elites 51, 149–51; and legitimacy 51, 67, 78, 158–61, 164; non-government 55–6, 57, 58, 61, 67; in post-Communist countries 65; and strong leader-figures 65
integration (elites): and confidence 58–62; and differentiation 12–16, 25–6, 58–62, 125–6; and imposed consensus 47; regional 170–1, 173–4, 177, 182–4
interviewing elites, selection and methodology 52

judiciary 53, 56

Kaliningrad Oblast 116, 117
Karachaevo-Cherkesiya 111
Karl, Terry 198
Katz, Richard 109
Kemerovo Oblast 111, 115, 116

Khakasiya Republic 110
Khodyrev, Gennadii 33, 40
Khrushchev, Nikita 17, 20
Kirienko, Sergei 23
Kliment'ev, Andrei 34–5, 36, 39, 40
Komsomol (Young Communist League) 142, 152, 162, 163, 174
Kondratenko, Nikolai 115
KPRF (Communist Party of Russian Federation) 41, 42, 46, 112, 113, 114, 115, 119, 120–1
Krasnodarskii krai 115, 116, 117
Kremlin 46, 93, 95; and governors 74, 75, 80, 81–2, 83, 85, 87
Kress, Viktor 174, 180, 181, 182
Krest'yaninov, Chairman 33, 36, 39
Kryshtanovskaya, Olga 130, 169, 188, 196, 197
Kuhn, Thomas 200

labour regulation 102
Lane, David 6, 19, 62, 130, 132, 169
Lapina, Nataliya 194
Lebedev, Yurii 39, 40
legislative bodies 161, 162
legislature/legislation: constitutional 102; electoral law 26, 121; federal 80, 106; judiciary 53, 56; regional 121–2, 183
Leningrad Oblast 8, 152, 162, *164*
Levada, Yurii 195
Liberal Democratic Party 26
Ligachev, Yegor 172, 173, 174, 178
Linz, Juan 47, 128
Lipset, Seymour Martin 127
local issues: elites 125–7, 132–3; government 56, 83, 106–7; and power 143–4; and transition 131, 132–3
Lukin, Alexander 65
Luzhkov, Yuri 25

Magomedov, Arbakhan 194
Makarov, Alexander 175, 180
Mal'tsev, Boris 175, 177
Marii El Republic 116, 117
market economy: development 148; failure 131; and regional elites 149, 154–8, 163–4
Marvick, Roger 22
Mawdsley, Evan 17, 19–20, 21
McAuley, Mary 172
media: attacks on 46–7; and elite's confidence 55, 56, 60; and federal laws 102
Media-Most companies 46

Meisel, James 150
Mikul'skii, Konstantin 193
military 53, 57, 110, 125, 126, 134, 160, 193; elites 5, 12, 17, 27, 45, 191, 195; industrial groups 173, 174, 175, 176, 177, 178; and Putin era 25–6, 44, 45, 76
Miller, Arthur 64
Mills, C. Wright 187, 193, 194
Mishler, William 54, 65
Montero, Jose Ramon 158
Mordoviya 111
Morlino, Leonardo 158
Moscow 26, 97, 101–2
Mukha, Vitaly 134, 141, 142

Nathan, Richard P. 94–5, 103
national elites 3, 4, 5, 6, 7, 8–9, 25, 32, 40–9, 52, 81, 82, 128–9, 149, 199; and consolidation 40–9, 128, 129; and politics 120, 121, 152; research on 190, 192, 195, 196, 199, 200; and transition 130, 131, 132, 170; under Putin 44–7
national parliament (1993–1999) 46, 174, 179
Nazdratenko, Yevgenii (governor of Primore) 81
Nemtsov, Boris 33–7, 48; leadership style 41–2; regime 37–8, 44
Nemtsov–Sklyarov pact 33–4, 37–8
Nizhnii Novgorod Oblast: case study 29, 33–40, 47, 48; Coordinating Council 35, 38; Council of Entrepreneurs 34–5; decision-making process 34, 38; elections 35–7, 39, 40; Legislative Assembly 35; party system 37–8; post-Nemtsov period 39–40
nomenklatura 4, 5, 7, 8, 16, 18, 21, 58, 160; networks 196–7; and post-Communist transition 130, 162, 169, 174, 196
non-government sector 60–1; institutions 55–6, 57, 58, 61, 67
North, Douglass 151
Novosibirsk: case study 124, 133–7; local administrative hegemons 141–3; old/new elites attitudes 137–41; post-Soviet elite definition 134–7

Offe, Claus 53, 65
oligarchs/oligarchy 22, 23, 24, 25, 47, 197, 198
Our Home is Russia Party 112, 119, 141, 175

Pareto, Vilfredo 126
patron/client relationships 38, 82–6, 88, 170, 177–8; Putin era 8; under Soviets 192; vertical focus 84; Yeltsin era 6, 72, 75
People's Power Party 115
perestroika 19, 72, 159, 160, 162, 169, 173
PK (Provincial Komitetchiki) elites: networks 17–18
pluralism 2–3, 5, 6, 53, 126, 128, 162, 172; and democracy 7, 66, 67–8; and elites 12, 13, 58, 127, 133, 137, 149, 190; trends 143–4
Poland 21, 128, 149, 170
police 55, 56, 57, 102
political elites 92, 97, 120, 152, 164; and decision-making 12, 63; definition and typology 12–16, *15*, 30–2; development research 188–90; integration and differentiation 12–16; and power-sharing 97–101, 106; research themes and perspectives 190–4; research theory/methodology 194–6; and Russia's transition 197–200; and social restructuring 162–3
political institutions: and differentiation 161; and elites 1, 8, 30, 31, 36; and federalism 94; legitimacy 92, 158; and Putin's era 68; and Yeltsin's era 42, 101
political parties 26, 56, 57, 60, 67; affiliations 113, 114, 120; at regional level 118–19, 175–8; development 109, 113–19, 120, 131; extinction of 110–12, 119, 122; and proportional representation 116–18; studies 109, 110–22
political regime(s) 2, 6, 7, 151; and 'cartel of anxiety' 32, 42, 43; contestation and participation 37–8; and democracy 53–5; and elites 31; and imposed consensus 47–8; regional 33–40, 41, 42, 43, 47–9, 118, 182–4; typology and patterns 14–16, 30, 171
politics/politicians 12, 46, 64, 199; party deputies 112–13, 117; post-Communist 21, 41; regional 172–84; rise in localism 132; studies 199
post-Communist era 170; and institutions 65; politics 21, 41; Russian transition 1–2, 130, 132, 133, 144–5, 162, 169, 174, 196; studies 128

Potanin, Vladimir 22
Power Elite, The (Mills) 187
power(s): devolution 80–1, 83–4; and elites 2–3, 125–6, 194; federal 100–1, 105; governors 74, 75–7, 80–1, 87
power-sharing 92, 97–101, 106
presidency: and 1993 putsch 33, 40, 72, 73, 78; administration 55, 56, 58–9, 96; elections 22, 23–4, 25, 42–3, 44, 85; popularity 55, 56, 59, 61, 66–7; and power-sharing 106; and regional elites 82; and Russian Constitution 93
presidentialism 117, 119
press *see* media
Primakov, Yevgeny 23, 25
private sector 56, 57, 58, 60–1, 126; and public utilities 156; and regional elites 133, 135, 137–8, 156–8
privatization 64, 155, 194; and old/new elites 130, 131, 135, 136, 137, 138, *139*, *140*, 143; and Putin era 24; and transformation 162, 174; and Yeltsin era 22, 36, 102
Przeworski, Adam 128
Pskov Oblast 117
Putin administration 3, 44–7; economic reforms 45, 67, 68; and elites 51; federal reforms 46, 76, 80, 81, 82, 86, 87, 88; and leadership dilemma 6; and political parties 121; and power-sharing preferences 98–100; and stabilization 5, 45; taxation reforms 104–5
Putin, Vladimir 5, 23, 43, 44–7, 48; confidence in 56; and 'Dictatorship of Law' slogan 47, 77, 80; and Duma election (1999) 26; and national elites 24–5, 26–7, 44–9, 66, 93; popularity 55, 56, 59, 60, 95–6; and presidential election 44, 45, 85, 95; and recentralization 105–7
Putnam, Robert 62, 194
putsch (October 1993) 33, 40, 72, 73, 78

Radaev, Vadim 196
Rasteryaev, Vyacheslav 37
reforms: economic 45, 51, 67, 68, 95, 100, 148, 157, 171, 174, 177; federal 46, 76, 80, 81, 82, 86, 87, 88; and regional elites 151; taxation 25, 46, 104–5
regime(s): authoritarian 65; definition and typology 14–15; legitimacy 34, 42, 43, 63, 65, 68; representative 14; transformation 113, 168–70, 184;

transitional 29, 47, 124, 127–9, 171; unstable unrepresentative 14–15, 16–20, *see also* political regime(s)
regime transitions: and elite transformations 113, 168–70; and political elites 198; regional perspective 171
regional elites 82, 83; case studies 133–7, 152–65, 171–84, 193; and democratic institutions 149–51, 158–61; integration and differentiation 170–1, 173–4, 177, 182–4; intra-elite relations 178, 199; and market economy 149, 154–8, 163–4; and political values 163; role/influence 32, 33–7, 150–1, 152; and Russian identity 149, 153–4; transformations 168–70, 177
regional government 56, 58, 60, 63, 95–7; appointments/elections 35–7, 39, 40, 80–1, 109, 180–1, 183–4; and central government 95–7; and decision-making 97, 178, 182–3; and 'Dictatorship of Law' 47, 77; Dumas 74, 175, 179–80, 183–4; establishment of governors 72–3; legislatures 121–2, 183; and market economy 149; and politics 175–8, 181–2; and power-sharing 80, 97–101; presidential systems 114–15; and proportional representation 116–18; regimes and legislature 114–15; taxation control/collection 104–5
resources 11, 17, 23, 53, 133, 195; control 93, 103–5, 107, 150; distribution 68, 94, 101; economic 40, 44; exchange system 34–40, 42, 44, 45, 47; oil and gas 21, 25, 172, 178, 181–2
Roeder, Philip 38
ROMIR, Russian Public Opinion and Market Research 68
Rose, Richard 54, 65
Ross, Cameron 19, 62, 106, 130, 132, 169
Rostov Oblast 115–16
'rule of law' 47, 80
Russian Academy of Sciences (RAS) 188
Russian Communist Workers' Party 112
Russian Constitution (1993) 3, 40, 68, 79, 92, 93, 94, 105; and political institutions 101
Russian Federation 46, 94, 97; and centralized power 100–1, 105; and de-/recentralization 105–7; elections 41;

fiscal system 103–5; operation of 105–7; regions 110–11; resource control 103–5, 107; and special agreements 101–3; study data 93–5
Russia's Choice Party 112, 119
Rustow, Dankwart 127, 128
Ryabov, Andrei 24

St Petersburg 101, 115, 131, 149; case study 152–65; elite sample 152; and institutional legitimacy 158–61; and Russian identity 153–4; views on government and business 162–3
Saratov Oblast 116, 117
Schmitter, Phillipe 198
Schumpeter, Joseph 4, 128
Seleznev, Gebbadii 27
semi-democracy 31, 198, 199
settlements: and consensus 11, 45; and democratization 30, 33–40; and elite fragmentation 37–40; Nizhnii Novgorod case study 33–7
Shevtsova, Lilia 26
Siberia 132, 133–4, 143, 172, 174, 175, 181
Sklyarov Ivan 33, 37, 39, 40
Smith, Graham 54, 92
socialization 16, 53, 54, 125, 126, 140, 149; and generation differences 151, 159–61, 165
social science: and elite research 2, 7, 9, 188
society: crisis 64–8; and elite activity 150
Solnick, Steven 101, 103
Soviet Union 5, 80, 93; collapse of 1, 15, 17–19, 20, 31; current views of 159–60; decision-making system 4, 16; and elite fragmentation 19, 20–4
stability 94, 129; democratic 51, 65, 131, 151, 164, 168; economic 24, 45, 138, 151; political 7, 9, 14–15, 41, 48, 53, 64, 65, 92, 96, 170–1; post-Communist 1, 5, 43, 164; regime 5, 45, 148, 173, 184; regional 34, 36, 37
Stalin, Joseph 17, 18, 19
Stark, David 64
state: de-/recentralization 2, 6, 7, 71, 77, 81; and market development 149, 154–8; and oligarchs 47; and power devolution 80–1
State Duma(s): deputies' roles/preferences 101–3; elections 23, 26, 35, 41, 44, 46, 76, 110, 119, 121;